IMPROVING EDUCATION

Also available from Cassell:

Ronald Barnett and Anne Griffin (eds): *The End of Knowledge in Higher Education*

Christopher M. Clark: *Thoughtful Teaching*

David Scott and Robin Usher: *Researching Education: Data, Methods and Theory in Educational Enquiry*

John Smyth (ed.): *Critical Discourses on Teacher Development*

John White: *Education and the End of Work: A New Philosophy of Work and Learning*

Improving Education

Realist Approaches to Method and Research

Edited by
Joanna Swann and John Pratt

CASSELL
London and New York

Cassell
Wellington House
125 Strand
London WC2R 0BB

370 Lexington Avenue
New York
NY 10017–6550

First published 1999

British Library Cataloguing-in-Publication Data
A catalogue record for this book is available from the British Library.

ISBN   0-304-70553-5 (hardback)
      0-304-70554-3 (paperback)

Typeset by Kenneth Burnley, Wirral, Cheshire.
Printed and bound in Great Britain by Biddles Ltd, Guildford and King's Lynn.

Contents

Foreword   vii
Acknowledgements   ix
The Contributors   x

Part I   Context

1   The Crisis of Method   3
    John Pratt and Joanna Swann

Part II   Principles

2   Pursuing Truth: A Science of Education   15
    Joanna Swann

3   The Abdication of Reason: Postmodern Attacks
    Upon Science and Reason   30
    Richard Bailey

4   Testing Policy   39
    John Pratt

5   Making Better Plans: Problem-based Versus   53
    Objectives-based Planning
    Joanna Swann

6   Critical Realism: Post-Popper Realism for the Real World   67
    David Corson

Part III   Practice

7   Higher Education in Britain: Policy and Practice 1956–92   79
    John Pratt

8   Empowering Lecturers to Improve Assessment Practice
    in Higher Education   89
    Joanna Swann and Kathryn Ecclestone

9   Reconsidering the Prescribed Curriculum   101
    Ronald Swartz

10 The Logic-of-Learning Approach to Teaching:
    A Testable Theory   109
    Joanna Swann

11 Using Critical Realism in Policy-making at School Level   121
    David Corson

12 Equal Opportunities in Secondary Education: A Case Study   135
    John Pratt

13 Exploring Informal Practitioner Theory in Adult Basic
    Education   146
    Yvonne Hillier

14 Inquiry for 'Taught' Masters   156
    Tyrrell Burgess

Part IV Evaluation

15 The Popperian Approach to Raising Standards   167
    in Educational Research
    James Tooley

    References   181
    Index   192

Foreword

Karl Popper is famous as a philosopher of science. He has also made important contributions to political theory, to sociology, and to economics. But he wrote nothing about education, even though he was, for a time, a schoolteacher who dreamed – he tells us in his autobiography – of founding a school 'in which young people could learn without boredom'. Yet Popper's philosophy clearly has profound implications for education.

The central notion of his philosophy is human fallibility: we never know what we are saying, nor what we are doing – we never know all the implications of our statements, nor all the consequences of our actions. Traditionally, most philosophers have tried to escape from fallibility by discovering, or inventing, some means of attaining certainty. To this end they have conducted fruitless searches for a way to justify some statements as true, and a way to prove some actions as correct. Educators, for their part, have usually followed in the path of these traditional philosophers, struggling to justify that what they teach is true, trying to prove that the policies they adopt are correct, and seeking to confirm that their research findings are sound – all without success.

By accepting fallibility as part of the human condition – something we cannot transcend – Karl Popper launched a Copernican revolution in philosophy. For, although it may be depressing to admit that our knowledge and our actions can never be perfect, it becomes exhilarating when we realize this means that they can *always* get better, *always* be improved. So instead of vainly attempting to establish our statements as true, and our actions as correct, Popper directs us to the matter of improving them.

He explained that our knowledge and our conduct improves through trial and error-elimination, telling us to view any proposed solutions to a problem as tentative trials, to be subjected to criticism. Criticism will, if we are lucky, uncover mistakes, inadequacies and errors, which, when eliminated, will result in better – but never perfect – solutions.

Popperians stress criticism and critical dialogue: that is the message of this book. By applying the critical approach to all aspects of education, the contributors demonstrate how it can help to improve teaching practices, curriculum design, policy-making, and research. There are no panaceas here, merely the hopeful news that education can be improved through criticism.

Criticism, of course, is a threat to the way things are, and many people – including teachers, policy-makers and researchers – like things as they are. Popperians, ever conscious of their fallibility, aware that their criticism may be wrong, look for critical dialogue, not capitulation. Moreover, recognizing that reforms will always have unanticipated consequences, they abjure radical and total reform, favouring instead piecemeal gradual change through the elimination of the recognized concrete evils that criticism uncovers. Popperians are concerned critics who want to preserve and improve the existing arrangements, not destroy them.

Henry J. Perkinson
Emeritus Professor of Educational History
New York University

Acknowledgements

The editors are grateful to colleagues for helpful feedback on draft chapters: Elizabeth Atkinson (Chapters 2, 5 and 10), Richard Bailey (Chapter 2), Tyrrell Burgess (Chapter 10), Jenny Cumming (Chapters 2 and 10), Kathryn Ecclestone (Chapters 2 and 5), Mike Locke (Chapters 4 and 7), Brian Marley (Chapter 2), Gill Reay (Chapter 5), Bob Wass (Chapter 5). Our colleagues are not, of course, responsible for any errors or limitations that remain.

The Contributors

Richard Bailey is a lecturer in the School of Education, University of Reading, where he is subject leader for physical education and sport. His lecturing responsibilities include child development, special educational needs, and paediatric exercise science. He has taught in primary and secondary schools, and at a teacher training college. Currently, he is writing a book on the teaching of physical education in the primary school, and is directing a research project examining sporting opportunities for people with physical and learning disabilities. He also researches philosophical issues in education, particularly the application of the theory of knowledge and moral philosophy to educational practice. In 1998 he presented a paper to the US Senate on 'Values education in English schools'.

Tyrrell Burgess is Emeritus Professor in the Philosophy of Social Institutions at the University of East London. He was the first head of the university's School for Independent Study in which students were required to create their own programmes of higher education, and whose principles and practice he described in *Education After School* (1977). He has written extensively on education and public institutions, and has acted as consultant to governments and such organizations as the World Bank and the United Nations Development Programme. He has recently been involved in a project to establish a professional institution and learned society for teachers. Since 1993 he has been chairman of Spitalfields Market Opera.

David Corson is Professor in the Department of Theory and Policy Studies, and in the Modern Language Centre at the Ontario Institute for Studies in Education, Canada. He has also taught at universities in England, Australia and New Zealand, and has been a teacher at primary and secondary levels, a curriculum officer, and a school and system administrator at compulsory and post-compulsory levels. He is Founding Editor of *Language and Education: An International Journal*, and General Editor of the *Encyclopedia of*

Language and Education (eight volumes). He has authored/edited around twenty books including *Education for Work: Background to Policy and Curriculum* (1990c), *Discourse and Power in Educational Organizations* (1995a), *Using English Words* (1995b), *Changing Education for Diversity* (1998), and *Language Policy in Schools* (1999).

Kathryn Ecclestone worked in further education for eight years on vocational and access to higher education courses before moving into higher education to run teacher education programmes for further and adult education teachers and trainers in the public and private sectors. She now lectures in post-compulsory education at the University of Newcastle. Her research interests and publications encompass the policy and practice of assessment throughout the post-compulsory sector. At present she is researching how current policy and practice in the context of debates about lifelong learning affect learner autonomy and motivation. Publications include *How to Assess the Vocational Curriculum* (1996).

Yvonne Hillier lectures in continuing education at City University, London. Having worked in all sectors of education, from primary and secondary schooling to adult, further and higher education, and special needs, she now lectures on research methods, adult learning and independent learning. Her experience also includes the delivery of National Vocational Qualification programmes, external verification of teacher training qualifications, and consultancy on vocational qualifications to a range of voluntary and private-sector organizations. She has researched policy issues for women returners, funding mechanisms in higher education, and informal practitioner theory in adult basic education. Her current research interests lie in teaching and learning, research capability in further education, and the impact of policy on basic skills provision.

John Pratt is Professor of Institutional Studies and Director of the Centre for Institutional Studies at the University of East London. (The centre's work is based on the approach set out in this book.) He has undertaken an extensive range of studies of public policy, particularly in higher education, both in the United Kingdom and abroad. He has been a consultant to the Organisation for Economic Co-operation and Development, the governments of Finland and Austria, and for a range of organizations and institutions. He is the editor of *Higher Education Review* and author of more than a dozen books, the most recent of which is *The Polytechnic Experiment 1965–1992* (1997).

Joanna Swann has a background in initial teacher education, educational research, primary school teaching and educational support services. She is a senior lecturer in the School of Education at the University of Sunderland. Her research interests include: the improvement of education; philosophical theories of learning underlying the practices of teachers and students and implicit in the organization of teaching; the philosophy of Karl Popper;

problem-based planning and evaluation; assessment in higher education; teachers' theories of learning and teaching; developing and testing educational research methodologies; and the policy and practice of learner independence in formal education. Her publications include a book co-authored with Tyrrell Burgess, *Improving Learning – Improving Schools: The Art and Science of Education* (forthcoming).

Ronald Swartz is Professor of Education and Philosophy at Oakland University, USA, where he is Chair of the Department of Human Development and Child Studies. He co-authored *Knowledge and Fallibilism: Essays on Improving Education* (1980), and has published articles in a variety of academic journals including *The Teachers College Record*, *Educational Studies*, *Journal of Educational Thought*, and *Interchange*. In his writing he has developed a liberal, democratic, self-governing educational philosophy which draws on the work of John Dewey, Bertrand Russell, Karl Popper, Homer Lane, A. S. Neill and Paul Goodman.

James Tooley is Professor of Education Policy at the University of Newcastle. Prior to this he was Senior Research Fellow in the School of Education, University of Manchester. He is also Director of the Education Unit at the Institute for Economic Affairs, London. He has held research positions at the University of Oxford's Department of Educational Studies and the National Foundation for Educational Research. He has taught at Simon Fraser University, Canada; the University of the Western Cape, South Africa; and as a mathematics teacher at schools in Zimbabwe. He is a columnist for *Economic Affairs*, and is the author of *Disestablishing the School: Debunking Justifications for State Intervention in Education* (1995), *Education Without the State* (1996), *The Debate on Higher Education: Challenging the Assumptions* (co-authored with Adrian Seville, 1997), *Educational Research: A Critique* (with Doug Darby, 1998), *The Global Education Industry* (1999b), and *Reclaiming Education* (forthcoming).

Part I

Context

Chapter 1

The Crisis of Method

JOHN PRATT AND JOANNA SWANN

There is a crisis in educational research. In October 1998, the journal of the British Educational Research Association reported that 'Educational research is in turmoil' (BERA 1998:1). Such concerns are by no means unique to the United Kingdom, nor are they new. The President of the American Educational Research Association worried that 'current waves of educational policy are neither informed by educational research nor researchers' and 'educational research has low credibility among educational policymakers and practitioners, as well as the general public' (Peterson 1998:4). A review initiated by the Australian Research Council reported a feeling of 'lost focus and impetus' in educational research and lack of support from government agencies and higher education (McGaw *et al.* 1992:iii). The Organisation for Economic Co-operation and Development (OECD 1995:19) reported a 'crisis of confidence' in the value of the knowledge produced by educational researchers in a number of capitalist countries going back to the 1980s. It is possible to find parallels with wider concerns about education; for example, Bloom's (1987) account of the 'closing of the American mind'. Other authors (Gitlin *et al.* 1992, for example), although from different perspectives, have argued for research more closely related to the needs of pupils, teachers and schools.

The occasion for the alarm expressed in the BERA journal was the publication of a review of educational research relating to schools in England commissioned by the Department for Education and Employment (Hillage *et al.* 1998). The review was not, of itself, particularly damning of educational research, though it pointed out some familiar shortcomings; if anything it highlighted the failings of policy-makers to make good use of research generated by the academic community and others. The research community was alarmed partly because this review was published not long after an earlier study, undertaken for the Office for Standards in Education (Tooley with Darby 1998), which was critical of the quality and partisanship of a sample of papers in educational research. Both reports contributed to a sense of unease in the UK about educational research, and to alarm among its practitioners, because they were used by politicians and officials as an opportunity to seize control of the research agenda. Chris Woodhead, Chief Inspector of Schools in England, was reported in *The Times* (23 July 1998) to have said that research into education by academics amounted to little more than biased and irrelevant 'dross', and that the education research budget should fund only work of use in training teachers and formulating government policy.

This book does not attempt to rebut the criticisms of specific reports, contentious books or an intemperate Chief Inspector of Schools. Its purpose is to challenge assumptions about educational research, and to present ideas that are new or, more accurately, not widely known. While not necessarily agreeing with the reports, we recognize the importance of the issues they raise, and address what we see as some key questions about educational research and the way in which it can contribute to the improvement of policy and practice.

THE PURPOSES OF RESEARCH

The heatedness of the debate engendered by the reports illustrates the importance of some of these issues. They include concerns about the purpose of educational research and how far it can or should contribute directly to policy or practice, locally, nationally, institutionally or in any specific classroom. These concerns relate to critiques of the increasing 'instrumentalism' of education; the critiques take an apparently polar stance to those of the government and some of these reports. The reports also raise fundamental issues about the intellectual and academic independence of research (and researchers). Research, as we argue later, is essentially a critical activity that will almost inevitably cause offence to the bigoted or complacent. There is an extensive literature – supported by, among others, the Higher Education Funding Council for England (1995) – that argues for the critical role of higher education (where much, though not all, research is carried out), and the importance of pluralism in democratic societies.

None of this can be taken to justify partisanship or inadequacy of research. Indeed, the function of the researcher as a 'critical friend' in the development of any society and its education heightens the need for integrity and quality in educational research. The reports indicate that there are concerns about these issues, and we are bound to agree with them where they are justified. The problems arise, in our view, from misapprehensions about the nature of research, its functions and the way in which it can advance knowledge and understanding.

KINDS OF KNOWLEDGE

Many texts on educational – and, more generally, social – research set out two broadly different views of its nature. One view reported as widely held by political authorities (though in our opinion mistakenly) is that social science is 'positivist' – that is, independent of context, neutral with respect to social values, generalizable to many situations, and thus able to be 'applied' by policy-makers, teachers and others in policy and practice. Nevertheless, there is a view that the aim of social science should be to produce what, in a more sympathetic understanding of this approach by Eraut (1994), can be described as 'propositional knowledge'. The other view, more often held by those working in education institutions (according to the OECD), is that relevant knowledge is a product of reflective practice, dependent on context and related to specific values. In this view, applicable knowledge is 'locally embedded . . . arising from reflection on experience and the art of practice' (OECD 1995:29). Unsurprisingly, the OECD went on to note that the relationship between knowledge production and knowledge use is problematical.

Indeed it is, though not necessarily only because of this apparent dichotomy. As the report notes, policy-makers and practitioners in education legitimately use knowledge additional to that derived from research (educational statistics, for example). More importantly, not all educational research is meant to inform policy or practice directly. The OECD ministers, and the report that their remarks spawned were, not unreasonably, concerned mainly with the contribution of educational research to policy. More narrowly, the main reason for their interest was 'the recurring belief that knowledge is an increasingly important factor in innovation and economic growth' (OECD 1995:9–10). However, the report identified a variety of kinds, uses and aims of educational research. At its broadest, educational research is 'aimed at understanding certain fundamental relations such as structures, processes and contexts involving human learning and development' (OECD 1995:31).

Because all learning takes place in a context, and usually for some purpose, the relationship between education and society as a whole is central to educational research – particularly its function in socialization. Thus educational research considers learning at several levels including societal, structural, operational and individual. Some research is undertaken to explore fundamental conceptual issues within education, and sometimes in other disciplines (such as sociology). Such concepts may not have immediately obvious applicability (though you never know when they might). Some research (towards PhD, for example) is directed more to the training of researchers (often as potential academics) than to policy change. These are legitimate, even though different, purposes.

There is some validity in the distinction between different kinds of knowledge. Lyotard (1984) argued that science generates a particular kind of knowledge, and, since all knowledge is context bound, there are other knowledges that may be more apt, useful, benign; the object may be to understand rather than predict and control, and this understanding is of the inevitably different experiences and perceptions of different actors. Much of the dilemma arises from the inductive approach often assumed by the protagonists of both camps. If a realist problem-centred and fallibilist approach is taken (see Chapter 2), some of the difficulties do not arise. What the OECD sees as different kinds of 'knowledges' are better viewed as attempts to solve different types of problem; for example: 'What is the case?' and 'How can we get from one state of affairs to another?' As will be discussed in Chapter 5, a solution to the second type of problem is qualitatively different from a solution to the first.

Moreover, we do not believe that the kinds of educational research identified by the OECD (1995) are entirely incompatible. Locally embedded knowledge can include the testing of general propositions, as examples in this book show. Indeed we would argue that it unavoidably does so. What it further offers is an identification of particular circumstances or conditions under which the general propositions are found to be supported or to fail (see Chapter 4). As Edwards (1999:19) says, 'Universal theories do not . . . mean universal solutions'. And propositional knowledge, while it can be couched in the form of value-free statements ('If you do this, then that will happen'), cannot be value-free – for example, in the choice of propositions for testing.

These issues in educational research reflect broader debates about the nature of social science. Typically, it is said that social science is not capable of generating laws that state unvarying relationships between variables, that there is an element of irrationality in human affairs that precludes scientific analysis. This is argued in particular by those who advocate the 'locally embedded' view of knowledge. Much has been written about the problem of generalization in social and educational research (Cohen and Manion 1994; Yin 1994), reflecting the dichotomy expressed above between generalized propositional and locally embedded knowledge. Bassey (1998:5), for example, has argued that there are few generalizations of the kind 'If you do this, then that will happen' which tell teachers anything worthwhile. This may well be true, but it may be no less true for many natural science generalizations. What is worthwhile generally depends on context. The theory of gravity, describing the inverse square relationship between bodies of particular masses, is not often thought of as telling anyone anything worthwhile. Stating it as 'If you drop things they will fall' would usually be thought banal; but it matters if you are in an aircraft.

Another objection to the validity of the social sciences (and indeed of all science) is that they cannot be 'objective'. This criticism proceeds usually from an assumption of the positivist nature of natural science as neutral, and proceeding by the inductive accumulation of facts to generalize and verify laws (Thomas 1998). Yet all knowledge, including both social and natural science, is context-bound. More sophisticated critiques note that the study of social phenomena is unavoidably different from that of physical phenomena, since the knowledge generated by the study itself becomes a factor in social behaviour; social science is simultaneously the object and the process of study. The notion of reflexivity in human and social affairs is clearly an element that complicates their study, though complexity is by no means unique to the social world (think of cosmology). Recent work on both physical and social phenomena has introduced ideas that attempt to explore such notions as chaos, complexity and turbulence (for example, Eve *et al.* 1997). Nor does this reflexivity invalidate the pursuit of tested propositions about social and individual human behaviour.

Some of the ideas now associated with interpretive and hermeneutic approaches and postmodern analysis can be seen as a development of the argument about the impossibility of objectivity in social (or all) science. Central in this development is the role of language or discourse – reality is in the discourse or is the discourse – and this is a human construct. Given that there is no theory-free observation, there are, of course, multiple discourses and each may be valid; but some discourses become dominant, reflecting power relations in society. In this view, the task of the social scientist is to deconstruct the discourse, to understand the circumstances and in particular the power relations that led to its construction.

A REALIST APPROACH

This book sets out realist approaches to method and research in education. In proposing a realist methodology, we reject as sterile and misconceived much of the debate about different approaches in the social sciences; some is even ill-informed – as when Habermas (1976:141–8) criticizes Popper as a positivist. In particular, we see the dichotomy between 'objective' or 'positivist' approaches and other interpretive, even postmodern, approaches as simplistic and sometimes unnecessary. We agree with Pawson and Tilley (1997:55) that a realist epistemology offers an approach to scientific explanation which 'avoids the traditional epistemological poles of positivism and relativism'. A fuller account of our approach is set out in Chapter 2, and a particular development of this synthesis is offered in Chapter 6. Here we make some summary points (drawing to some extent on those set out by Sayer, 1992).

The world exists independently of our knowledge of it. This might seem unexceptional to many people, but it stands in contrast to extreme postmodern interpretations that discourse is the (only) reality. We share, however, with many postmodernists, the idea that knowledge is a human construct. It is a description, interpretation, account, explanation, under-standing of reality – but not therefore the reality it describes. It is fallible not least because it is linguistic, and depends on the nature of language and how we communicate. It is socially constructed in that our view of it depends on our perception or understanding of it and who we are. Its linguistic construction invariably embodies assumptions or prejudices, usually reflecting power structures in society. More importantly, it is fallible for logical as well as social reasons.

We cannot be sure whether our constructions accurately describe reality (see Chapter 2). Our observations are inevitably theory-laden, and in any case no finite number of observations can confirm the truth of a universal statement. But in realist philosophies the relationship between knowledge and its object is crucial; and relativism – the idea that all points of view are equally valid – is not only frivolous and dangerous in reality (in an aircraft you ignore the theory of gravity at your peril) but fallacious, since there are some explanations that are more successful than others (as the previous parenthesis illustrates). This is not to say that different points of view should not be considered, but a key issue in realism is that of why one statement about knowledge is preferable to another. It is desirable that the preference takes account of as many statements as practicable. But, in our experience, a significant difference between realists and others lies in the emphasis placed on interpretations of reality typical of postmodern and other discourses, and the realist concern with the critical testing of the statements so generated.

In practical terms, the realist approaches advocated in this book emphasize rigour in the analysis of physical, social or education phenomena; they are concerned with the logic and validity of the methods employed, and with the development of a rational basis for preferring some knowledge statements to others. This in turn enables knowledge to be developed that can be used with an understanding of its validity and limitations. Some ways of doing things are better than others. We can select what seems to be the best available method by reference to reason and evidence, never knowing for sure whether we have chosen wisely, but often having good reasons to reject some methods because of the anticipated consequences. When disputes occur over what is to be done and how, then we can have recourse to reason and evidence rather than coercion or whim.

POPPERIAN AND POST-POPPERIAN METHOD AND RESEARCH

This book presents ideas about learning and the growth of knowledge that derive from the philosophy of Karl Popper (1902–94). Popper's reputation was established by his contributions to the philosophy of science from the 1930s onwards (for example, Popper 1972a [1959]), in which he radically challenged conventional views about the nature of science and the development of scientific knowledge. Later he extended some of his analysis to issues in the social sciences (for example, Popper 1966a and 1966b [1945]).

A key idea in Popper's epistemology is that learning and the growth of knowledge necessarily involve the discovery of error and inadequacy in existing theories or expectations. Criticism (specifically, that which is constructive) is crucial to any endeavour designed to develop knowledge and improve practice. Our task as learners (as teachers, students, educational inquirers, researchers or policy-makers) is to discover and eliminate our mistaken ideas, and modify and develop those which are inadequate.

It may seem surprising to present a book about method and research in education based on ideas about the philosophy of science that were first argued some half-century ago. The validity of an argument does not, however, depend either on its provenance or its age. What is remarkable is how little attention has been paid to Popperian ideas in education, although interest, as David Corson notes in Chapter 6, is increasing. It is embarrassing that a profession devoted to learning and knowledge should have so neglected one of the major contributors to epistemology. However, many scientists have failed to grasp the significance of Popper's work for science; even they rarely think about epistemology (Medawar 1969:1).

Furthermore, on the occasions when Popper is mentioned in educational texts, his ideas are often misrepresented or cursorily dismissed. And, for many people, a Popperian approach to learning and knowledge is difficult to comprehend because it is fundamentally different from that of the prevailing hegemony. Given this, it is perhaps not surprising that many readers are resistant to pursuing a deeper understanding of his work, although papers on Popperian themes generate considerable interest at conferences. A Popperian approach is also difficult to adopt in practice because, quite simply, the discovery of error and inadequacy can be an uncomfortable experience. Nevertheless, if we are committed to learning and the growth of knowledge, we must strive to encourage such discoveries.

This book does not present a wide-ranging review of literature on educational research (some chapters contain only those references thought by the authors to be essential to their argument); rather it develops specific arguments directly relevant to research practice. The arguments, though diverse, share a realist approach, and in general take a broadly Popperian view of the nature of knowledge and the logic of learning. However, we doubt whether Popper would agree with some of the ways in which his ideas have been interpreted and developed. Our intention, as editors, is to stimulate debate rather than present a unified view, and we are not intent on having the last word. Readers will doubtless reach their own conclusions as to the strengths and weaknesses of the various arguments.

Part II of the book discusses and develops the philosophical ideas that underpin these arguments. Key Popperian theories are set out by Joanna Swann in Chapter 2. Richard Bailey offers a critique of postmodern ideas in Chapter 3. John Pratt develops a Popperian approach to policy in Chapter 4, and in Chapter 5 Joanna Swann offers a problem-based alternative to objectives-based planning and evaluation. The final chapter, by David Corson, offers an approach to social science that builds on Popper's ideas to create a critical realist conception of discovery.

The chapters in Part III present examples of the application of Popperian and post-Popperian philosophy to method and research in primary, secondary, adult and higher education.

Part IV comprises a chapter by James Tooley (one of the initiators of the current debate in the UK) in which he explores connections between the issues raised in his report for the Office for Standards in Education (Tooley with Darby 1998) and a Popperian approach to educational research. He concludes with a critique of the approach developed in this book, and suggests an alternative.

WHERE NEXT?

The ideas contained in this book have implications for governments, as well as researchers and practitioners. We, like Tooley with Darby (1998) and Hillage *et al.* (1998), do not approve of – though not always for the same reasons – all that passes for educational research. We also reject uncritical analysis and untestable diatribes. We believe that educational researchers should adopt rigorous methods and standards of analysis. Pursuit of these standards requires an understanding of the nature of knowledge and the way it is generated. We believe that the crisis of method in educational research has arisen because many researchers (and those who fund their work) have failed to address these issues.

None of this means that we believe the educational research agenda should be dominated by narrow concerns about relevance and applicability; nor should it be under government control. It is often impossible to judge in advance what will or will not be relevant to practice. Good research (that associated with learning and the growth of knowledge) is open-ended; it is not possible to predict what all the outcomes will be.

In a Popperian model the purpose of research is to promote learning. Learning is a creative activity involving the discovery of error or inadequacy. It is not about the development of certain or secure knowledge; nor is it about creating or supporting dogma, though it may be construed in this way. Good research requires diversity – of people, opportunities, approaches, funding – to generate new ideas.

But the ideas generated by research are no less conjectural than those they challenge or supersede. The growth of knowledge can best be characterized as the progressive rebuilding of ideas out of the discovery of error and inadequacy. Research can, of course, generate knowledge for technical application (as in, 'If you do x then y will happen/not happen'), but it should not lead, as Reynolds (1998:27) appears to believe, to the uncritical application of a 'codified scientifically established body of knowledge' to teacher practice. *All* knowledge should be regarded as conjectural, and subject to amendment. Often, what passes for knowledge has not been tested; rather, it is derived from the uncritical acceptance of common practice. (Governments, moreover, tend to adopt ideas that are politically expedient.)

To be effective, researchers require freedom to engage in constructive criticism of the *status quo* and accepted knowledge. They require the opportunity to play with ideas – to create and consider diverse hypotheses. They need to acknowledge that research and learning are open-ended creative processes, and both have the same implicit logic. Good research requires enthusiasm and commitment on the part of a team of researchers or an individual researcher.

The preceding discussion raises a number of important questions for governments. How can central government and its agencies best make decisions about the allocation of funds for research? How can diversity and rigour in research be promoted? Indeed, why does research need to be regulated? An even better question might be: How can good research be supported? Criticism, problem-formulation, and the generation of trial solutions and tentative theories, are creative activities requiring individual initiative. Yet the OECD (1995), Tooley with Darby (1998) and Hillage *et al.* (1998), overlook the extent to which small-scale educational research is undertaken through the goodwill of the researchers. People often undertake research because of their interest in and commitment to particular values. Hillage *et al.* (1998) appear to offer a central control agenda, rather than an empowerment agenda designed to support individuals and groups according to their perceptions of what they or their clients need.

The issues for government are broader, even, than this. The urge of governments generally to prescribe and control education is both inappropriate and dangerous and, paradoxically, incompatible with their stated policy aims. Policy statements increasingly refer to the need to establish a 'learning society' (Department for Education and Employment 1998a). Governments recognize that post-industrial societies will be increasingly 'knowledge based', and that knowledge is changing so fast it is no longer possible to conceive of education as a one-off activity; 'lifelong learning' is the new mantra of education.

Many of the implicit (or even explicit) epistemological assumptions underpinning government policy are inappropriate. There are no secure bodies of knowledge to be imparted. Learning does not take place by induction. Criticality rather than corroboration is the key to learning and the growth of knowledge. People with widely differing interests and experiences will need to learn different things at different times throughout their lives, but increased central control inhibits individual initiative and diminishes the diversity essential for genuine learning. A learning society is quintessentially Popperian because it recognizes the conjectural and changing nature of knowledge, and the need to refine and improve it. A Popperian approach will be essential for method and research in education in the twenty-first century.

Part II

Principles

Chapter 2

Pursuing Truth: A Science of Education

JOANNA SWANN

> All acquired knowledge, all learning, consists of the modification (possibly the rejection) of some form of knowledge, or disposition, which was there previously; and in the last instance, of inborn dispositions...All growth of knowledge consists in the improvement of existing knowledge which is changed in the hope of approaching nearer to the truth.
>
> Karl Popper (1979:71)

This chapter constitutes an argument for a science of education based on the philosophy of Karl Popper. Emphasis is placed on the logic of the growth of knowledge and the logical analysis of science. This does not mean that factors such as imagination and persistence are thought to be insignificant – on the contrary; nor that learning and the growth of knowledge can be fully explained in logical terms (see Swann 1999). However, logical analysis shows that knowledge cannot grow without the discovery of either an error or an inadequacy; thus, one of our principal tasks as learners is to seek to discover our mistaken and inadequate ideas.

Given the need for brevity, complex ideas have been simplified, and there is, of course, no substitute for reading Popper (1979, in particular). Anyone who has been swayed by criticism of Popper is urged to consult Miller (1982, 1994). See also Popper's replies to his critics in Schilpp (1974). In general, while acknowledging that Popper's theories should not be accepted uncritically, I urge teachers, researchers and policy-makers in the field of education to address his critiques of widely accepted ideas and consider the alternatives he developed.

A POPPERIAN ACCOUNT OF KNOWLEDGE

Science and metaphysics

In the natural sciences Popper's reputation as a philosopher is well established. Because of this, some people have concluded, mistakenly, that his philosophy does not apply to the social sciences or education. It is often assumed, again mistakenly, that he sidelined metaphysics. However, while it is true that Popper differentiated between scientific and metaphysical theories, he never suggested that the latter are meaningless or unimportant.

Popper suggested that in contrast to metaphysical theories, scientific theories are those universal statements which are, in principle, refutable (testable) by reference to statements of observation. In Popper's account, a universal theory is no less scientific for being about social practices such as education rather than about magnetism. A significant distinguishing factor is whether a theory can be, and has been, formulated in such a way that it may in principle be falsified by reference to observation statements. Some ideas are necessarily metaphysical – they cannot be formulated as falsifiable theories. Commonsense realism (discussed below) is one such theory. In more general terms, Popper talked about metaphysical research programmes. These are important in the development of testable (that is, refutable) ideas, but they are not in themselves testable; they can, however, be critically discussed.

Other essentially non-scientific ideas are values (ideas about what is good and/or what ought to be the case in the world); these too are no less important for being irrefutable. According to Popper (1966a:Chapter 5), questions of fact and questions of value emerge together within situations. He clearly rejected the idea that the latter can be reduced to the former. The logic of the growth of knowledge is, moreover, equally applicable to the development of theories of value and theories of fact; the difference is that statements of fact can be contradicted by statements of empirical evidence, whereas statements of value cannot. It is not always easy to distinguish between issues of fact and value in a specific context, but the presence of issues of value, which make the analysis of social practice a 'messy' business, should not divert us from developing and testing theories about the nature of the external reality.

Popper argued that any theory which purports to describe the nature of the external reality should, insofar as this is possible, be presented in a form whereby it may be subjected to the most rigorous criticism. Ideas which could be, but have not been, presented in a falsifiable form (astrological theories fall into this category), can be criticized on the grounds that they are non-scientific. The most rigorous criticism makes reference to empirical tests, and takes us beyond the question of 'Is this argument valid?' to 'Is this theory true?' (Our answer to the latter question may then be incorporated into our answer to the former.) The practice of self-consciously formulating and working with falsifiable theories is not widespread in educational research; indeed some researchers reject it. There is, moreover, another way in which most contemporary educational research falls outside of Popper's conception of science: he characterizes scientific theories in terms of their boldness, not merely their testability. This issue, discussed later in the chapter, is highlighted in the following quotation:

There is a reality behind the world as it appears to us, possibly a many-layered reality, of which the appearances are the outermost layers. What the great scientist does is boldly to guess, daringly to conjecture, what these inner realities are like. (Popper 1985a:122)

Realism

It would seem that, like Popper, most people believe in the existence of a shared external reality; they are commonsense realists. Commonsense realism can neither be demonstrated nor disproved. This is also true of the opposing idea, idealism. The most extreme form of idealism, solipsism, is represented by the assertion, 'The world is my dream.' When a person is convinced that what she experiences exists only in the mind, no amount of *empirical* evidence will convince her otherwise; all of her experiences will be interpreted as aspects of a lifelong dream.

Solipsism is not, however, as valid a theory as commonsense realism – there are strong *arguments* which support the commonsense realist view. These include the following (adapted from Popper 1979:Chapter 2): there is no good reason to reject commonsense realism, therefore we should be cautious about relinquishing it; denying the existence of an external reality means that the individual is necessarily the creator of her universe, which amounts to megalomania; most science and all descriptive human language imply an independently existing world, and if we abandon commonsense realism we must, if we wish to be rational, give an alternative (and convincing) account of the nature of human language and the practices of science.

Realism, as an isolate term, may be applied to various philosophical positions. Phillips (1987:205) defines realism as the belief that 'entities exist independently of being perceived, or independently of our theories about them', which may or may not be accompanied by the belief (metaphysical realism) that knowledge of these entities is possible. Despite a general acceptance of commonsense realism, there is little consensus about whether or to what extent knowledge of the shared external reality is possible and, insofar as it is thought to be possible, how such knowledge may be pursued. However, any theorist who rejects the notion that objective knowledge of external reality is possible has taken a significant step towards idealism (and, most likely, towards relativism – see Chapter 3). Some educational theorists, such as Ernst von Glasersfeld and other radical constructivists, maintain that all we can know directly are our own ideas; they argue that while external reality (including the social world) impinges on our knowledge and leads us to modify our thinking and actions, we cannot sensibly pursue true descriptions of it (see, for example, von Glasersfeld 1985; Driver and Oldham 1986).

The idea that we can sensibly set out to describe, explain or otherwise represent the world has been criticized on the grounds that we cannot be certain that our accounts reflect what is actually there. There is no way of checking, say, theory T_1 as an account of reality, except by reference to theory T_2, but, of course, theory T_2 is no more certain or secure than T_1. A number of theories may interrelate and support each other but nevertheless fail to provide secure knowledge of the nature of the external reality. As a criticism of the quest for certain or secure knowledge, this argument is valid; but abandonment of this quest does not inevitably mean abandoning the quest for true descriptions of external reality. Although we cannot be certain that our descriptions or other representations of external reality are correct, it does not follow that our attempts to represent it are worthless. Rather, we should recognize the conjectural nature of knowledge and, instead of trying to establish certain or secure knowledge, we should focus on the processes by which knowledge grows.

We need only give up the question of how to establish certainty, substituting and addressing in its place, 'How can we best pursue truth?' We can engage in procedures which, logically, are likely to create better descriptions of the world, even though the success of our endeavours must remain conjectural. These procedures are no less applicable to the growth of knowledge about the human world than they are to the growth of knowledge about non-human phenomena. (There are, of course, differences with regard to research methods and tools, limitations and difficulties concerning research design and, in particular, ethical issues.)

Truth

In addressing the question of how we can best pursue truth, Popper (1979:Chapter 9) drew on Alfred Tarski's account of the correspondence theory of truth, the idea that truth is correspondence with fact (that is, reality).

Popper emphasized the importance of using the two-value system of logic, in which a statement is declared to be either true or false (not to be confused with the idea of *knowing* whether a statement is true or false). The two-value system enables valid inferences to be made which transmit the truth of the premises to the conclusion, or re-transmit the falsity of the conclusion to at least one of the premises. The application of the two-value system can be illustrated by means of an example: if we take the universal theory, 'Children with temperatures over 38°C will be absent from school', and the specific condition, 'This child's temperature is over 38°C', it leads to the conclusion, 'This child is absent from school.' If the conclusion is false, and the child is not absent from school, then one or both of the premises must be false. It might be the case that children sometimes come to school with temperatures over 38°C and/or the child's temperature is not over 38°C.

A true conclusion does not, however, prove the truth of a universal theory: the child may be absent from school and have a temperature over 38°C, but would have come to school were it not for a heavy fall of snow that blocked the road.

Popper also distinguishes between two questions concerning truth. The first question is, 'What is truth?'; the second, 'Is this theory true?' He rejects the first question as it invites a diversionary argument about the meaning of 'truth'. Instead, he focuses on the second question, which leads to the following problem: 'can there be such a thing as a statement or a theory which corresponds to the facts, or which does not correspond to the facts?' (Popper 1979:312). The answer to this question is 'Yes', and providing that a metalanguage is used it is possible to talk about the correspondence between a statement and a fact without getting embroiled in paradoxes and contradictions. The metalanguage must, however, be rich enough to be able to refer to statements and describe facts within the original (object) language. Once a distinction has been made between metalanguage and object language, it is valid to say that a statement is true if, and only if, it corresponds to the facts. In short, 'truth and falsity are essentially regarded as properties, or classes, of statements' (Popper 1979:44).

It should be noted that the idea that a statement is true if, and only if, it corresponds to the facts does not provide a criterion or method for determining whether or not a statement is true or false. Truth is a standard at which to aim, but we can never know for certain whether it has been reached.

In addition, this version of the correspondence theory of truth requires an understanding of the idea that there are

> two different senses of knowledge or of thought: (1) *knowledge or thought in the subjective sense*, consisting of a state of mind or of consciousness or a disposition to behave or to react, and (2) *knowledge or thought in an objective sense*, consisting of problems, theories and arguments ... (Popper 1979:108–9)

Most epistemologists have concerned themselves with knowledge in the first rather than the second sense, and this, Popper argues, has led to a good deal of philosophical discussion that is irrelevant to the growth of knowledge.

Popper accepts the idea that there is an external world, and suggests that ideas in the mind (the subjective realm, which he calls World 2) can, at least conjecturally, represent or correspond to features of this external world. The external world, moreover, is comprised of two different kinds of entity: physical objects and events (World 1); and ideas, such as those made public in the world of speech, books, radio and television, music and the arts in general, and in particular, critical argument (World 3). The world of public ideas (of objective knowledge) exists as a consequence of the descriptive and argumentative functions of language. These functions enable us to describe, explain and argue about features external to our subjective experience. As we are also able to describe our internal subjective states, such descriptions may then become part of the world of public ideas. Truth is pursued within the critical discussion of competing theories; theories may compete as accounts of how the world is or how we want the world to be.

Empiricism and rationalism

Before turning to the logic of the growth of knowledge, it is useful to consider the extent to which Popper's theories are situated within the epistemological traditions of empiricism and rationalism.

Traditionally, empiricism has been contrasted with rationalism. In modern thinking, however, these 'isms' have been modified to the point where a coherent epistemology may be both empiricist and rationalist. Put simply: to an empiricist, knowledge and sensory experience are inextricably linked. Knowledge is thought to start with experience (naïve and classical empiricism), or be justified by experience (an implication of pragmatism), or be criticized by experience (the Popperian view). Rationalists, on the other hand, elevate reason above the senses in the acquisition of knowledge (Cottingham 1984:6). Empiricists do not inevitably deny the importance of rationality in learning (on the contrary), nor do rationalists deny the importance of sense-experience, but their emphasis is different. Although naïve and classical empiricists either reject or do not attribute importance to the idea of *a priori* knowledge, this is not true of modern empiricists. Similarly, whereas classical rationalists assert the existence of infallible *a priori* knowledge, modern rationalists regard such knowledge as fallible.

Popper is 'a rationalist of sorts' (1972b:6) in that he believes in *a priori* knowledge; however, he departs from classical rationalism in that he regards such knowledge as conjectural and fallible rather than absolute. He is also 'an empiricist of sorts' in that he argues that 'we learn from experience – that is, from our mistakes – how to correct them' (1972b:406), but he nonetheless rejects the idea of pure observation and pure sense-experience. In Popper's account, experience includes our internal subjective state, the external physical and social environments, and the world of public ideas.

The term 'positivist' is sometimes used incorrectly as a synonym for 'empiricist'. Without digressing into a debate about positivism (see Phillips 1987 and 1992, for illuminating discussion), it is, put crudely, the view that things which cannot be measured or, at least, directly observed are non-existent, meaningless or of little or no importance. Although most positivists are empiricists, not all empiricists are positivists. There is no inherent conflict between empiricism and the idea that there are (some) features of the world (particularly the human world) which are important yet not readily measurable or even directly observable. (Popper is, emphatically, not a positivist – see Popper 1976b.)

HOW KNOWLEDGE GROWS

The invalid logic of induction

Popper's account of the logic of the growth of knowledge derives from criticism of the empiricist theory of induction. (Note: the focus is on logic rather than sociology or psychology.) According to this theory, repeated acts of observation lead to expectations and a belief in specific regularities. Eventually, these beliefs take the form of more substantial theories or, in the case of scientific knowledge, laws (certain knowledge). People 'know', for instance, that the sun will rise tomorrow because it has always done so. The theory of induction proposes that universal theories, which describe general features of the world, are abstracted from singular observation statements.

When, following Francis Bacon, a scientist adopts induction as a method, she makes carefully recorded observations on the assumption that a universal theory may eventually emerge. Corroborative evidence is then sought to strengthen the theory, possibly to the point where it functions as a law.

David Hume, the eighteenth-century Scottish philosopher, discovered a major flaw in the theory of induction: there is no logical reason for assuming that the future will be like the past. For an inference to be logically valid, the conclusion must not go beyond the evidence presented in the premises, thus inductive inference – reasoning from repeated instances of experience to other instances (conclusions) of which there is no experience – represents a logically invalid argument. No number of true singular observation statements of the kind, 'This is a five-year-old child who enjoys stories about animals' can entail the general theory, 'All five-year-old children enjoy stories about animals.'

The discovery of error provokes new problems. One problem following Hume's discovery of error within the theory of induction is, 'Why . . . do all reasonable people expect, and *believe*, that instances of which they have no experience will conform to those of which they have experience?' (Popper 1979:4). Hume's criticism of induction was devastating, but he was unable to answer the question it raised, except to say that while repetition is powerless in terms of logical argument, people are nonetheless conditioned to believe that the future will be like the past, and this is an important biological factor for survival. Although Hume's original intention was to establish a secure foundation for knowledge, his critique of the theory of induction undermined the empiricist enterprise and led to irrationalism: there was no longer any justification for accepting repeated observation as the basis for knowledge, yet such repetition remained central to scientific method.

Humean and post-Humean criticisms of the pursuit of certain knowledge are compelling; however, 'certain knowledge' has largely been replaced by 'secure knowledge', which is only marginally different, and the inductivist idea of abstracting generalizations from data has been widely retained. Many people continue to view science as an 'accumulation of highly confirmed, or highly probable, or well-supported hypotheses' (Miller 1982:19–20). In general, inductive process is compatible with the view that ideas can be abstracted from experience, whether this experience is characterized as the observation of natural phenomena, the 'observation' of ideas in books (through reading), or the 'observation' of ideas presented in a teacher's instructive talk (Swann 1998a). And even though the idea of theory-free observation has been discarded, significance is often not attributed to ideas which exist prior to data collection.

In short, although induction is recognized to be problematic, the idea of an inductive process is still commonly accepted at an implicit level, and corroboration is thought to be an essential part of learning.

The logic of the growth of knowledge

Popper, following Hume, accepted that the theory of induction is logically invalid but, unlike Hume, he denied that induction ever takes place, psychologically or otherwise. Popper demonstrated an asymmetry between verification and falsification: while no number of true singular observation statements can verify or prove the truth of a universal theory, one true singular observation statement can refute it. To continue a previous illustration: although no number of true statements of the kind, 'This is a five-year-old child who enjoys stories about animals' will prove the truth of the universal theory, 'All five-year-old children enjoy stories about animals', the statement, 'This is a five-year-old child who does not enjoy stories about animals', if true, will falsify it. Thus a universal theory is always provisional and unverifiable; it can, in principle, be refuted. On a daily basis, the idea that the sun will rise tomorrow is accepted as secure; nonetheless, it is open to question. Many of our unrefuted conjectures can be (and have to be) acted upon, though one day they may be refuted.

Popper's discovery of an asymmetry between the ideas of verification and falsification led to a new theory of how knowledge grows, and a new theory of what happens when an individual learns (Swann 1999). A singular statement is significant insofar as it relates to a universal theory which, potentially, it may refute or contradict; so too an individual's observation is relevant and possible *only* in the context of an expectation, assumption or theory which that individual holds about herself, the physical and social environment, or the world of public knowledge.

An observation requires both an observer and a thing observed, and for the observer to observe this thing there must necessarily be some prior expectation or idea (Popper 1979, in particular Chapter 7). For instance, if a child is asked to observe a tree the question arises, either implicitly or explicitly, 'What is to be observed about the tree?' In this situation, identifying which features are to be observed becomes a problem. It may be tackled by asking the question, or by the child identifying something to observe based on expectations created in prior learning. It is, of course, possible to guide observation by suggesting features to be observed, but even so, the child's understanding of what is suggested, and her awareness of the tree, will be dependent on existing ideas. Whatever is seen (heard, read or cognitively assembled) in any situation is not only dependent on what is actually there, but also on the prior expectations (implicit assumptions or explicit theories) of the observer: there is always something prior to an observation. All observation is theory-laden. This is no less true for observations of the physical world than it is for the social world.

The idea of *belief in regularity* may, Popper argued, be exchanged for the idea of an inborn *need for regularity* (Popper 1992:48–52). Regularities are needed, expected, even sought, though often not found. Following Popper, learning and the growth of knowledge are characterized not by the acquisition of true or almost certainly true information, but by the discovery of erroneous or inadequate expectations.

Thus, every incidence of learning and all growth of knowledge begins with a problem. In the case of learning (an individual activity), a problem occurs when an individual experiences or anticipates a mismatch between expectation and experience, and when she desires to resolve the mismatch in some way. (Note: in the animal world in general, most learning involves only minimal levels of consciousness; even for humans, most learning is unself-conscious, haphazard, accidental and implicit in situations.) The growth of public knowledge is similarly rooted in problems – mismatches between ideas which individuals and groups working at the boundaries of their problem area desire to solve. A problem triggers the search for a solution, and the creation of a trial solution brings with it a new set of expectations (which may or may not be explicit). These expectations may subsequently be found to be flawed, and new problems may then be created.

This process has been summarized by Popper in the simplified schema of conjecture and refutation (Popper 1979:243):

$$P_1 \rightarrow TS \rightarrow EE \rightarrow P_2$$

In this schema, P_1 represents an initial problem, TS is a trial solution applied to the problem, and EE is the process of error elimination to which the trial solution is subject, giving rise to P_2. P_2, the new problem which emerges from the attempt to solve the initial problem, is always different from P_1. In most representations of the schema, Popper uses TT for tentative theory rather than TS for trial solution, reflecting his greater interest in theoretical rather than practical issues: a tentative theory is proffered as a trial solution to a theoretical problem. The use of TS is, in my opinion, preferable because it encompasses the idea of tentative theory; it is also more appropriate when learning and other practical activities are being discussed.

The schema is a simplification of what happens when learning takes place and knowledge grows (a problem, for instance, may generate multiple trials); but the logic is essentially the same wherever and whenever there is learning and the growth of knowledge. (The logic of learning is discussed further in Chapter 10.)

Criticism is fundamental to the growth of knowledge; the identification of error (or inadequacy) in the world of public ideas is the basis for its subsequent elimination. By discovering where our ideas are mistaken or inadequate, we are able to improve theoretical accounts and practical policies. This process is accelerated in the scientific realm by the deliberate formulation of ideas in a manner which encourages falsification (that is, refutation). The falsification of an idea is not, however, unproblematic; we may be mistaken in thinking that we are mistaken.

Error and inadequacy

Popper stressed the importance of the discovery of error, rather than the discovery of inadequacy. His concern with theoretical rather than practical problems led him (as discussed earlier) to emphasize the two-value system of logic: the most rigorous test of a theory is one which leads to the (conjectural) judgement of 'true' or 'false'. In day-to-day learning, however, a useful distinction can be made between error, where an idea is false, and inadequacy. (This parallels the distinction between theoretical and practical problems discussed in Chapter 5.)

A teacher would be expressing the discovery of an error if she said, 'I thought the students understood my explanation but realized I was wrong when I questioned them afterwards.' In contrast, the discovery of an inadequacy would involve a mismatch between what the teacher knows and what might be known, as in 'I want to convey this idea to the students but I don't know how.' Both scenarios involve a mismatch, but in the second (a case of 'wanting to know but not knowing') a practical mistake may be anticipated and avoided by the recognition of an inadequacy. The implications of this distinction can be illustrated by an example of learning from reading. (Note: the ideas of learning from reading and learning by conducting an inquiry in its broader sense are interchangeable.)

There are three main ways in which reading a book can help someone to learn; two are direct, the other is indirect. These ways of learning are not mutually exclusive; all three functions of a book may come into play at any reading.

First, a book may challenge the assumptions or existing theories of the reader (the would-be learner). On reading a book, the reader may discover a mismatch between the ideas she brings to her reading and the ideas in the book. The book may (a) contradict the reader's current ideas or (b) expand upon them. In the case of (a) there is potential for discovering error, and in (b) an unforeseen limitation is potentially revealed. An individual may thus be encouraged to think, 'Are my ideas correct? Are my ideas adequate?' If the answer to either question is 'No', reading the book may result in learning by provoking the reader to formulate one or more new problems.

Secondly, the reader may bring to a book a question (or set of questions) to which she seeks an answer (or answers). The reader has previously experienced a mismatch between what she knows and wants to know; she has identified an inadequacy in her current knowledge. On the basis of a desire to resolve the mismatch, a problem may be formulated, such as 'How can I find an answer to the question: what is wood made of?' In this situation, reading a book may provide part of a solution to a pre-existing problem. What the reader 'observes' in the book will still be dependent, though not wholly, on prior expectations. Reading will not necessarily result in good learning; it may endorse prior, or generate new, erroneous assumptions. When reading for learning it is, wherever possible, better to formulate one's principal expectations in advance; expectation- or hypothesis-testing is more conducive than question-answering to bold and critical thinking.

Thirdly, the reader may find in a book ideas which correspond with those she already holds to be true or valid. In this circumstance, insofar as there is no mismatch, no direct learning will take place; logically, the discovery of corroborative evidence is not a necessary feature of learning. Corroborative evidence may, however, make the reader feel good, and can boost confidence. This feel-good factor may provide an individual with encouragement to continue working on ideas. (It may also, of course, lead to complacency.) Thus, corroborative evidence may have a significant, though indirect, impact on future learning.

SCIENTIFIC ACTIVITY

Critical preference

The fact that no theory can be proved to be true did not lead Popper to relativism, even with regard to choosing between unrefuted scientific theories. In discussion of how best to choose between theories competing within a problem situation, Popper introduced the idea of critical preference; this is discussed in the context of persons concerned with the development of theory, and those concerned more with practical action (Popper 1979:Chapter 1; Popper 1985a).

A logical preference can be proposed whereby some theories are arguably better than others (although they remain conjectural). The pursuit of truth is maintained by searching for and eliminating false theory, and this is supplemented by the idea of 'growth of informative content'. For a theoretician, any theory with a great deal of informative content is interesting, even prior to testing (which entails the search for falsifying evidence): bold theories, those which entail a large number of consequences, are preferable to theories which predict or imply little. A bold theory is nonetheless required to stand up to tests, to be subjected to the risk of refutation, but even when such a theory is refuted the act of refutation can lead to more learning than if a theory with fewer consequences is falsified. In short, the task of science is to produce bold universal theories that are difficult to refute. Note: refutation should not be evaded by 'immunizing tactics or stratagems' (Popper 1985b:126), though some kinds of auxiliary hypotheses are valid (Popper 1992:42; 1985b:128–30).

The refutation of a theory does not automatically lead to a new theory (in the same way that Hume's criticism of the theory of induction did not readily lead to a replacement). Refutation, in the first instance, leads to a new problem, and any subsequent theory is a product of imagination in the context of that problem. (Popper does not suggest or otherwise imply that the search for refutation is an alternative means of achieving certainty. The discovery of falsifying evidence is itself a conjectural business.)

In a situation where an individual is concerned more with practical decision-taking than theory development, Popper argues that preference should be given to the best-tested theory, one not shown to be false despite refutations having been sought.

The logical analysis of science

Scientific activity thus has two related aspects: the provision of theoretical explanations, and a practical function of offering either predictions or technical applications. The logical schema in Figure 2.1 is relevant to both aspects (Popper 1979:351).

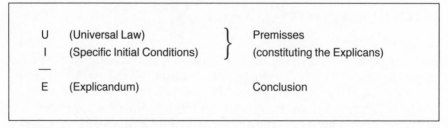

Figure 2.1: Schema of explanation

Although the form of explanations found acceptable by scientists and others has changed during the course of history,

> all consist of a *logical deduction*; a deduction whose conclusion is the *explicandum* – a statement of the thing to be explained – and whose premises consist of the *explicans* (a statement of the explaining laws and conditions) . . . an explanation is always the deduction of the *explicandum* from certain [that is, specific] premises, to be called the *explicans*. (Popper 1979:349–50)

An explanation involves the search for the appropriate universal theory and a set of initial conditions: the search for the U (universal theory/law) and I (specific initial conditions) of the schema to account for E, the *explicandum* (that which is to be explained). In the derivation of predictions the process is reversed; the universal theory is assumed to be known and is coupled with specific conditions (known, or assumed to be known, by observation) to formulate logical consequences which are then to be observed (or not, as the case may be). The prediction takes the place of the *explicandum*, E, in the schema.

Put simply, a prediction may be expressed as, 'It is the case that [universal theory]; therefore, given the observable conditions that [specific initial conditions], then [prediction] will be the case (or will not be the case).' The prediction fails if it does not agree with what is subsequently observed, in which case either the universal theory is false, and/or the specific initial conditions have been erroneously perceived. Note, however, that if the prediction is fulfilled, it may not be for the reasons suggested. Nothing is proved in science; there is no scientific verification.

Using this analysis, it can be seen that not all explanations are satisfactory. It is important, for instance, to avoid explanations that are circular. The reasons given in support of an hypothesis should be other than, and independent of, the *explicandum*. If it is only possible to adduce the *explicandum* itself as evidence, the explanation is circular.

In the case of technical applications of science, what is given are specifications which take the place of E in the schema. A classroom example might be encapsulated by a teacher as, 'I want a model bridge to be built in the classroom without the use of adhesives.' The task would involve the use of (probably implicit) theories about construction and bridge building, and about specific materials and resources. Here, specific universal theories are presumed to be true; often they have been corroborated by previous testing. Even so, something unexpected may occur. Thus, both predictions and technical applications can be viewed as tests of scientific theories.

Prohibitive hypotheses

In discussing explanatory theories, Popper makes a recommendation which I adopted in my classroom research (Swann 1988); it has subsequently been taken up by one of my doctoral students. The recommendation is useful in the development of theory, though it is invariably difficult to apply:

> There is a way of formulating scientific theories which points with particular clarity to the possibility of their falsification: we can formulate them in the form of prohibitions (or *negative existential statements*) . . . It can be shown that universal statements and negative existential statements are logically equivalent. This makes it possible to formulate all universal laws . . . as prohibitions. (Popper 1979:360–1)

Popper points out that negative existential statements (prohibitive hypotheses) are of use to technologists (engineers and anyone engaged with practical problems), but for the scientist 'they are a challenge to test and to falsify; they stimulate him to try to discover those states of affairs whose existence they prohibit, or deny' (1979:361).

In the context of classroom practice, a prohibitive hypothesis may be derived from a (preferably bold) universal theory about how, for instance, student attainment or competence may be increased. The universal theory might take the form, 'Students will make more progress with regard to [specified] attainments or competences if this [specified] set of ideas is adopted in practice rather than [specified alternative].' This universal theory, accompanied by the condition, 'This [specified] set of ideas is not being adopted in practice', constitutes an explanation for perceived limitations in student progress.

The conventional prediction derived from this explanation takes the form, 'If this [specified] set of ideas is adopted in practice, then students will make more progress with regard to [specified] attainments or competences in comparison with students who are subject to [specified alternative].' Such a formulation does not encourage the search for refutations. However, when the universal theory is formulated prohibitively – 'There does not exist a situation in which this [specified] set of ideas when adopted in practice does not lead to greater progress with regard to [specified] attainments or competences in comparison with [specified alternative]' – it challenges the researcher to look for situations in which the practice is unsuccessful; where, in other words, the prediction fails. (Note: in educational research it is also important to be alert to the possibility of unexpected, unintended and undesirable consequences – see Chapter 5.)

If falsifying evidence is found, either the universal theory (the statement of how student attainment or competence may be enhanced) or the initial conditions (statements about what the students experienced), or both, are in error. The observation of what ensued from the practice may also be mistaken; for instance, we may be wrong in thinking that we have found falsifying evidence.

Of course, what is considered to be a worthwhile attainment or competence, etc., is value-laden, but this does not stop us from testing the application of various theories *vis-à-vis* predicted outcomes. The value of using prohibitive hypotheses can only be understood by reference to the idea that the discovery of error (or inadequacy) is the basis for the growth of knowledge, and that secure knowledge is a chimera. (A proposal for testing a Popperian approach to teaching is outlined in Chapter 10.)

CONCLUDING DISCUSSION

Although the pursuit of certain or secure knowledge is misguided, we should not feel embarrassed or be apologetic about pursuing truth; that is, attempting to create better (conjectural) descriptions of our shared external reality. If we wish to pursue truth we must welcome the discovery of error and inadequacy as a prerequisite to eliminating or modifying mistaken and inadequate expectations (assumptions and theories).

Whether or to what extent the methods used by natural scientists are applicable to learning and the growth of knowledge in the social sciences and in the field of education has been widely debated. While there are significant difficulties in, and limitations pertaining to, the study of human phenomena, such constraints should not lead educationists to reject as irrelevant ideas derived from analysis of the natural sciences. In particular, following Popper, scientific theories are characterized as those bold theories of what is the case in the world which are, in principle at least, refutable by reference to empirical evidence. The development and testing of such theories is not, however, what professional educational researchers have hitherto been funded to do, nor is it characteristic of educational research in general.

Much educational practice is based on assumptions that could be, but have not been, formulated in a way which encourages the search for refutation. Formal education rests largely on ideas which have not been subject to rigorous testing of the kind discussed in this chapter. Thus, there is considerable scope for the development of a Popperian non-inductive science of education. Researchers should be encouraged, for example, to develop bold theories of what is the case about classroom practice; to formulate these theories in such a way that they can be tested (by the search for refuting evidence); and to devise situations in which these theories can be put to the test. In general, I urge educationists to formulate ideas about the policy and practice of education in such a way that counter-evidence is conceivable, and then to search for it (see Chapters 5 and 8 for discussion about testing solutions to practical problems).

It should be noted that I am not in favour of limiting educational research to the models advocated in this chapter and in Chapter 8. In particular, there is clearly a place for research which addresses mismatches between what is known and what is desired to be known, and where hypotheses have yet to be formulated (exemplified in the discussion of learning through reading). Of questionable value, however, is educational research which implies that generalizable theories can be abstracted from data collection by a process which assumes induction. When guided by the 'logic' of induction, the pursuit of generalizable theories tends to result in theories with limited informative content; because the researchers have failed to consider situations in which the theories do not apply, the theories are of little practical use or, worse, they may be harmful. If researchers and funders of research wish to promote the growth of knowledge, they must be prepared to discover where their theories fail. Both research and policy development properly involve the reconstruction of ideas from the discovery of error (and, to a lesser extent, inadequacy). Some occasions for discoveries of this kind are, of course, better than others; it is better to discover error in a research model, scale model, prototype or pilot study, rather than in a widely distributed artefact or far-reaching policy.

David Miller relates how 'Popper prescribes revolutionary thinking in science because its products, imaginative new theories, are easily relinquished if they are mistaken', and how 'he proscribes revolutionary activity in society' on the grounds that 'its consequences, which are rarely possible to foresee, are almost always altogether impossible to overcome' (Miller 1985:12). While agreeing with this thesis at the macro-level, I suggest there is value in the introduction of micro-revolutions in society, specifically in formal education. An implication of Popper's logical analysis of the growth of knowledge in general, and science in particular, is that we need not shy away from reasoned small-scale radical change, provided that its introduction is used rigorously to test the theories which underpin such change.

NOTE

This chapter draws on discussion in Swann 1995, 1998a and 1999.

Chapter 3

The Abdication of Reason: Postmodern Attacks Upon Science and Reason

RICHARD BAILEY

> There is one thing a professor can be certain of: almost every student entering the university believes, or says he believes, that truth is relative ... The relativity of truth is not a theoretical insight but a moral postulate, the condition of a free society, or so they see it.
>
> Allan Bloom (1987:25)

THE POSTMODERN POST-MORTEM

We live, we are told, in postmodern times. Many of the ideas in our intellectual environment have been challenged and rejected. Science and rationalism, in particular, including the kinds of ideas set out in this book, have been the victims of sustained attacks from cultural critics, sociologists, educationists and an array of others proclaiming a new era of uncertainty, complexity and change.

The first barrier facing anyone who wishes to consider postmodern thought is the difficulty of identifying quite what it is. There exists no standard definition, no pivotal text, and no agreed founding father. Yet it is a fashionable movement whose influence can be discerned in almost every field of academic inquiry. The term 'postmodernism' originated in 1960s literary criticism; writers identified the demise of the modernist movement and heralded postmodernism as its successor. It was then quickly adopted by intellectuals in other areas. Key figures within the movement – Michel Foucault, Jacques Derrida, Richard Rorty, Sandra Harding, and others – have achieved worldwide fame (or infamy), but their influence has been felt most forcefully among members of the intellectual left of continental Europe and America.[1]

Clarity of expression is not a quality immediately associated with postmodern theorizing. Indeed, its supporters recognize (and at times celebrate) this: 'the corpus of postmodern theorizing, read as a single discourse, is definitionally incoherent and even contradictory' (Billig and

Simons 1994:5. See Tarnas 1991, and Rabinow 1986, for similar boasts of opacity). As a result, there exists a certain slipperiness to the position that exposes any criticism of it to claims of misunderstanding and misrepresentation.

Fortunately, there seem to be themes common to the position. Most fundamental of these is a general assumption of the breakdown of established forms of knowledge and inquiry, specifically those associated with the Enlightenment's self-confident pursuit of truth and reality: science and rationality. Lather (1994:102) summarizes postmodernism as a 'codename' for the crisis of confidence in the Western conceptual system. The different schools accepting this general position – post-structuralism, deconstructivism, cultural constructivism, eco-afro-feminism – share an assumption of this crisis. Use of the generic descriptor, postmodernism, therefore does not imply any unanimity of views but rather a shorthand for a style of theorizing that is common to a cluster of viewpoints.

Earlier critics of the Enlightenment 'project' condemned it for failing to provide an adequate representation of the world and its underlying objective truth. Thinkers such as Theodore Adorno and Herbert Marcuse went to great lengths to expose its superficial objectivity, and while they did not provide a generally accepted alternative, there remained an implicit assumption in their work that an alternative could be found. The postmodernists have taken the criticism a step further, and claim that the pursuit of such objectivity will always be doomed to fail as the pursuit presupposes that objectivity exists (Gellner, 1992). The world does not exist as a thing-in-itself, independent of human interpretation, but as an 'historically contingent product of linguistic and social practices of particular local communities of interpreters' (Tarnas 1991:399). Moreover, since all human experience is linguistically bound, and the different linguistic structures have no evident foundation in an external reality, the mind is forever forced to assume the particular form of life of its community. Thus, the mind does not perceive reality, but constructs it. In case this position is thought to be one of metaphor or poetry, Rorty states:

> it is pointless to ask whether there really are mountains or whether it is merely convenient for us to talk about mountains ... Given that it pays to talk about mountains, as it certainly does, one of the obvious truths about mountains is that they were here before we talked about them. If you do not believe that, you probably do not know how to play the usual language-games which employ the word 'mountain'. But the utility of those language-games has nothing to do with the question of whether Reality as It Is In Itself, apart from the way it is handy for human beings to describe it, has mountains in it. (Rorty 1994:56–7)

PLAYING THE LANGUAGE GAME

For the postmodern mind, 'objectivity' is not merely elusive, but unattainable. There is no Archimedean point from which it is possible to judge the veracity of statements about the world. Knowledge, as it is conventionally understood, amounts to no more than an interpretation of 'meanings'. No interpretation can claim final authority, since it must, in turn, be dependent upon other interpretations which are further dependent upon others, leading to an infinite regress. All meanings, therefore, are ultimately undecidable. What we mistakenly take to be experience and knowledge are 'narratives'; they are fictions we create to satisfy a need for meaning, and the 'objects' of our experience are 'texts' ('Il n'y a pas de hors-texte' – 'There is nothing outside the text' – is the oft-cited motto of Jacques Derrida).

Rather than undertaking the fruitless quest for reality, the wise man 'deconstructs' the meanings of the different texts that confront him. The literary roots of postmodernism are, therefore, not insignificant since the method (if that is an appropriate term) takes on many of the characteristics of that subject, but carried out on a grand scale. Each author's (or object of observation's) meaning is distinctive and subjective, and forever open to analysis and criticism; so too is the reader's (or observer's) response. Rather than chasing the illusory 'objective truth', we are led to pursue 'hermeneutic truth', acknowledging the subjectivity of both the inquirer and the inquiry itself (Gellner 1992:29). Subjectivity, therefore, is doubly potent, since it conditions not only the object of inquiry, but also the inquirer. The subject can never transcend its subjectivity, it can only attempt to bring together perspectives in a continuous interplay between the subject and the object: 'Instead of commenting on a text or a practice in ways that define it, a deconstructive approach links our "reading" to ourselves as socially situated spectators' (Lather 1994:124[2]).

DECONSTRUCTING SCIENCE

The postmodern approach is thus claimed to be as applicable to science, logic and mathematics as it is to literature, because every form of human experience is meaning-laden and textual by nature. Scientists' claims of objectivity are self-deceiving: they are no better able to detect objective reality than anyone else. (Presumably, they are less able, as they remain blissfully unaware of their ignorance!) The concepts that scientists use to structure their view of the world – such as gravity, causality, truth and falsity – are purely metaphors that give meaning to their task. What scientists naïvely think of as facts are really 'events to which we have given meaning' (Hutcheon 1989:57), and this applies to every feature of their work, no matter how seemingly neutral. Presumably, this is what Luce Irigaray means by the following:

> Is $E = Mc^2$ a sexed equation? Perhaps it is. Let us make the hypothesis that it is insofar as it privileges the speed of light over other speeds that are vitally necessary to us. What seems to me to indicate the possibly sexed nature of the equation is not directly its uses by nuclear weapons, rather it is having privileged what goes the fastest . . . (Translated and quoted in Sokal and Bricmont 1998:100)

Science has succeeded, however, in giving its narratives a mythical sense of objectivity, while de-legitimizing alternative language games (Redding 1986). Science and its associated sense of rationality have become central to the ideology of the modern age (Billig and Simons 1994:4). They cannot be used to deconstruct that ideology because they are central to it. The objectivity that science proclaims amounts to a tool of domination. Alternative forms of inquiry and understanding are necessarily suppressed and disempowered, and their adherents are forced to accept the dominant ideology along with its inherent bias in terms of gender, class, race and ethnicity: '[science is] not only sexist but also racist, classist, and culturally coercive ... Physics and chemistry, mathematics and logic, bear the fingerprints of their distinctive cultural creators no less than do anthropology and history' (Harding 1986:9, 250).

Postmodernism is a subversive response to this oppression, and deconstruction is framed as an act of liberation and empowerment. Unorthodox perspectives receive sympathetic consideration while those endorsed by the establishment are subject to sustained and radical attack. It is implicit in the nature of science, rationality, logic, mathematics and innumerable other aspects of thought that this should be so. Indeed, the entire Western intellectual canon, defined by a white, male, middle-class elite, has been vigorously attacked and rejected by postmodernists:

> Under the cloak of Western values, too many sins have been committed. Disenchanted eyes are now cast onto the West's long history of ruthless expansionism and exploitation – the rapacity of its elites ... its systematic thriving at the expense of others, its colonialism and imperialism, its slavery and genocide, its anti-Semitism, its oppression of women, people of color, minorities, homosexuals, the working classes, the poor, its destruction of indigenous societies throughout the world, its arrogant insensitivity to other cultural traditions and values, its cruel abuse of other forms of life, its blind ravaging of virtually the entire planet. (Tarnas 1991:400)

A 'WHIFF' OF RELATIVISM

The postmodern critique of Western culture presents a startling image. It may come as something of a shock to some readers to discover that they are victims, and in some cases perpetrators, of such crimes against humanity. Despite his enlistment of almost every marginalized group within society, Tarnas' indictment of Western imperialism and oppression is not persuasive, and is entirely at odds with the values endorsed by the vast majority of Enlightenment thinkers.

So how should we respond to such a proclamation? To begin with, perhaps, we should point out that it is nonsense. A great deal of postmodern theorizing alternates between banality and absurdity, between triviality posing as revelation and bizarre claims that conflict with common sense. That, in itself, is not unusual: anti-scientific and anti-rational philosophies are an ever-present feature of life. But, while these are mostly harmless follies, postmodernism has managed to find a place in the university curricula of social scientists, philosophers and, most alarming of all, educationists.

Nevertheless, it would be wrong to dismiss every aspect of the postmodern position. There is, of course, an element of truth to the relativistic claim that there is a large subjective element in science and rationality. There is a 'whiff' of relativism inherent in any human enterprise; however, this is not a flaw, it is a necessary condition for science's success. An individual's background constrains and directs his knowledge, so that his interests are influenced by his training and the perceived problems of the day. Observations are conditioned by systems of classification and expectation that must be (provisionally) assumed, therefore some basic assumptions relating to knowledge and method are treated as immune from criticism. Thus, science insists upon a degree of conformity and control in its members, just as the wider society enforces acceptance of specific basic values and standards of behaviour of its citizens. However, just as a society can be unjustifiably restrictive and intolerant of dissenters, so can science, or any area of human life. Rather than being an argument against the institution of science, the recognition of this fact should be taken as a warning against an abuse of that institution.

Sociologists of science have long recognized that politics and other human affairs impinge upon scientific practice. Scientists, like the rest of us, are prone to pride, jealousy, dishonesty and greed. Anthropological studies of 'laboratory behaviour' provide fascinating insights into the idiosyncrasy, irrationalism and petty politics that sometimes interfere with scientific practice. In their observations of scientists at work, Latour and Woolgar (1979:237) noted that 'The negotiations as to what counts as a proof or what constitutes a good assay are no more or less disorderly than any argument between lawyers or politicians.' This observation will be familiar to anyone who has worked in a laboratory.

However, it is not a valid logical step from the recognition that science is a social process that takes place in a social setting to the conclusion, drawn by postmodernists and others, that scientific theories are so because of social and historical forces acting in this process (Weinberg 1993:149). Whether a scientist or a group behaves in a particular way is not the central issue, because science is a public inter-subjective activity in which all findings must be repeatable, and thus all science, however flawed its individual practitioners might be, is ultimately accountable. If an individual fabricates evidence, or presents an erroneous argument, he has to undergo the conventional series of trials by peers, both formal and informal, before his work can enter the public domain. If the work gets that far, it then has to survive the pressure of fellow scientists trying to replicate the results. Moreover, scientific theories are usually expected to have applicability to the world of everyday observation; they can then be evaluated outside the cosseted realms of the initiated.

TU QUOQUE?

> It is usually a good strategy to ask whether a general claim about truth
> or meaning applies to itself.
>
> (Nagel 1997:15)

The leap of logic from the commonsense recognition that all human practices, including the most hallowed realms of objectivity, occur within social, historical and cultural situations, to the claim that all is subjectivity, condemns postmodernists to self-contradiction and paradox. If 'everything is subjective', then a distinction cannot be made between what is the case and what is not, between right and wrong; if the distinction can be made, then the subjectivist position must be incorrect.[3] In practice, therefore, even if postmodernists choose to analyse the world in relativistic terms, their proposals must be understood as non-relativistic accounts of how the world really is (Gellner 1992:81). Similarly, the standards against which the wildly inaccurate and simplistic claims regarding the inherent oppression and imperialism of the Eurocentric mind-set are compared (as in the indictment made by Tarnas 1991, and quoted earlier) use a language of morality that is derived from that very same mind-set.

Postmodernists are unable to meet the standards that they themselves set. The influential advocate, Jean-François Lyotard (1984) defined the essence of the postmodern stance as a loss of faith in the grand meta-narrative. In the words of Tarnas (1991:401): 'Any alleged comprehensive, coherent outlook is at best no more than a temporarily useful fiction masking chaos, at worst an oppressive fiction masking relationships of power, violence and subordination.' However, the postmodernists' assumption of superiority over scientific, rational views, and their advancement of an alternative approach, presuppose a meta-narrative of their own. It is difficult to see how a recognition of this 'unstable paradox that permeates the postmodern mind' (Tarnas 1991:402) is capable of rescuing it from fatality.

ANYTHING GOES ... EVERYTHING STAYS[4]

The character of the postmodernists' non-relativistic outlook is generally moral. A great deal of their writing proclaims a defence of under-represented and oppressed groups within society, such as women, non-Western ethnic groups, the working class, homosexuals, and so on, and this often overshadows its other epistemological and ontological aims. Paul Feyerabend, the 'anarchist' philosopher of science, admits as much in the introduction to *Against Method* (1988:3): 'My main motive in writing the book was humanitarian, not intellectual. I wanted to support people, not to "advance knowledge".'

A positive contribution that could be claimed on behalf of the writers discussed is that they have reiterated (but not introduced) the importance of challenging narrow and unrepresentative conceptions of science and rationality. It would be foolish to deny that large sections of the population have distinctive and valuable talents that have, to some extent, been neglected. It may well be the case that science and our pursuit of knowledge have suffered as a result, and that increasing access to women and members of currently marginalized cultures would offer us richer, more innovative ways of looking at the world.

A difficulty is that those who propose a postmodern slant on the matter often proceed from coherent arguments about equality of opportunity, and the recognition of under-valued contributions to the growth of knowledge, to statements condemning the inherent andro-centric or Eurocentric bias of science and rationality.[5] Assertions that logic, mathematics and science are inescapably sexist, classist and racist, if believed, create a barrier to participation and success among marginalized groups far more impregnable than currently exists. They are also offensive to those groups (Pinker 1998:50).

Though imperfect, and practised in a social environment that is prone to prejudice, scientific and rational approaches offer the most successful methods yet discovered by which truth may be pursued. Postmodernists are able neither to explain the success of science nor provide a viable alternative. By blurring the distinction between fact and fiction, and by dismissing evidence, logical argument and rigour, as relics of an imperialist and repressive past, their rhetoric disempowers the very people they aim to save:

> It is . . . pretty suicidal for embattled minorities to embrace Michel Foucault, let alone Jacques Derrida. The minority view was always that power could be undermined by truth . . . Once you read Foucault as saying that truth is simply an effect of power, you've had it . . . But American departments of literature, history and sociology contain large numbers of self-described leftists who have confused radical doubts about objectivity with political radicalism, and are in a mess. (Ryan 1992:21. See also Hobsbawm 1993, and Chalmers 1990.)

It must be annoying to anti-science theorists that cultures which have apparently been most alienated and oppressed by the scientific world-view, such as Third World countries, are those which are now most desperate to embrace it.

CONCLUSION

> All our science, measured against reality, is primitive and childlike – and yet it is the most precious thing we have.
> (Albert Einstein, quoted in Sagan 1996:6)

It is easy for ideas as successful and institutionalized as science and rationality to become cosy certainties, seldom questioned and threatened. One positive effect of the postmodern movement has been to raise some doubts. As it emphatically rejects the core elements of traditional reasoning, its critique is necessarily radical and potentially challenging. Another consequence has been to raise awareness of a number of important issues for society, not least of which involve groups that continue to be under-represented and alienated.

Sadly, postmodernist attacks upon science and reason have rarely been constructive. Nor have they been fair. The typical presentation of their opponents is little more than a crude caricature: knowledge becomes certainty; criticism becomes repression; the only considered alternative to radical relativism is tyrannical absolutism. Consider, for example, Richard Brown's (1994:27) words of comfort to those who fear the consequences of non-judgemental relativism: 'Which is worse, the possibility that evil will be tolerated in the name of cultural relativism, or the promise that atrocities will be justified by some group's assurance that they are absolutely right?' Presumably the latter. This is, however, a naïve and misleading argument.

A fascinating thought-experiment would be to turn postmodernism's deconstructive armoury upon itself, to begin to understand the 'narratives' of its advocates: their backgrounds, their motives, their ideologies. It may be significant that postmodernist discourse is only accessible to a small number of inductees who have learned the peculiar patois that constitutes the characteristic form of 'inquiry'. It might also be interesting to note that despite the great sympathy expressed towards under-represented groups, postmodernism is practised largely by white middle-class Western academics living comfortable and protected lives.

Another explanation has been offered by Wilson (1998:46), who mischievously suggested that part of the attraction might be the relief it offers 'those who have chosen not to encumber themselves with a scientific education'. A startling example of scientific illiteracy is found in the work of the celebrated postmodern philosopher of science, Bruno Latour. In discussing the discovery that Pharaoh Rameses II died around 1213 BCE of tuberculosis, he asks: 'How could he pass away due to a bacillus discovered by Robert Koch in 1882?' (quoted in Sokal and Bricmont 1997:88, note 123). The highly publicized 'Sokal Affair' is also informative in this respect: an American physicist produced a hoax article, full of absurdities, contradictions and bizarre leaps of logic, which was nevertheless accepted and published by a leading journal sympathetic to postmodern thought (Sokal and Bricmont 1998:Appendix A). Despite the fact that Sokal loosely linked a series of passages that were 'absurd or meaningless' (Sokal and Bricmont 1998:3), they authentically represented the views of leading French and American intellectuals on mathematics and physics.

It would be easy to dismiss the current popularity of postmodern thinking as a passing fad, owing its appeal to its seeming novelty and genuine obscurity (Gellner 1992:71). This may be the case, but it fails to acknowledge the mis-education that could result from such a fad. By systematically training students in the use of empty jargon and cryptic language games, postmodern teachers and theorists threaten the knowledge and understanding of a generation of students.

NOTES

1. Of course, a history of the development of postmodern ideas is beyond the remit of this chapter. An admirable, uncharacteristically clear and sympathetic attempt is made by Richard Tarnas (1991).
2. Lather (1994) offers an interesting portrayal of her research into education practice. Abandoning the 'fetish of documentation or legitimation' (Van Maanen 1988:23) typical of the discredited scientific methodology, she built up her 'database' from 'interviews, research reports, journal entries and my own insights/musings' (Lather 1994:102). As a postmodern teacher she recognizes that pedagogy is itself a text. Her duty, therefore, is to initiate the deconstruction by herself and her students of that text. Rather than envisage teaching as involving the transference of knowledge, she sees it as 'the transformation of consciousness that takes place in the intersection of the teacher, the learner and the knowledge they together produce' (1994:104). (A revealing analysis of possible models for postmodern teaching is offered by Simons, 1994, in the edited book in which Lather's chapter appears.)
3. This resembles very closely the famous 'Liar's Paradox' which dates back to the time of Plato or before (Musgrave 1993:269–71).
4. This is an abridgement of John Krige's (1980:142) comment that '*anything goes* ... means that, in practice, *everything stays.*'
5. See, for example, the contributors to Garry and Pearsall (1989); also Harding (1986:113), who famously and bizarrely argued that Isaac Newton's *Principia Mathematica* could be described as a 'rape manual'.

ACKNOWLEDGEMENTS

I would like to thank Richard Harris, Tony Macfadyen and Elizabeth Atkinson for some very useful comments on an earlier draft of this chapter. None should be held responsible for either content or errors.

Chapter 4

Testing Policy

JOHN PRATT

A policy is a hypothesis which has to be tested against reality and
corrected in the light of experience.

Bryan Magee (1973:75)

One of the aims of educational research (discussed in Chapter 1) is to affect
the development of education policy. The relationship between the two,
however, is not straightforward; it raises the same kinds of questions about the
purpose of research, and about epistemology and method, as those generated
by research into any other social (or indeed physical) phenomena. Debate
about policy-making (both generally and in education) and into research into
policy has reflected the controversy about the nature of social and
educational research (summarized in Chapter 1). In this chapter I discuss
some of that debate, and set out an approach to the study of policy which is
explicitly based on the realist epistemology advocated in this book.

POLICY AND EDUCATIONAL RESEARCH

The Organisation for Economic Co-operation and Development report
(1995), discussed in Chapter 1, drew attention to the different purposes for
which educational research may be undertaken. Not all of these purposes
serve policy-makers – and there is no reason why they should. Some research
is designed for those in education who have no role in policy-making; some
research is, in effect, the academic community talking to itself, developing new
concepts or critiques of existing ones. Educational research also legitimately
explores issues of education in its wider social context, often to the dislike or
discomfort of policy-makers. Educational research nevertheless can, and
should, contribute to policy in several different ways. It can serve instrumental
ends, such as the improvement of decision-making in the classroom or school,
and actual educational practice. More generally, it can contribute to
policy-making through its ability to problematize and inform issues faced by

policy-makers and practitioners. In a democratic society, it has a vital function in offering a critical challenge to conventional beliefs and practices. This does not mean it offers 'the answer' on any policy issue: 'It is in the very nature of research to raise more questions than it can answer, or to seek to answer questions that have not been formulated yet' (OECD 1995:30). Understanding what kinds of questions these are assists us to understand how research, and particularly a realist approach, can help to make better policy.

Policy is predominantly concerned with what my colleagues and I at the Centre for Institutional Studies at the University of East London have come to refer to as 'How to . . . ?' questions. In education, for example, policy is greatly concerned with such questions as: 'How can we best educate children of different abilities?' and 'How can higher education be made accessible to a wide range of students?' We distinguish these kinds of questions from 'What is the case?' or 'Why . . . ?' questions (see Chapter 2), which are the predominant concern of social and physical science and which, generally, produce 'propositional knowledge' (Eraut 1994). (We also distinguish them from other kinds of question such as the formal problems of mathematics, or the moral ones of ethics – see Chapter 5.) This has a number of implications.

The distinction raises questions about the relationship between theory and action. Whilst policy may rely on explicit theory or implicit assumptions about *why* things happen, such as that children learn best in small groups because they receive more attention from a teacher (which may or may not be true, but is a testable proposition susceptible to social scientific analysis), establishing answers to theoretical questions is not the purpose of policy. For the policy-maker in the 'real world' of time, financial constraint and public pressure to act, the empirical statement may be enough (provided it is accurate). Developing and testing the explanatory theory may be more the concern of the policy analyst, or social scientist, producing the empirical result as 'knowledge' for use by policy-makers (and with luck, policy-making might be improved by this). *That* it happens, in policy, is what matters. Children cannot wait for educational research to test all conceivable propositions about learning, or explore all conceivable contexts; they need to be educated *now*. Uninformed or ill-informed action is dangerous, but so too is inaction.

In the practical world of policy, we need to act on whatever knowledge-base is available. It may not be necessary to know exactly why things work, if we are reasonably assured that they do. The method of trial and error, and versions of it, as we shall see below, is advocated by policy analysts (as well as by Popper and other philosophers of science). The method can have practical advantages – certainly of time – over an approach which concentrates on 'Why . . . ?' questions. Researchers (and policy-makers) have been known to argue that we should not act to remedy some pressing ill until we understand all the underlying issues. Indeed, Corson in Chapter 6 appears to do so, and a government working party in the 1970s chaired by Professor David Donnison argued that no action should be taken about social deprivation until 'the theoretical framework for the understanding of the whole phenomenon' was 'firmly constructed' (quoted in Tunley *et al.* 1979:10). This can condemn a generation. Trying different solutions, with care, may identify helpful courses of action.

Yet policy-makers need theoretical knowledge – knowledge about the likely consequences of alternative courses of action. But in this they face some difficulties that scientists do not. They almost invariably have to act in circumstances which they may not fully be able to control. This is a far cry from the traditional (though largely misleading) view of science as the controlled experiment in a laboratory, under rigorous conditions of safety and elimination of extraneous variables. Policy is much more like engineering than science. Many criticisms of social science and educational research arise from the failure (often on the part of social scientists themselves) to understand this distinction.

Policy is a social artefact, more analogous with a physical artefact than it is with a scientific theory such as the law of gravity. Whilst the law of gravity explains and predicts the behaviour of a mass of metal such as an aircraft in its relation to the mass of matter called the Earth, it does not exactly predict (even leaving aside human factors) all the consequences of operating this complex artefact. There are many variables, some unanticipated (metal fatigue, for example, in the ill-fated *Comet*); some, like the weather, will probably remain unpredictable; and they may all interact in unpredictable ways. You have to test the aircraft to identify its actual behaviour, for example in stalling, landing at high speed and so on. The physical sciences offer far less convincing and all-embracing explanations and predictions of complex real-world phenomena than is often thought; answering 'Why . . . ?' questions does not necessarily provide answers to 'How to . . . ?' questions, least of all quickly. The development of chaos and complexity theory in both the physical and social worlds reflects this (see, for example, Eve *et al.* 1997). In policy, there are similarly many variables interacting unpredictably. One need only think of the complexity of the classroom – with such variables as teacher attitude, pupils' backgrounds, imposed curricula, school ethos, resource limitations – to understand why predictability is difficult to achieve.

Since ill-informed action is dangerous, research can be undertaken to generate knowledge that can be applied in particular circumstances and on which policy-makers may draw, though the evidence is that they do not do so sufficiently (Lampinen 1992). Moreover, policy-makers require knowledge about which there is some security regarding its validity, and an understanding of its limitations. Research can develop understanding and explanation, a knowledge-base which can inform policy-makers. This knowledge can be of many kinds – it is as likely to be locally embedded (and arising from reflection on practice) as it is to be formal theory. In educational policy, knowledge of particular aspects of the social world is needed. Realist research can help to provide this.

APPROACHES TO POLICY-MAKING

The literature on policy-making and policy analysis has reflected the general debate about social science and the problems it presents, and has thus gone through a number of paradigm shifts. There was a burgeoning of literature on policy-making, and in particular the decision-making process, in the decades after the Second World War. The war had shown how effective 'scientific' approaches – such as operations research – could be managed by military (and also civil) programmes. Later, in the 1970s, in the United States in particular, there was a series of efforts to link scientific knowledge and policy development in such programmes as Lyndon B. Johnson's 'Great Society'. It was during this period that many of the classical 'rational' and 'ideal' models (for example, Simon 1947, 1957, 1960) were posited, and – equally – rebutted (for example, Lindblom 1959). Both Simon and Lindblom described these 'ideal' models, which focused on the process of decision-making and choice of policy options. Though different, they contained common elements, including comprehensive information-gathering, the identification of values, the specification of objectives, generation of all possible options for achieving these objectives, and finally the choice of which options would maximize the values defined as being the most important. The literature tended to see this technical–rational approach as an ideal rather than an achievable goal, assisting in a move towards more rational behaviour. Later, in the 1980s and 1990s, very similar elements could be seen in the fashionable strategic planning approaches transferred from the private sector to public policy, although these covered more than just the decision-making process (for example, Stewart Howe 1986; Bryson 1995).

Lindblom (1979) went on to show that policy-makers are unlikely to follow this ideal process and that, in fact, 'muddling through' (a method of trial and error) is a far better description of reality. He argued that the pursuit of some unattainable ideal was actually detrimental to 'good' policy-making, and advocated a variety of incremental approaches. Simon (1960), too, discussed the limits to rationality in real-life policy-making, but believed that policy-makers could move towards more rational policy-making through use of the 'new science of management decision'. This view was, to some extent, supported by Dror (1968, 1971) who argued for an 'economically rational model' in which rational analysis in decision-making is pursued only as far as the benefit outweighs the cost.

The debate about policy-making shifted as stress was gradually placed on the importance of policy implementation. Ideal-type models seemed to assume that implementation would work automatically if policy decisions were made in the 'right' way, but the publication of Pressman and Wildavsky's (1973) study generated interest in the need to understand policy 'failure', which was seen as the outcome of many of the ambitious programmes adopted by governments during the 1960s and 1970s to deal with complex social problems. Quade (1975:1), for example, writing of the United States' experience, recorded that 'solutions have often been announced, but when they have been tried out, they are disappointing at best, and frequently seem to leave the situation worse off than if nothing had been done . . . Dissatisfaction with the results of the decision-making processes in use by government is apparent.' He argued that policy analysis should 'help public decision-makers make better choices' (Quade 1975:13).

The concept of policy failure assumes, of course, that there are problems which prevent a particular policy from being implemented successfully. It draws a line between the decision-making process, the outcome of which is a particular policy, and the implementation process, the outcome of which is seen as the success or failure of the policy. Failure can thus arise for different reasons. In their synthesis of approaches to policy-making, Hogwood and Gunn (1984) distinguished between 'non-implementation' and 'unsuccessful implementation'. In the former case, a policy is not put into effect as intended. In the latter, a policy is carried out in full but fails to produce the intended results. Failure, according to Hogwood and Gunn (1984:197), can in this case be attributed to 'bad policy'.

This view still implies an ideal-type approach to policy-making. It assumes that policy is a set of objectives which will be implemented, provided that the preconditions necessary for them to be achieved are present. This assumption suggests an obvious parallel with a scientific hypothesis. But numerous authors have acknowledged that there are unavoidable practical limitations to ideal-type policy-making. The classical rationalists, such as Simon and Lindblom, identify, for example, the lack of time and resources to undertake the laborious iterative process of generation and analysis of alternative solutions, human limitations and failings, and organizational constraints. Others, like Allison (1971), reflecting the more general argument about the 'relativity' of social science, showed how different people's 'conceptual lenses' lead to different interpretations of events, and hence different outcomes. Dror (1986), characterizing 'policy-making under adversity', showed how governments react irrationally to adverse circumstances. Putting these concerns another way, Hogwood and Gunn (1984:199–206) identified eight preconditions for 'perfect implementation' covering external circumstances, time and resources, agreement on objectives, compliance by those involved, and so on.

One of Hogwood and Gunn's preconditions for successful policy was that the policy is based on a valid theory of cause and effect; that is, the policy to be implemented is, in fact, an appropriate means for achieving the policy-makers' goal. (This typically Popperian idea is expanded below.) If this is not the case, policy failure can be the outcome. But one problem with ideal-type models is that what might be seen as bad policy from the point of view of analysts may be regarded as an excellent result from another point of view. In practice, policy is rarely underpinned by a clear or fixed set of objectives which come out of the decision-making process. Simon's (1957:198) and Lindblom's (1979:518) acceptance of limitations on ideal policy-making ('bounded rationality') reflected this. Lindblom (1979:523) referred to a process of 'partisan mutual adjustment' in decision-making whereby the various actors or organizations in a 'polycentric' system negotiate. In 'disjointed incrementalism' (Lindblom 1979:518) the outcome and the process are intertwined. Nor, as Barrett and Fudge (1981) pointed out, is implementation necessarily a logical step-by-step progression from policy intention to action. They augmented this criticism with an attack on what they saw as the top-down or managerial approach of ideal-type models, which tend 'to be associated with hierarchical concepts of organization; policy emanates from the "top" (or centre) and is transmitted down the hierarchy (or to the periphery)'. The policy is 'translated into more specific rules and procedures as it goes to guide or control action at the bottom (or on the ground)' (1981:12).

Barrett and Fudge's critique was an example of a general shift in policy analysis to one which sees both policy-making and policy implementation as processes of interaction and negotiation, and which emphasizes wider social, political and organizational factors. Habermas (1976:146), for example, saw the ideal-model approach as dangerously utopian. Others recognized the local embeddedness of policy and of knowledge about it; they sought in research to understand social phenomena by recognizing the different experiences and perceptions of different actors. Barrett and Fudge presented an alternative 'action-centred' approach, which observes what actually happens or gets done and seeks to understand how and why; this involves, in particular, '*power relations* and different mechanisms for gaining or avoiding influence or control' (1981:13). In educational research, this approach is typified by studies, such as those of Ball (1987) and Blase and Anderson (1995), into the micro-politics of schools. Shore and Wright's (1997) anthropological approach to policy is a further development of this idea, whilst Marsh and Rhodes (1992) and Marsh (1998) describe and analyse 'policy networks' – the links between actors in any particular policy domain.

Yet policy, and public policy in particular, does, explicitly or implicitly, involve an assumption of the kind, 'If you do this, then that will happen' – however much it may be modified in the course of events. For this reason, Hogwood and Gunn (1984) reject the criticisms of the top-down perspective. They express concern with Barrett and Fudge's ready acceptance of the tendency of lower-level actors to take decisions which effectively limit hierarchical influence, pre-empt top-level decision-making or alter policies. They maintain that while implementation necessarily involves a process of interaction between organizations, the members of which may have different values, perspectives and priorities from one another and from those advocating the policy, much of this interaction can and should take place before policy formulation. They argue that 'those seeking to put policy into effect' are usually elected, while 'those upon whom action depends' usually are not (Hogwood and Gunn 1984:207), though this argument clearly applies only to policy of particular kinds (mainly that of public authorities), and it imports a value preference into a discussion of empirical issues.

As this argument makes clear, one problem with the shift of focus in policy analysis to micro-politics and negotiating processes in policy-making and implementation, however valuable it may be in understanding and explaining practice and outcomes, is that it tends to lose track of some important questions, such as whether the policy accomplished what was intended, either in the first place or as it was later amended, and what its consequences have been. The shift in focus may be illuminating for analysts of policy, but for those making it, carrying it out, and particularly those on whom it acts – the beneficiaries (or victims) – knowing whether or not it actually works is of some importance. In Hogwood and Gunn's own terminology, 'unsuccessful implementation' occurs when policy 'fails to produce the intended results (or outcomes)' (1984:197). Is a policy which is altered in the course of implementation, but which produces the intended results, a 'worse' policy than one which is implemented in its original form but does the opposite of what was intended by policy-makers? As with much of the wider debate in the social sciences, the two views are not mutually exclusive: knowing how policy intentions get amended is of importance to those making and carrying out policy.

A REALIST APPROACH

An approach which focuses on the policy process in terms of outcomes and the impact of policy avoids the normative trap of putting any intrinsic value on either top-down or bottom-up implementation. Such an analysis can still be directed at improving policy implementation, but the benefit would come from its concern with how the policy actually worked in practice. An approach of this kind was developed as far back as 1970 at the Centre for Institutional Studies at what was then North East London Polytechnic. The CIS approach has proved useful in a number of studies of public policy in the United Kingdom and elsewhere (see Chapters 7 and 12). It is based on the realist empiricist ideas set out in this book, and draws on and substantially develops some of Popper's work on social science (Popper 1961, 1966a, 1966b, 1976a). Further comparable (though by no means identical) developments are found in the work of Corson (see Chapter 6), and we can identify with aspects of the work of Sayer (1992) and Pawson and Tilley (1997) on realism and realist explanation in social science and evaluation.

The approach focuses on the problems that policies can be seen to be designed to solve. It has the virtues of a 'rational' approach in that it makes policies susceptible to a similar kind of critical analysis to that of scientific theories (see Chapter 2), and offers grounds for policy choice in terms of their effectiveness in solving problems. But it also recognizes that various actors have different definitions of rationality. By analysing policies in terms of their success or failure in problem-solving, it allows researchers to assess the effectiveness of policies without accepting that what policy-makers do is necessarily rational. It is essentially pluralist, allowing alternative formulations of the problems to be tested. It is able to deal with the conflicts or anarchy which often occur during the implementation process.

Unfortunately for students of this approach, Popper was never as interested in social science as he was in the natural sciences (1992:121), and his views are spread inconveniently in discussions of other topics. He offers no direct discussion of a theory of policy analysis. His epistemology is nevertheless particularly apt. The CIS approach relies on Popper's critical rationalism, embodied in the logic through which intellectual progress is made. His simplified schema of conjecture and refutation – starting with the formulation of a problem for which a trial solution is proposed, rigorously tested to eliminate error, and leading to a new situation with new problems – was discussed in Chapter 2. Scientific method (whether in the social or natural sciences) is thus one of trial and error, of inventing hypotheses which can be tested, and submitting them to tests. In policy, as Magee (1973:75) points out, 'All government policies, indeed all executive and administrative decisions, involve empirical predictions: "If we do X, Y will follow: on the other hand if we want to achieve B we must do A."' In this sense, as Magee goes on, 'a policy is a hypothesis' (though it might be more appropriate to say that a policy embodies a hypothesis) since the empirical statements above imply explanatory theories (Y follows X because . . .). Thus policy relies on what Pawson and Tilley (1997:65) refer to as 'explanatory mechanisms' – an '*account* of the make-up, behaviour and interrelationships of those processes which are responsible for [a] regularity' (1997:68). For them, a realist explanation is summarized: regularity = mechanism + context (1997:71). The mechanism consists of propositions about how the interplay between structure (the stratified nature of social reality) and agency (people's choices) constitutes the regularity, and whether or not the regularity occurs depends on the context.

This realist approach has a number of significant implications for policy-making, not least in challenging in significant respects the ideal-type models of the classical policy analysts (as well as the objectives-based approaches that have become fashionable as a result of the application of the 'science of management' in policy and in educational practice – see Chapter 5). As Magee (1973:75) notes in his discussion of Popper's epistemology in policy, 'it is *normal* for [empirical predictions] to have to be modified as their application proceeds'; the policy hypothesis 'has to be tested against reality and corrected in the light of experience.' In this sense, the Popperian view offers epistemological support for the incrementalism of Lindblom (1979) and advocates of process models like Barrett and Fudge (1981). Thus in policy-making as in science, trial and error is an essential part of the process – not a reluctant concession to 'limitations' on an ideal.

Others have extended this argument. Whilst accepting the idea of policy as theory, Majone (1980:153) proposes a craft analogy as more apt, arguing that both science, but even more, policy, uses 'a repertoire of procedures and judgements' and knowledge that is 'less explicit than formalized theoretical knowledge, but more objective than intuition'. It is hard to see some policy-making in any other terms. The radical reorganization of secondary education in England and Wales in the 1960s, for example, was achieved without legislation or regulation. One of the more subtle civil servants of the period, Wilma Harte, knew from experience that, in the circumstances of the time, when the government barely had a majority in Parliament but broad support for the measure, a circular from the Department of Education and Science would be sufficient – and possibly more effective – than a legal sledgehammer. The reorganization was achieved by a civil servant writing to local authorities merely 'requesting' reorganization plans. Such understanding of the nuances of policy-making would not seem to be formal propositional knowledge, though it could be elaborated, as Tyrrell Burgess did, into Harte's Law: 'If you want something done, you must give someone a job to do.'

Elsewhere, Popper (1966a) extended the logic of trial and error to an advocacy of what he called 'piecemeal social engineering' – a process of trial and error in social policy – rejecting as dangerous, tyrannous and ineffective the alternative utopian approach. In this he, again, anticipated later policy analysts, particularly Lindblom (1979). Utopian engineering is an ideal-type in the extreme, though Popper's rejection was on political as well as empirical grounds.

The implications of this stance are more far-reaching than initially they appear to be. Even Popper took an unduly limited view of the implications of his own epistemology to policy and social reform. As Magee said, 'My longest-running argument with the older Popper is about . . . his failure to accept, in . . . practical politics, the radical consequences of his own ideas' (1973:84). One consequence is, as Magee notes, that the approach is 'devoted to change' (1973:85); it draws attention to solving problems, and to the critical testing of policies.

Further, bound up as the approach is with Popper's problem-based theory of knowledge, it focuses attention on the way in which the policy problem has been formulated. This, in turn, raises a number of issues. The ideal-models of policy start with a phase variously called 'issue search' or 'scanning', which implies that the problems are simply there to be 'discovered'. This implies a failure to recognize that problems are *formulated*, and different people may formulate them differently. It is a common experience to find that little attention has been given to problem formulation in specific policy-making. Often the urge is to act, or to be seen to act. The cry is 'the government should do something about . . . '. When it does so without paying attention to the nature of the problem, the result can be characterized as 'knee-jerk policy-making', and can be not only ineffective but damaging. Examples abound in educational policy, as the repeated changes to education legislation in Britain in the 1980s illustrate.

But even less hasty policy-makers often fail to formulate clearly the problems they seek to tackle. Government policy frequently fails to make clear what the problem was – at least in any meaningful way, as several examples in Chapter 7 show. Policy documents often start with some vague, value-laden generalizations, and then set out a series of measures that will be taken. Here the researcher is faced with a number of options. One is to take the formulations as they stand and examine the outcomes. It is important in a democratic society to take seriously what governments say they are trying to do, and to see if they do it. This is a basic Popperian approach to policy, and surprisingly little done, even today in an age of accountability. There are a number of reasons for this. Governments tend not to like critics (recent contracts issued by the Department for Education and Employment require researchers to incorporate the department's amendments to their research studies). More fundamentally, neither policy-makers nor researchers have fully grasped the importance of learning through trial and error. The aim of research is often to show that things work (implying an inductive process) or, at the other extreme, to understand deep, underlying processes – undoubtedly adding to social theory but not always helping to advance policy or practice. (Understanding that we are, probably, in a postmodern age does not of itself tell us what or how to teach.)

Typically, too, governments act to address not the 'real' problem, but what might be called 'problems of the solution'. In education, for example, there is now much national policy about the curriculum, prescribing in tiresome detail what children should be taught, for how long, and so on. Yet the national curriculum was a response to a concern about the alleged power of the teaching profession and of 'producer capture' (Maclure 1989:vi). Such disputes over relativities of power are, in turn, problems of the way in which education policy in general has been implemented, involving allocations of responsibilities, powers and duties variously between central and local authorities, schools and their stakeholders. This elaborate superstructure is a national attempt to address what might be thought of as the 'basic' problem (P_1 in the Popperian schema set out in Chapter 2) of how best to educate children. In this simplified analysis, the imposition of such requirements as a 'literacy hour' is nearer to P_5 than P_1, and it is far from clear to what extent P_1 was part of the formulation of the problem this policy was meant to address.

It is important to note that the approach to policy research outlined here does not limit the researcher to official statements of policy. One advantage is that it opens up a pluralistic approach to policy analysis. Researchers can and should test alternative formulations of the problem. One important contribution of research to policy can be the analysis of the problem. Researchers can help to test whether the evidence supports the public formulation of the problem in a policy document, or whether some other formulation is more consistent with the data. It may well be, as Dror (1986) argued, that the painstaking, incremental 'rational' approach to policy formulation is inapt and ineffective. Imaginative (even irrational) leaps may be needed to see issues and formulate problems in new ways.

SITUATIONAL LOGIC

A Popperian approach enables us to take this idea further. Researchers can look at the problem the policy could be seen as designed to solve, and assess the situation in which the actors find themselves. In this kind of analysis, another of Popper's concepts is useful. The idea of situational logic or situational analysis was developed by Popper in relation to historical explanation, but it applies to public policy as well:

By a situational analysis I mean a certain kind of tentative or conjectural explanation of some human action which appeals to the situation in which the agent finds himself ... [We] can try, conjecturally, to give an idealized reconstruction of the *problem situation* in which the agent found himself, and to that extent make the action 'under-standable' (or 'rationally understandable'), that is to say, *adequate to his situation as he saw it.* (Popper 1979:179)

This technique involves conjecturing what would happen if people follow the logic of their situations. Rationality lies in problem-solving, rather than in a model of 'perfect administration' which assumes that only the rationality of top policy-makers is at issue. Situational logic, in some respects, resembles (and pre-dates) the idea of 'deconstructing' social phenomena. However, its use generates propositions about how people are expected to behave, and thus explanations of their behaviour, which are testable against their actual behaviour. For a Popperian, the wealth of interpretations of social phenomena that are generated by deconstructing may be interesting, but they are also hypotheses for testing. In policy, preferences have to be made between competing policies, and testing alternative hypotheses offers a basis for such preference. Yet one advantage of deconstruction is its imaginative approach, its capacity for formulating innovative interpretations, liberating researchers from testing hypotheses based on accepted authority. Popper, in his concern for the testing of hypotheses, tended to understate the importance of imaginative alternative interpretations. He was less interested in the generation of ideas than in the logic of their criticism.

Using the concept of situational logic has proved helpful in cases where policy did not have a direct impact on institutions or practice, and where policies themselves were unclear. The task for researchers here is to assess the constraints and opportunities within which institutions or actors are placed. Chapter 7 offers one example where the advantages of this approach were evident; Pratt and Silverman's (1988) study of higher education institutions' responses in a period of financial constraint is another. The implementation of cuts is such a political process that models of perfect administration seem particularly inappropriate. It was not surprising that institutions facing cuts tried to alter policies in the course of their implementation, or that policy-makers preferred to avoid becoming identified with declining services. The concept of situational logic is helpful because it focuses on institutions' or actors' assessments of their interests. Such an approach is consistent with understanding the interaction between policy and action, and the negotiations and political struggles which occur in the course of implementation. It does not assume that altering policies is in itself bad, since the outcome is more than a matter of whether it conforms to the intentions of the policy-makers. It reminds us (or those on whom policies act) that the policy is only one element in the situation.

Situational logic offers a further tool for policy-makers and policy research. Whilst, in the end, policy must be tested by its outcomes, it is preferable to detect mistakes and inherent dangers beforehand, using the predictive theories generated by policy analysis and the study of institutions. In CIS we have come to call these 'paper tests' of policy. Situational analysis offers a way of predicting some of the likely consequences of policy before it is implemented. It allows researchers and policy-makers to ask: 'Are the proposed solutions *prima facie* apt?' We can ask: 'What, on the evidence of past experience, and given what we know about the logic of the situation in which actors are placed, are the likely actions of, say, teachers if the government were to introduce a national curriculum of a particular kind?' The use of situational analysis with predictive theories based on past policy can enable solutions to be proposed that might otherwise be rejected. In a recent example, Austria introduced a new policy for vocational higher education, drawing on British experience of the (now defunct) accrediting body, the Council for National Academic Awards. Much informed opinion in Austria assumed that a body composed of university academics and their social partners would act conservatively in course validation. British experience indicated that such an institution's behaviour is not predictable solely from its members' self-interests; so it has proven in practice (Pratt and Hackl forthcoming).

Popper saw the accumulation of evidence and tested hypotheses as the development of a kind of social technology. As with piecemeal social engineering, some of the connotations of the terms he used have tended to distract commentators from the value of the ideas. As noted earlier, policy is more analogous to engineering than it is to science, in that policies and institutions are social artefacts, designed or used to achieve particular purposes and solve problems, similar in conceptual terms to those of the engineer in the physical world – 'to achieve a transformation from one state of affairs to another', as Krick (1969:3) describes the kinds of problem the engineer faces.

One implication of situational logic for reformers or public administrators is that the potential for change in institutions consists not so much in issuing instructions as in setting up the situations, the logic of which will make desired outcomes more likely. It draws attention to the importance of social institutions, which constitute a large element of any social situation, and which are usually the elements most susceptible to change. As Popper (1966b:93) says, 'institutions and traditions are neither the work of God nor of nature, but the results of human actions and decisions, and alterable by human actions and decisions.'

POLICY AS A TRIAL SOLUTION

Policy is implemented through social institutions, and creating and running these institutions can be seen as a social technology. This draws attention to the allocation of powers and responsibilities. We have, too, to ask of institutions, as we do of physical devices, whether they are fit for their purpose, whether they are achieving what is required of them. Again, the process is one of problem formulation, trial solution and testing. As a result, we can adjust the institution or use it differently.

The realist approach places importance on testing predictions against evidence. Policy-as-trial-solution can be tested against its outcomes, in much the same way as a scientific hypothesis is tested. When, in the 1960s, my colleagues and I first began to study the outcomes of policy, such ideas were not only radical but rarely implemented. Since then there has been a burgeoning of monitoring and evaluation of policies, reflecting the development of the 'contract culture' and increased demands for public accountability (Scott 1995), and the increased use of strategic planning approaches in policy and institutions. Yet these evaluations are still often misconceived. Chapter 5 offers a criticism of the failings of an objectives-based approach in education, and these apply with similar force in policy-making. One of the key features of strategic planning and strategic management approaches is the setting of objectives. Typically these are second- or third-order components of a hierarchical process which starts from a statement of 'vision', and for an institution usually involves a 'mission statement'. From these may be derived strategic objectives or key objectives, and from them a sequence of operational objectives. These in turn may be used to develop 'milestones' and statements of expected 'outputs', against which actual performance is to be assessed – usually, for outputs, on an annual basis, with shorter intervals for milestones. Elaborate monitoring and review procedures are usually proposed to secure this assessment.

What such procedures usually achieve is an assessment, but only of the extent to which the programme, the chosen solution, has been implemented. This may or may not result in the problem(s) that the programme was set up to tackle being solved. The realist approach espoused here makes clear that the testing of a solution must be in terms of solving the policy problem(s). One does not test the theory of gravity simply by counting the number of experiments carried out, or how well they have been conducted, but by examining the implications of the results for the theory. For example, a policy to improve housing would be assessed not just in terms of the number, kind and quality of houses built or refurbished, but in terms of the impact on homelessness, 'quality of life', tenant satisfaction and so on, depending on the nature of the initial problems. Britain has, after all, built and refurbished millions of homes in the last 50 years, but homelessness is still a problem. The data suggest not only that there is a mismatch between the outputs (kinds of houses) and people's needs, but that the problem may be inappropriately formulated (it may be one of poverty, not housing).

A further reason for the emphasis on testing outcomes in practice is that it is, in any real situation, almost always impossible to predict all the outcomes of the complex interactions between institutions, people and other factors. Much social 'science' rejects the possibility of this kind of deterministic prediction. But as Magee (1973:75) puts it, 'it is often only by critical examination of the practical results [of policy] . . . that some of the mistakes are to be identified.'

This draws attention to another aspect of a realist analysis of policy: any action may have unintended consequences. Human action is not always consciously defined or explicable in terms of needs, hopes or motives. Even consequences which arise 'as the result of conscious and intentional human actions are, as a rule, *the indirect, the unintended and often the unwanted by-products of such actions'* (Popper 1966b:93). Magee (1973:75) uses a simple economic example – that any purchaser entering a market automatically increases the market price of the commodity he intends to purchase. This outcome, whilst a direct consequence of the action, is not the intended one. It is nevertheless a predictable, if unintended, consequence. There are likely to be unintended but largely unpredictable consequences of most policies, not least because of their very complexity. Boudon (1973:17), for example, showed how even a deterministic, mathematical model of relative educational level and social mobility generates a high degree of apparent randomness. Press criticism of Prime Minister Tony Blair's holiday arrangements in late 1998 illustrates the difficulty of predicting all the consequences of policy. Blair's new government in 1997 enthusiastically continued the practice of publishing 'league tables' as part of its policy of school improvement. Blair's holiday in the Seychelles involved taking his children out of school for a few days. The criticism arose in part because such absences depress a school's ranking in the league tables. Blair could reasonably feel he was a victim of an unpredictable consequence of his own government's policy.

Of course, as with many such minor scandals, the concern missed the point; neither the policy nor the criticism necessarily had much connection with education. Publishing league tables may or may not improve educational attainment; the holiday might well have had educational outcomes. But the example illustrates some of the benefits of taking a realist approach to policy.

A realist approach is concerned with outcomes, whether they are intended or not. It is through this that we may learn how policy works, and what works. By starting with the problems that policies are designed to solve, by testing policies as trial solutions to problems, by formulating alternative problems and alternative solutions, and by examining the outcomes, intended or not, a realist approach to policy and to studies of policy can offer hope of improvement.

Chapter 5

Making Better Plans: Problem-based Versus Objectives-based Planning

JOANNA SWANN

> We do not *have* objectives: we choose to conceptualize our behaviour
> in terms of objectives – or we choose not to.
>
> Lawrence Stenhouse (1975:71)

This chapter offers a problem-based approach to planning and evaluation, and contrasts it with the commonly accepted model which is, I argue, significantly flawed. The flawed model is used in the planning and evaluation of education policy at macro- and micro-levels, including the planning and assessment of learning, and curriculum development in general. When it is applied, 'targets', 'objectives' or 'intended learning outcomes' are used to describe its operation. In this chapter, 'objectives' has been adopted as the generic term.

The argument focuses on the main characteristics of the flawed model and its application, rather than on specific examples. Of course, teachers and other practitioners tend to work with a composite of methods, thus my account of objectives-based planning and evaluation is an approximation of what actually takes place. (For a discussion of the gap between espoused theory and teacher practice, see Clark and Yinger 1987, and Swann and Brown 1997.) The thrust of the argument, based on situational logic, is that planning and evaluation practices which adhere to the objectives model tend to incorporate specific flaws, particularly in complex situations where significant learning is required. These flaws are less likely to occur when a problem-based method is adopted.

WHO MAKES PLANS, AND WHY?

All humans engage in planning. The planning may be undertaken by individuals, pairs or groups, and may or may not be documented. It may be comparatively trivial, such as making a shopping list, or more profound, as in planning to get married or planning an undergraduate degree programme. The plan may not be designed specifically to advance learning, but merely get something done; even so, learning may take place. Planning a meal, for example, often necessitates a change from 'not having all the ingredients' to 'having all the ingredients'. While the process of securing the ingredients may result in *ad hoc* opportunities for learning, learning may not be an intended outcome. However, when a meal is based on a new recipe, the planning will either explicitly or implicitly involve some expectation of learning.

In general, people plan for two main reasons. First, they want a state of affairs to improve, or they want to achieve a specific state of affairs in the foreseeable future. In the former instance, they judge the current situation to be deficient or problematic and wish to bring about an improvement, though the precise nature of the improvement may not be specified or known. In the latter, the desired state of affairs is also regarded as an improvement, although the idea of improvement may not be explicit. In both circumstances, there is a belief that planning is necessary to achieve desirable change.

Second, people make plans because they are obliged to do so (for instance, by their employers). A formal requirement to make plans may be regarded as intrinsically worthwhile, viewed cynically as a purely bureaucratic activity, or perhaps a bit of both.

THE UBIQUITOUS APPROACH TO PLANNING

The objectives model

According to the objectives model of planning, the first stage in any planning process should involve the formulation of one or more aims or broad goals. These are determined by answering a question of the kind, 'What am I (are we) trying to achieve?' The result is a description of a desired future state, such as, in the context of school students, 'lively, enquiring minds and a love of learning' (Croydon Education Authority 1985:5). The next stage involves the formulation of a series of objectives which, if met (or 'delivered') collectively, will result in the achievement of the aim(s). Objectives are more specific than aims, although some people's objectives are so vague or broad that they are indistinguishable from other people's aims.

Debate in the late 1960s and early 1970s about 'instructional objectives' focused on the relative merits of non-behavioural and behavioural objectives, the latter being demonstrable and measurable by reference to specific changes in student behaviour (see, for example, Popham *et al.* 1969). As an illustration, 'To further the class's understanding of Hardy's "The Darkling Thrush"' is a non-behavioural objective, whereas 'At the end of a forty-five-minute lesson on Hardy's "The Darkling Thrush" the class will be able [to] detail the images which conjure up a landscape of winter and death' is a behavioural objective (Cohen *et al.* 1996:61). Objectives may also be distinguished according to vagueness or specificity – as in, respectively, 'The students will develop an understanding of events leading up to the Second World War' or 'The students will put into the correct sequence six events leading up to the Second World

War.' Currently, in the United Kingdom, students in initial teacher education may be required to distinguish between learning objectives (intended changes in pupils' skills, knowledge, understanding, values, confidence and other attitudes) and teaching objectives (what the teacher intends to do in order to bring about the specified learning).

In general, policy targets, curriculum objectives, and intended learning outcomes are associated with measurable, or at least clearly demonstrable, achievements.

Once objectives have been formulated, the courses of action that follow are evaluated according to whether or to what extent the objectives have been met. The link between the objectives and the initial aim(s) is not usually reconsidered at the evaluative stage.

Historical background

In the 1960s, initial support for objectives-based teaching in the UK came largely from the United States of America, with Bloom's *Taxonomy of Educational Objectives* (1956) providing the most influential illustrated argument. The classification of Bloom and his associates was probably more talked about than applied in UK schools, but elements of it were adopted in the further education sector (Technician Education Council 1976). During the 1970s, people who favoured the use of objectives in curriculum planning often felt obliged to argue in support of this practice, referring not only to Bloom's *Taxonomy* but also, for example, to Tyler (1949), Kerr (1968), and Popham *et al.* (1969). The controversial nature of objectives-based planning was usually acknowledged (for a notable exception see Schools Council Publications 1972), and arguments against the use of objectives (as in Stenhouse 1975, and Dearden 1976) were given serious consideration, even if ultimately they were rejected.

From the early 1970s, the formulation of objectives was increasingly favoured by curriculum organizers and examining bodies, and by the end of that decade public debate about the validity of objectives-based planning had largely ceased. Despite the later critiques of authors such as Blenkin and Kelly (1987), the current assumption is that objectives provide the only sound basis for educational planning. In mainstream education in the UK, professionals are obliged to work with objectives. (It is, of course, possible to employ a different method and present one's plans and achievements as if the objectives model had been adopted.)

The influence of the objectives movement is evident in General National Vocational Qualifications and National Vocational Qualifications in the post-16 sector. In the compulsory sector, the national curriculum for state-maintained schools presents teachers with teaching objectives, in the form of programmes of study, and attainment targets which 'set out the expected standards of pupils' performance' (Department for Education 1995:v). The objectives model has been incorporated into the design of higher education courses, and is deeply embedded in teacher training. Although there is greater flexibility in higher education, the recently introduced national curriculum for initial teacher training (Department for Education and Employment 1998b), and moves to introduce benchmarking for subjects common to a range of higher education institutions (Quality Assurance Agency for Higher Education 1998b), suggest that this flexibility may not be maintained. There is also a growing interest among lecturers in the use of elements of Bloom's *Taxonomy* to specify criteria for undergraduate levels.

In support of objectives

In their simplest form, arguments in support of objectives-based planning and evaluation include the following:

- Objectives-based planning and evaluation is the only rational approach.
- The alternative to the use of objectives is a *laissez-faire* approach which often results in chaos.
- We need to know where we are going.
- If our objectives are clear, we are less likely to be side-tracked by trivial *ad hoc* suggestions.
- Objectives-based planning helps us to focus on important and worthwhile achievements.
- The formulation of objectives is consistent with democratic principles. For example, outcome-based assessment makes the teaching and learning process transparent; consequently the assessment of student attainment is fairer and more equitable, because students (and their assessors) know the criteria against which the work is to be judged.
- Practitioners can be guided in their work by means of objectives set by policy-makers. This results in higher standards of performance, and greater consistency within and between institutions.
- The use of objectives is consistent with establishing systems of accountability. People know what they are required to do and achieve during a specific period, and it is relatively straightforward to assess whether the objectives have been met.

Against objectives

While the objectives model of planning and evaluation can support the achievement of goals in situations that are unproblematic, in more complex situations its usefulness is questionable. Ten specific criticisms are outlined below. (They refer to the above arguments in support of objectives, but the order of the supporting arguments has not been followed systematically.) Some of the criticisms are applicable when the model is adopted badly; others refer to the model's inherent limitations. For discussion of some of these and other criticisms, see Stenhouse (1975), Dearden (1976), and Blenkin and Kelly (1987).

First, the two initial arguments in support of objectives-based planning and evaluation are flawed because, quite simply, there are rational options that are clearly distinguishable from a *laissez-faire* approach. This chapter offers one such option.

Second, the objectives model fails to address the open-ended nature of human endeavour and, in particular, social change. Although we may wish to know where we are going, this knowledge is rarely available except in the most general terms. Even when it appears to be available, our expectations may be mistaken. Thus, when advocates of objectives-based planning ask, 'How do you know where you are going if you haven't formulated aims and objectives?', a valid answer in all but the most mundane situations is, 'You don't – but you can have some idea of where you are (through problem formulation), of where you and others have been (by being aware of previously tested ideas), and what you are travelling with (a method).' The future, unlike the past, is open; people cannot, with any degree of certainty, know what will take place.

Third, although the use of objectives can help people to avoid being side-tracked by trivial *ad hoc* suggestions, it tends to encourage a blinkered view of what will be possible and successful in practice. In particular, the unforeseen consequences of action may go unnoticed. Planners should be mindful that the unintended consequences of policy are often more far-reaching than those which are intended; this is particularly true of social planning. (For a critique of far-reaching objectives as a form of utopianism, see Popper 1961, 1972b, 1985c; and Little 1981.) Rather than using objectives, a method is needed which encourages us to make reflective judgements about *ad hoc* ideas (rather than dismiss them out of hand), and discover and address the unexpected and undesirable consequences of action.

Fourth, given the open-ended nature of human endeavour, it makes sense to begin our planning by focusing on the present rather than on a desired future state of affairs. A critical response to questions such as, 'What am I going to do?' and 'What am I trying to achieve?' is, 'Why do or try to achieve anything?' This may sound facetious, but a serious point is being made. Any action or desire to act is best understood in relation to its problem context. Arguably, people formulate questions about what is to be done and what is to be achieved because of experienced or anticipated difficulties (see Chapter 10). The belief that good planning starts with the formulation of aims and objectives is mistaken; rather, it is important to focus initially on the problem context and the formulation of one or more pressing problems.

When a plan is required to address a problem, the context should be scrutinized before launching in with a solution. Good planners will do this whether or not they are working with objectives. The objectives model does not, however, encourage such good practice. People are often inclined to concentrate on a solution, because acknowledging a problem can be uncomfortable. But, in the context of a well-formulated problem, all proposed solutions can be critically discussed in terms of whether or to what extent they are likely to solve the initial problem. The evaluation of policy is directed towards the question: 'To what extent has the problem been solved, and have there been unexpected consequences?' This is in contrast to evaluation within an objectives-based process, which tends to focus on the questions: 'Have our stated objectives been met?' and 'If not, why not?'

A fifth flaw in the use of objectives-based planning is that the task of implementing policy to achieve the stated objectives tends to take priority over the issue of whether or to what extent the aims and objectives were worthwhile in the first place.

Sixth, objectives-based planning discourages the expression of contention. But what frequently happens is that disagreement, having no legitimate outlet, is suppressed or sidelined. We need to find ways of legitimizing conflict and working with it, and in this regard a problem- rather than objectives-based method is enabling.

When a group convenes to develop policies and/or plans, trying to achieve a consensus about aims often results in the selection of the lowest common denominator of the group's ideas. This is why statements of aims are generally so banal (though they can prove more controversial than their formulators anticipate). Focusing on aims means that the initial starting point for the group – a shared and often pressing problem – may be ignored.

Thus, seventh, objectives-based planning generally promotes mediocrity because it provides no social mechanism by which bold and potentially valuable ideas may be discussed and subsequently tested.

Eighth, the objectives model of planning – or, rather, the corrupted, ubiquitous version of it – often generates lists in which the objectives are not prioritized, and there is an unwitting mix of problems and solutions (highlighted in Pratt 1976), and/or different types of objective (for example, policy targets, teaching objectives, and intended learning outcomes).

Ninth, when objectives are set by one group of people for others to adopt, ideological and empirical issues are raised. For example, a national curriculum, by denying individuals the right to determine important features of their formal learning, is essentially authoritarian. Thus, although outcome-based assessment can be used to make teaching and learning transparent, and its assessment seemingly fair and equitable, it nonetheless exemplifies the organizational form of authoritarianism (as described by Meighan and Siraj-Blatchford 1997:203). Teachers' professional judgements about curriculum content – for instance, in light of their students' individual learning problems (see Chapters 9 and 10) – are supplanted by the decrees of politicians and their appointees. Empirically, there is no sound evidence to suggest that good teachers and lecturers cannot be trusted to take responsibility for the content of their work. While it is proper to legislate against bad practice (for instance, to ban physical punishment from schools), it is not possible to plan for excellence by insisting that everyone follows identical guidelines.

This is not to imply that practitioners should be unaccountable to their clients, their employers, the tax-payers, etc., but the model of accountability associated with objectives-based planning is flawed: it constrains creativity and (despite expressed intentions to the contrary) diminishes the practitioner's sense of responsibility. The use of centrally agreed objectives may well result in greater consistency within and between institutions, and clarify what people are required to do and achieve during a specific period. It is, however, far from clear whether overall standards of performance are improved by this means. Consistency and control are achieved at the expense of diversity and responsibility.

Tenth, as suggested earlier in the chapter, the objectives model is particularly flawed when it is applied to learning – not least because of its failure to address the open-ended nature of human endeavour. Only the most trivial and basic learning can be planned in detail and predicted with accuracy.

For example, learning to play a musical instrument well requires interpretative skills which cannot be fully encompassed by a list of targets or 'intended learning outcomes' (unless the intended learning outcomes are so broad that they are, to all intents and purposes, aims). In a guitar master class, the teacher helps the musicians to refine their technique and improve their understanding of the instrument and its potential. In the pursuit of excellence, there is no question of trying to make all students play in exactly the same way; rather, they are encouraged to interpret the music individually.

Within compulsory education, learning objectives are generally devised by policy-makers and teachers; thus, major decisions which shape the experience of students are made without their involvement. This practice reflects misconceptions about the nature of learning. Although learning is often an unself-conscious process, it is never passive (see Chapter 10). Learning necessitates autonomous activity on the part of the learner, and it is always based on the skills, knowledge, values and attitudes which the learner brings to the situation. It is, of course, possible to encourage learning, and it is often possible to get people to do specific things through forms of coercion; but learning is something for which the individual learner is uniquely responsible. When we set learning objectives for others, we ignore important aspects of what would-be learners bring (desires and values, etc.) to the learning environment.

Moreover, the use of objectives usually focuses attention on performance rather than learning. Performance is a product of learning (and other factors), but it is not synonymous with learning, which is a process. We may assess students in terms of our stated objectives, but what they learn in a broader sense is beyond our control and the scope of our assessments (their learning may even be contrary to our intentions). The objectives model of educational planning is associated with the idea that the assessment of educational provision is largely synonymous with the assessment of student performance. However, performance refers to what the student can be observed to do, and learning is merely inferred.

The use of behavioural objectives focuses attention on readily observable events, and treats learning as a linear process. These objectives, in particular, fail to address the development of attitudes, and changes in long-term dispositions and potential.

This leads to the question: 'If we do not use objectives how can we plan to promote learning?' Instead of asking, 'What educational purposes or objectives ought the school or course seek to attain?' (Bloom 1956:25; following Tyler 1949:1), we should address the question, 'What are the students' most significant and pressing learning problems?' (see Chapter 10).

PROBLEM-BASED PLANNING

Practical problems

The problem-based approach to planning and evaluation discussed in this chapter is derived from the philosophy of Karl Popper. Following Popper, it can be argued that the starting point for any incidence of learning is a problem (see Chapters 2 and 10). A problem – which, like the process of learning, need not be experienced self-consciously – involves the discovery of a mismatch between expectation and experience, actual or anticipated, and a desire (or will) to resolve the mismatch in some way. A problem triggers the search for a solution. As stated in Chapter 10, the creation of a solution brings with it a new set of expectations (which may or may not be explicit), and these too may subsequently be found to be flawed. Once an attempt has been made to solve a problem, the trial solution, whether it is successful or not, exists within the history of the situation; for instance, if we try to do something and fail, we may recognize what not to do in future, even though we may remain unsure about what to do for the best.

Useful distinctions can be made between different types of problem, in particular between practical problems and theoretical problems (see Chapters 2 and 4). Practical problems are those of how to get from one state of affairs to another, and they arise when someone wants to *do* something (Burgess 1977, 1979). Decisions about such problems entail, either implicitly or explicitly, issues of fact and of value, but the results of attempts to solve practical problems are that things get done (or decisions not to do specific things are taken). A practical problem is not solved merely by the formulation of theory.

Theoretical problems include those of: what is the case (including scientific problems), what is good (general questions of value), what we ought to do (ethical problems), what was done in the past (historical problems), what is logically valid (logical and mathematical problems), and what is aesthetically pleasing. Solutions to these problems are statements of theory, which may nonetheless influence changes in practice.

As an illustration, 'How can I make this bread into toast?' describes a fairly low-level practical problem. Its solution is a situation in which a slice of bread is toasted. In contrast, 'How does this toaster work?' is a problem of what is the case, solved at a simple level by the statement: 'This toaster works by converting electrical energy into a source of controllable heat by means of which slices of bread may be toasted.'

Practical problems stimulate planning, whether or not planners are aware that this is so. Generally, they are best formulated using one of three sentence openings:

- 'How can I ... ?' – used for a personal practical problem, such as, 'How can I successfully complete this course of study?'
- 'How can we ... ?' – suitable for a group practical problem, such as, 'How can we construct a model bridge without the use of adhesives?'
- 'How can ... ?' – used for general practical problems of the kind, 'How can classroom practice be improved?'

Methodological principles and procedures

In light of this analysis of practical problems, the process outlined below is recommended as (conjecturally) the best method to adopt when engaging in planning where learning is either a desired outcome or necessary in order for a desired change to take place. Most planning for social change falls into this category. The first two stages in the procedure constitute an analysis of the problem context (raised earlier in the chapter).

First, address the questions: 'What is going well in the present situation?' and 'What do we want to defend, maintain and develop?' Focusing on what is going well may help to make us more confident and positive about our endeavours; more importantly, it can help to prevent us 'throwing the baby out with the bath water'. Too often planned change results in the achievement of something thought desirable, but at the expense of losing other desirable features that were taken for granted prior to the change. Logically, one would expect to start with what is problematic but, psychologically, it is better to begin by focusing on what is going well.

Second, formulate one or more practical problems (How can ... ?) by addressing the questions: 'What is not going well in the present situation?' and 'What aspects of the current state of affairs do I/we want to change?' These questions can be interpreted loosely; what is not going well in the present may be contained within our expectations about future events. For example: 'I think this four-year-old child will have difficulty transferring from the nursery to the reception class; how can he become ready for this transition?'

Third, address the question: 'What seems to be stopping (or inhibiting) these changes from taking place?' Or: 'What can be expected to stop (or inhibit) these changes from taking place?' To continue the previous example: 'This child is insufficiently independent' and 'I do not seem to have enough time in which to help him.'

The focus is clearly directed towards the present situation and the removal of impediments to change, rather than on a specified future state. If you are wearing a straitjacket it does not really matter whether you want to take a shower or go shopping; before you can do anything the straitjacket must be removed. This is not to suggest that the idea of a desirable future state of affairs should play no part in planning, but (as discussed earlier) there are dangers in making desired future states the focus.

Given the significance for learning of the discovery of error and inadequacy (discussed in Chapters 2 and 10), when we try to do something (or imagine ourselves trying to do something) and find that our efforts are disappointed or thwarted in some way (or we anticipate that this will be the case), it makes sense to formulate and address a 'What is stopping . . . ?' or 'What is inhibiting . . . ?' question in order to identify the difficulty. Consider the example of a bridge which collapses unexpectedly. A valid question to ask (and have answered) is, 'What in the construction of the bridge led to its failure: what stopped it from remaining standing?' This contrasts with the response of simply building a new bridge which, though different, potentially replicates the fault which caused the first bridge to collapse.

One way of tackling a problem is to generate numerous trial solutions in the hope that some will be successful, but it is not the best way to proceed where failed trials (such as a series of collapsing bridges) may be life-threatening. This is not an argument against creating a variety of theoretical solutions to problems; rather, caution in practical endeavours is advocated. People involved in education should be wary of addressing disappointed expectations by introducing a series of new practices which may implicitly contain the same flaws as those which have generated concern.

Fourth, having identified one or more impediments to change, decide which of these impediments lie within your sphere of influence. (This is not to deny the value of discussing socio-political issues beyond our control.) At this point, sub-problems may be formulated.

Fifth, formulate tentative theories about how these impediments can be removed, or how their effects may be alleviated. This is, so to speak, the brainstorming stage in the planning process, where it is appropriate to experiment with ideas, to consider a range of possibilities from a variety of sources. At this point, a person's underlying aims and ideals may provide a valuable stimulus for creative thinking.

Sixth, on the basis of critical discussion, select one or more trial solutions arising from these tentative theories. How many empirical tests of solutions can be made (distinct from how many can be considered) will depend on the specific situation. For instance, in the context of a shared problem, various practitioners within an institution might be able to adopt and test competing ideas with different groups of students.

Seventh, state what would count as a failure of any trial solution (that is, the policy to be adopted). For instance, the loss of some of the positive features of the initial situation (identified at the first stage) may be regarded as an undesirable consequence.

Eighth, test each chosen trial solution by implementing it and being alert to the possibility of unintended consequences (desirable or undesirable). By treating policies as trials, we are encouraged to discard policies which are failing. It is crucial to bear in mind that the solutions we adopt do not always improve situations. When we keep the initial problem in mind and consciously look for undesirable consequences, we are far more likely to avoid an intensification of difficulties.

Ninth, carry out a review process (an evaluation), with reference to the questions: 'To what extent, if at all, has (have) the initial problem (or problems) been solved?', 'What unintended and unexpected consequences (desirable or undesirable) have arisen?' and 'With the benefit of hindsight, might other strategies have been preferable?' In some contexts – for instance, where significant social change has been planned – it is appropriate at this stage to write a formal account of what has taken place and, in particular, what has been learned.

These stages (presented here in a generalized form) can be worked through by individuals, pairs or groups. In some situations it is important to focus on the most pressing and important practical problems; in others, it may be preferable to address the most manageable problems first. Either way, problem formulation is a creative activity, requiring time and concentration. In many situations, the primary impediment to change is lack of knowledge.

In social planning, what counts as a pressing and important problem is potentially controversial. Moreover, as suggested earlier, while consensus may be reached about what is wrong in a given situation, there is usually far less agreement about ultimate aims or ideals. When a group reaches agreement about what is wrong, a shared problem can be formulated, and a variety of solutions can then be sought, subjected to critical discussion and, possibly, tested. Thus, people's conflicting ideas about solutions are acknowledged and addressed. In contrast, when people try to formulate an agreed list of objectives, the offer of different viewpoints, which may postpone or otherwise inhibit the required unanimity, is likely to be unwelcome. Some participants at planning meetings stifle their misgivings about proposals in order to speed up or smooth the process; but such misgivings do not simply go away.

It follows that we should ask individuals and groups to give an account of their activities, rather than seeking a statement of their aims and objectives. It is preferable to ascertain which problems are being given priority and to ask for an account of process. The rejection of an objectives-based approach to planning may be difficult when it comes to explaining proposals and adopted policies, because people are unaccustomed to formulating accounts of process. Moreover, it may be intrinsically harder to describe a process than a product. But if better planning and evaluation procedures are desired, these difficulties must be faced.

Researching practical problems

Given that problems are the starting points for learning, then their formulation becomes the key activity for people self-consciously engaged in an attempt to advance knowledge and/or accelerate their own learning. On this basis, every researcher should formulate a problem that is central to her or his research programme. The core research problem (an over-arching question) stimulates the formulation of other problems (research questions) and hypotheses.

When planning research, researchers should identify the type of problem which provides the impetus for their work. The considerations brought to bear on research with a practical problem at its core will be different from those in which the primary concern is to address a theoretical problem. Many people embark upon research because of the desire to bring about change in their work environment; the initial stimulus for their research is not so much to learn more about the world, to explain it better; rather they want practical improvements. In developing their research, however, some researchers lose touch with their initial stimulus; they become more knowledgeable within a particular field of inquiry, but not better able to bring about improvements in practice.

Accounts of action research generally make an explicit link between this approach and the desire to change practice (for example, Carr and Kemmis 1986:165), and many accounts explicitly refer to the term 'problem'. The analysis derived from Burgess (1977, 1979) facilitates the process of deciding which problems will be best addressed by action research, because it draws attention to the distinction between practical and theoretical problems. All action research addresses practical problems, even though these may be ill-defined.

Chapter 8 provides an account of action research in which the problem-based principles and procedures, discussed in the present chapter, were adopted. See also Swann and Ecclestone (1999) and Swann and Arthurs (1999).

DISTINGUISHING BETWEEN PROBLEM- AND OBJECTIVES-BASED PLANNING

I am aware of the argument that the formulation of a practical problem (a 'How can ...?' question) is in itself an objective, because a state other than the present is sought. For instance, the practical problem 'How can I become a reader?' may be seen to imply the objective 'To become a reader'; and 'How can classroom practice be improved?' implies the less specific objective 'To improve classroom practice' (though it may also be thought of as an aim capable of being translated into a set of objectives). This argument can be countered in the following way.

In formulating a practical problem, attention is necessarily drawn to the current situation and what is wrong with it. Hopes or aims may be considered but, in contrast to the objectives model, they are not the starting point of planning. The fulfilment of a hope and the achievement of an aim may or may not be possible, and there is no certain route to success; but, by formulating problems and seeking to identify impediments to progress, there is the (uncertain and undefined) possibility of *creating* a route. The problem-based method encourages a critical consideration of hopes and aims, which may be modified and developed along with other ideas that an individual or group holds to be true or valid.

It has been suggested, during my conversations with colleagues, that the term 'objective' may be applied to the linguistic encapsulation of a practical problem. However, as illustrated in this chapter, methodologies designed to address practical problems are very different from those associated with objectives. To call a practical problem an objective is to fudge this important distinction.

A further distinction between the approaches arises when ideas generated within a problem-based methodology are tested. A particular method or process may be developed and adopted, and, in seeking to test this method, statements about its possible consequences will be formulated. For instance, in seeking to make an empirical comparison between problem- and objectives-based approaches to teaching (see Chapter 10), 'better spelling' might be highlighted as a desirable outcome of both. An exponent of objectives-based planning might then conclude that 'better spelling' was an objective of the problem-based approach.

This indicates a misunderstanding about both the nature of problem-based planning and the idea of testing a *process*. One of the ways that processes may be distinguished empirically is by their observable outcomes; however, the status of some of these outcomes may be that of a by-product. For instance, success in formal tests and examinations may be construed as a desirable by-product of better classroom practice, rather than as a goal of better classroom practice. Part of the evidence in support of a process lies in observable outcomes, but a process entails more than can be specified. There is, for example, more to better classroom practice than better spelling. Moreover, treating 'better spelling' as a specified objective distracts attention not only from the more significant general problem, but also from the difficulties of making changes and, most importantly, from the potential for unintended consequences.

If we wish to test problem-based processes, we must attempt to formulate ideas for the identification of *some* tangible results; these ideas can include both desirable and undesirable outcomes. But when desirable outcomes are formulated, they do not represent goals or objectives – their role is that of test statements. Individual practitioners may, of course, turn test statements into goals or objectives, but, in the context of a problem-based approach, this inclination should be resisted.

IMPLICATIONS OF THE DISCUSSION

This chapter offers no general solution to the social and political dilemmas of anyone who wishes to challenge the practice of objectives-based planning and evaluation in the workplace. In the field of education studies in the 1970s, the intellectual battle about the assumptions and efficacy of objectives-based planning was won by those who opposed this approach. However, the success of the arguments against the use of objectives had little impact on subsequent events, specifically in the UK.

If we wish to improve educational planning policy we must challenge the orthodoxy of the objectives model, and adopt and test problem-based methods such as the one offered in this chapter. For many of us this will be difficult; the procedures we are permitted to adopt are limited. Where the requirement to present plans using the objectives model is inescapable, we may decide to use a problem-based approach in private and then present our plans and any subsequent evaluations as if objectives had been used. But this does not provide an adequate solution to the problem of how to make better plans. Apart from the time-consuming nature (and bad faith) of this approach, it fails to address the problem of how to challenge the current orthodoxy, and it provides inadequate scope for testing ideas.

The large-scale abandonment of the objectives model will require a considerable ideological shift but, as an immediate strategy, we can at least keep the debate alive by not colluding with the idea that no rational alternative exists. We can remind ourselves, and others, that learning is an open-ended activity in which new ideas are generated. Learning involves the discovery of error or inadequacy in our existing assumptions, and a creative or inventive response to difficulties. If we really want to promote learning, we must (a) accept and work with uncertainty, and (b) value systems and procedures which are open rather than closed. In short, when we set objectives for other people to adopt, and when we uncritically accept the objectives that others set for us, we participate in procedures which militate against learning.

NOTE

This chapter draws on Swann (1997, 1999), and Swann and Ecclestone (1999).

Chapter 6

Critical Realism: Post-Popper Realism for the Real World

DAVID CORSON

Karl Popper's theory of knowledge was the earliest reaction against the distorting world-view that positivism offers. But his theory extends only the first word in opposition, not the last. This chapter updates Popper's realism by showing how an influential and current approach to the philosophy of the social sciences builds on his ideas to create a critically real conception of discovery that is sensitive to human needs and interests, while also having emancipatory potential for the social world.

POPPER'S THEORY OF KNOWLEDGE

As earlier chapters in this book indicate, Popper's impact on educational thought has increased, if only in recent years. Near-complete bibliographies of his works are available in two sources (Popper 1992; Schilpp 1974). Like Dewey and Wittgenstein, Popper had early life experiences as a school-teacher, and these early associations were critical for his later scientific views and for his epistemology (Bartley 1974). His formal training was in education and Gestalt psychology, under the supervision of Bühler; and there is a direct connection between the trial and error approach to teaching and learning that was common in Vienna during Popper's training in education, and his use of error elimination as the central idea for his epistemology. This idea is simple and quite radical: knowledge grows by a process of conjectures and refutations, by a method of trial and the elimination of error (Popper 1925, 1927, 1931, 1932).

A theme underlying his theory of knowledge is that all aspects of the universe, including knowledge about those aspects, can only be properly understood if we accept that they are in a constant state of evolutionary change. By reapplying Darwin's theory of natural selection to his own theory about the growth of knowledge, Popper accepted this evolutionary first principle as a template for his own theory. The process of progressive error elimination, in response to trials in their environment, is the way that organisms evolve; and this process provides the paradigm for the growth of knowledge. Indeed, the 'stages' in his epistemology represent the non-temporal, overlapping stages through which evolution is thought to proceed. These are captured clearly in his often-cited formula: an initial problem provokes a tentative theory, which is subjected to error elimination, leading to a new problem.

Popper's theory changed over time, in detail and in character, notably during the early 1960s when the idea of an 'evolutionary epistemology' (Campbell 1959) began to gain currency in discussions about knowledge. His earlier theory was based on 'falsificationism' as a reaction to positivism and that doctrine's quest for a principle of verification. Popper was also much interested in marking off 'knowledge' from non-knowledge. Even in his very early work (1934:109–11), he made it clear that we accept test statements not conventionally but critically. They are subject to the same processes of formulation and error elimination as theories. As a consequence, statements of the results of inquiry are provisional, rather like the verdicts handed down by juries. We erect weighty consequences upon those verdicts for individuals and groups, but the verdicts themselves, and the truth tests used in reaching them, are always open to quashing or revising in the light of later evidence.

Later, he moved away from falsificationism as the central dialectical principle in his research process, and began to stress 'error elimination' instead, speaking more of a 'theory about the growth of knowledge'. However, error elimination is not as well known as his original idea, although this gradual change from falsificationism to error elimination matches the changing theory of evolution. Theories, like natural species, are usually modified in minor ways by exposure to the trial and error testing of their environments. In other words, their errors are 'eliminated'; they rarely become extinct or falsified. Error elimination allows us to accept knowledge claims tentatively, once they have 'proven their mettle'. This is a phrase Popper uses as the criterion for deciding whether or not a theory has been 'corroborated'. For him, the corroboration of a theory or a finding of any kind – including a policy response to some social problem – means that it has survived the most rigorous processes of trial and error testing presently available.

GOING BEYOND POPPER

Strengths and weaknesses in Popper's account

My early applications of Popper to educational research (Corson 1981, 1985a) convinced me that the main value his theory had for a social science was in creating a certain mind-set in researchers themselves. This mind-set left one open to other theoretical possibilities and to a whole world of potential evidence. This contrasts with the alternative research world confined by the narrow theorizing, methodologies, and range of evidence available in any single discipline. After thinking about his writings, I found myself more ready to identify research problems that straddled disciplinary boundaries. These were problems much closer to the 'real world' problems that educators face. I also found myself less emotionally attached to the tentative theories that I developed in response to these problems; I found myself more interested in improving my theories, or killing them off, by admitting new evidence and methodologies from any relevant source, regardless of its disciplinary provenance.

However, my early application of his theory to educational policy-making (1985a, 1987, 1989a) found the theory wanting in two main ways (1990a, 1990b). Firstly, and not surprisingly for a theory developed by a philosopher-scientist to describe the growth of scientific knowledge, it lacked a sense of human sociality when applied to a human science field like education. There was little in Popper's writings that was useful for guiding the actual, human, policy process of 'problem identification', or the process of 'tentative policy design', or the process of 'trial and error testing' of a tentative policy. Popper says a great deal about the harmful and inhumane consequences of holistic policy-making in social systems (Corson 1986), but apart from advocating trial and error testing, he says nothing about specific ways of 'doing' policy-making so as to avoid these consequences.

Secondly, and relatedly, Popper's writings offer little discussion of the other 'voices' that must be heeded in social planning and policy-making – voices whose interests and needs are regularly suppressed, misunderstood, or overlooked by dominant individuals at the centre of webs of power. Again, Popper's academic background isolated him to a certain extent from these voices. Yet, when he discusses the purpose and point of education, including the poverty of didacticism (Corson 1985b, 1989b), he seems fully aware of the vastly different theories that students and other people bring with them when they interpret the world, theories whose diversity and incompatibility make holistic policy-making of any kind a dangerous practice indeed.

As mentioned too, Popper talks of 'discovering the real world' while still remaining tentative about our discoveries. This seems a reasonable approach to the impenetrable mysteries of the physical world, but his hesitant epistemology creates a problem for researchers in the human sciences. On Popper's account, we must always doubt what it is that we have discovered. So this kind of scepticism can mean in practice not just that 'anything goes' but that 'everything stays'. In other words, it can support tacit acceptance of almost any unjust *status quo*. Yet, in furthering his own liberal political aims, and despite his scepticism, Popper would still have us use our discoveries to improve the human condition, even while he asks us to doubt the reality of those discoveries.

Bhaskar's critical realism

In contrast, the influential contemporary philosopher of science and the social sciences, Roy Bhaskar, cuts through the Gordian Knot of his own scepticism. He talks about 'reclaiming reality' by eliminating the prejudices, errors, unsupported claims, and philosophical false trails that have covered or disguised reality for us. And he talks of using this reclaimed reality as the only basis for emancipatory social practice (Bhaskar 1989). Emancipation, for Bhaskar, occurs when we make the move from unwanted to wanted sources of determination. His focus is on changing the relations between action and structural context in order to promote the development of this type of emancipation (1986:194–211). The relevance of this kind of 'critical realism' to policy reform and school improvement seems straightforward; and it also complements and builds on Popper's own project (Corson 1991a, 1991b).

In contrast to Popper, Bhaskar extends his ideas directly and compellingly from the sciences so that they have a comparable impact in the social sciences. His critical realism is an elision of two earlier conceptions, one for science and one for the human sciences (1989). He describes his philosophy of science as 'transcendental realism'. This realism is transcendental in that, while sustaining the idea of the independent existence and action of the causal structures and things investigated and discovered by science, it asks what it is that our scientific practices presuppose about the world, because really it is these presuppositions that provide the subject matter of science (1978). This realism is in direct opposition to an 'empirical realist' position, the valid subject matter of which is exhausted by atomistic facts and their conjunctions. Alongside this philosophy of science, Bhaskar's philosophy of the human sciences is a 'critical naturalism': an explanatory critique of structural sources of determination and their emancipatory transformation (1979).

In some respects, Bhaskar either stands firmly on the shoulders of Popper or disagrees sharply with him. Bhaskar finds error in Popper's 'methodological individualism' (1979:34–9), in his blanket denial of the possibility of prediction in the social sciences (1978:138), and in his claim to have solved the problem of induction (1978:217–18). We can see Bhaskar's position best by setting his form of scientific realism, 'transcendental realism', alongside Popper's form of realism, which for Bhaskar is a variety of 'transcendental idealism'. For Bhaskar, ontological objectivity is essential, rather than just conventional as it is for Popper. Yet Bhaskar's scientific claims, like Popper's, are still always tentative in case something better comes along. Our defining statements are 'fallible attempts to capture in words the real essences of things' (1978:211). However, while the imagined mechanisms in our theories remain tentative metaphysical existences for Popper, for Bhaskar these mechanisms may be *real* and may come to be established as such (1978:45–6).

So the basis for this critical realism is not a theory of knowledge (epistemology), but a theory of being (ontology), although an ontology is bound to have epistemological implications. This theory of being includes as real entities the properties of the social world – especially the reasons and accounts that people use or offer, to direct or effect social or individual behaviour or change. In line with other accounts of scientific realism, Bhaskar (1986) asserts that people's reasons and accounts are 'real' in the sense that their existence and activity as objects of scientific inquiry are absolutely or relatively independent of the inquiry of which they are the objects. They are an emergent or objective aspect of his ontology. The twin tasks of research are to show the existence and then to detail the operation of these mechanisms: to show the hypothetical reasons or accounts to be genuine indicators of the structures that affect people's lives. Bhaskar's critical realism insists that we will only be able to understand and change the social world if we can identify the structures at work that generate those special interests (1989).

While Bhaskar clearly differs from Popper in some ways, both theorists are consistent advocates of interdisciplinarity. They see the need to substitute a single coherent system of interlocking knowledge claims, a unifying system that would replace the 'mythical framework' of paradigms, disciplines and perspectives that troubled Popper so much (1974). This interdisciplinary field would match Quine's vision of science: a single sprawling system, loosely connected in some portions but disconnected nowhere, which we need to substitute in our thinking for the disciplinary boundaries that are only 'useful for deans and librarians' (Quine 1966:56).

Like Popper, Bhaskar highlights the centrality of language in the process of discovery in the human sciences. We cannot escape from our language, which he describes as 'that system of differences we exploit to produce meaning and in virtue of which meaning is produced for us' (1979:201). Language mediates between his realist ontology on the one hand, and his ever-sceptical epistemology on the other. It is the capacity for 'second order monitoring' by humans – that is, to monitor the monitoring of their performances and comment upon them – that sets the human sciences into a category of difficulty that is not remotely matched by the natural sciences (1979:44). Extending his discussion of this self-monitoring capacity to confront questions of 'fact and value' and 'theory and practice', Bhaskar sees his core argument as simple: 'It turns on the condition that the subject-matter of the human sciences comprehends both social objects (including beliefs) and beliefs about those objects' (1986:176).

On my reading, Bhaskar's account meets the objections to Popper's conception that I raised above, while still embracing the strengths of Popper's theory. Bhaskar's conception also goes much further in seeing the reality of the structural 'mechanisms' involved as the terminus of research, namely by asking the following four questions: Is the mechanism enduring? Is it operating? Are the results of the activity of the mechanism unaffected by the operations of others? Are the results of the activity of the mechanism perceived or otherwise detected by humans? (1978:246). Like Popper's account, this critical realism is still epistemologically cautious, allowing us only tentative grounds for prediction in the open systems of the social sciences. But unlike Popper's, it is ontologically bold (Bhaskar 1989:186). In other words, the reasons and accounts that people offer are basic facts that cannot be ignored in social policy-making. They tell us of the structures and mechanisms in people's lives that oppress them, or of the things that they value.

Because Bhaskar is concerned with 'emancipatory social practice', he shares ground with many social theorists on the political left. But in promoting this kind of social practice, his position inverts the famous dictum of Marx, who gave prominence in his programme to changing the world, even ahead of adequate interpretation. For Bhaskar, the world cannot be rationally changed unless it is adequately interpreted, so the urgent task for philosophy is to 'reclaim reality'. We interpret the world best by starting with the reasons and accounts of relevant actors in that world, whether or not their reasons and accounts seem rational, mentalistic, or irrational to those doing the interpreting. People's reasons and accounts are emergent phenomena: that is, they really exist. They are the best guide to understanding the material or immaterial structural influences that provide important controlling mechanisms in people's lives. They reveal what people perceive those mechanisms to be.

To interpret adequately all the structural influences that affect people's lives, the first object of research is to find what is really in people's minds about their world. Social reality is interpreted by discovering what people report its reality to be for them, and then by trying to confirm the reality for them of the things they report. Later stages involve explaining the operation of structural influences, and using that knowledge to promote emancipatory change of some kind. And this programme of change follows as a morally binding response for policy-makers. In a long and closely argued passage (1986: 103–211), Bhaskar shows that while social phenomena are conditioned by, dependent upon, and only materially manifest in natural phenomena, the same social phenomena remain causally, ontologically, and epistemologically irreducible to natural phenomena.

BHASKAR AND OTHER THEORISTS

In this section, I compare Bhaskar's conception of discovery with the ideas of three social theorists: Emile Durkheim, Jürgen Habermas, and Pierre Bourdieu. The section concludes with Ludwig Wittgenstein's key ideas, since these underpin the work of many recent social theorists and inform 'the interpretative alternative' to social research theory (Hughes 1990).

Durkheim and Bhaskar

Durkheim tried to create a unity between idealism and materialism as a basis for a science of sociology. There are strong similarities between his and Bhaskar's interpretation of social processes. Both see individual states of consciousness as due to the operation of social processes, and both assert the reality of collective phenomena: 'society is not a mere sum of individuals. Rather, the system formed by their association represents a specific reality which has its own characteristics' (Durkheim 1966 [1895]:103). Both also give priority to language in the determination of 'social facts' (in Durkheim's case) or 'structures and mechanisms' (in Bhaskar's). For Durkheim, these are 'a category of facts with very distinct characteristics: it consists of ways of acting, thinking, and feeling, external to the individual, and endowed with a power of coercion, by reason of which they control' the individual (1966 [1895]:3). These social facts are 'real' in the sense that they are external to the individual, and they are constraining, diffuse, and general. Durkheim's 'principle of correlation', which is at the base of all social scientific research, allows social researchers to learn about these facts, the effects of which are discernible in the world through the various sequences of sounds, movements of bodies, etc. that would not occur without their influence.

While Bhaskar's 'structures and mechanisms' are real for him too, their existence and range 'depends upon the intentional activity of human beings' (1989:81). In other words, 'Society is both ever-present *condition* and continually reproduced *outcome* of human agency' (1989:92). This seems to answer John Shotter's main objection to Bhaskar's conception. Shotter (1993) contends that Bhaskar's 'social structures' are object-like, and so not 'socially constructed'. However this seems no more than a misunderstanding by Shotter, who takes literally the analogy that Bhaskar draws between the 'objects' or 'mechanisms' of the world of science, and the 'social structures' of the world of the social sciences. On Bhaskar's account, like the rest of the social world, its structures *are* socially constructed. They are ontologically rooted in the everyday transactions between agents and their material transactions with nature (Bhaskar 1986:130). And this is a very important point for his critical realism. If structures were not socially constructed, emancipation from their effects through social action would be impossible. Indeed, these structures include a range of social phenomena: the semi-material structures, like rules, laws, and regulations; the immaterial structures, like cultural and personal values, ideologies, religious beliefs, etc.; and all the material structures that tend to constrain or liberate us.

All this takes Durkheim's ideas about 'social facts' much further. While human discourses and other activities are constrained by structures, for Bhaskar human activities and discourses also change and constrain the structures. In short, by consulting the reasons and accounts of relevant actors, we learn about the values, beliefs, interests, ideologies, and material conditions that create important structural influences in their lives. Using people's own accounts as *prima facie* evidence, we can set about confirming the reality of the structures themselves and explaining their operation.

Shotter also writes in high praise of Bhaskar: 'He has fashioned a wholly new context for argumentation about social ontology, and because of this, his "voice" merits enormous critical attention in all the human sciences' (1993:78). Yet Shotter overlooks the most important point in Bhaskar's account: namely its contribution to human emancipation. Bhaskar (1993) argues that his own critical realism and Shotter's social constructionism are quite compatible. But he sees one important contrast between the two: Shotter tilts his account in the direction of voluntaristic agency, not in the direction of Bhaskar's own transformative praxis.

Habermas and Bhaskar

Bhaskar makes bold claims for his critical realism and for the transformational model of social activity that follows from it. Coupling this with the emancipatory aims that he has in mind, we can see close parallels between his work and the critical theory of Habermas (1970, 1979, 1984, 1987). By any political yardstick, the applied effects of Bhaskar's model would be rigorously democratic, like the applied effects of Habermas's 'discourse ethic' in which the foundational status of human language gets priority. If some ideal society were to follow either theorist's conception of discovery, both of the basic requirements of democracy would be met: everyone's point of view and interpretation of the world would be consulted; and everyone's interests would be taken into account when shaping the dominant narratives through which the distributions of power, wealth, position, and privilege were accounted for and justified.

Elsewhere, I argue that an adequate approach to social justice needs to allow for the full possible range of 'human interests' (Corson 1998a). Habermas describes these as developed needs that are not naturally present in all people, but which are acquired by socialization and enculturation. His account provides for interests like the following: the need to recognize group values acquired by minority cultural, social, or linguistic groups; the need to provide social and organizational arrangements supportive of group values; and the need to recognize and value group orientations towards language and learning. Habermas offers his 'discourse ethic' as the most feasible way of discovering these things. Clearly then there is a strong link between Habermas and Bhaskar in their respect for acquired human interests; and both give people's reasons and accounts priority in social research and social policy.

Bourdieu and Bhaskar

Bourdieu (1982, 1984) explores the different types of relations to the world that different social groups possess. These relations are embedded in different sets of dispositions and attitudes towards the material world and other people. Like Bhaskar, Bourdieu acknowledges that there are many possible sets of ethnic, gender, and class interests that are very different from one another and require different and perhaps incompatible types of treatment. So research and policy-making that ignore the voices of sectional interests can do great harm. They amount to attempts to work out in advance, from the interests of dominant groups of individuals, what arrangements would be chosen under unknown conditions by other groups of people whose interests might not be readily detectable by anyone who is not steeped in the relevant class, gender, or minority culture.

Developing policy methods for taking into account very different sets of human needs and interests is not an easy thing to do. For Bourdieu, groups with cultural capital different from that given high status in society often provide accounts of their own behaviour and intentions in relation to the world that are quite different from dominant group accounts. They may seem inscrutable as a result, or even obtuse, perverse, or wrong-headed. So, often these accounts are discounted or stigmatized. Bhaskar wants to reclaim the reality of these and other accounts, and use them to give a more adequate interpretation of the social world.

Wittgenstein and Bhaskar

Bhaskar, Habermas and Bourdieu all show the influence of Wittgenstein's later philosophy, especially his interest in 'unravelling the fabrics of conceptual systems', a task which 'usually necessitates some excavation of the institutional matrices within which such systems are set' (Bhaskar 1986:20). As is well known, Wittgenstein replaced the objective realism of his earlier philosophy with a kind of sophisticated relativism (1961 [1921], 1953). Having realized that his earlier view, that knowledge is a linguistic picture of reality, was untenable, he put together quite a different philosophy: we are all participants in many different language games played within fairly closed linguistic circles. When we have knowledge or belief, we have it according to the linguistic rules that obtain in a given circle: in a discipline, a theory, or some other ideological framework.

To play in these games, we need to learn the special rules of the circles in which we operate or hope to operate. These rules are no more than conventions, laid down at some time by those who have power to decide the rules in whatever circle they happen to be. And these language games govern meaning. For example, the meaning of a word or a fragment of discourse is its 'use' within its own language game. But while norms, rules, and values govern word use, they do not dictate it. Rather, a norm or a rule is that which, once an action is done, can be said to display the meaning of that action. Indeed, putting a word or expression to use in a language game is an action that makes propaganda for a certain way of thinking: for a certain circle (Corson 1995b). In other words, just by participating in a language game we add to its influence in the world of discourse and ideas.

I think Bhaskar is looking at these ideas of Wittgenstein from the other direction. Like Habermas, he is asking us to use the language games that people inhabit as the best way of understanding their social reality. For Bhaskar, getting inside people's reasons and accounts means getting inside the circle of language games or meaning systems that people are caught up in. And this is what anthropologists try to do, and historians too, using different kinds of accounts. Below I summarize in point form the conception of discovery that Bhaskar offers.

CRITICAL REALISM FOR CRITICAL POLICY-MAKING IN EDUCATION

As mentioned, Bhaskar shows that people's reasons and accounts are the most basic evidence available to us for deciding anything about the social world, because they tell us the things that are in people's minds about that world. His approach to (policy) discovery follows from this:

- Human reasons and accounts are basic social scientific evidence.
- By consulting the reasons and accounts of people, decision-makers learn about the values, beliefs, interests, ideologies, and material entities that are important structures in the lives of those people.

- People's reasons and accounts offer evidence about what their beliefs, etc. are, and also about what they believe about those beliefs, etc.
- By using people's reasons and accounts as the starting point, we can begin to work out the reality of influential structures in people's lives: the things they value, and the things that oppress them.
- Action to keep wanted structures, or to replace unwanted with wanted structures (emancipation), can then be taken.

As this summary suggests, the first step in changing anything is to consult the reasons and accounts of participants who have interests at stake. Clearly this sort of consultative process involves carefully devolving real decision-making power to the people whose interests are at stake: those who are really in touch with the structural factors that oppress them, or with the structures that they value.

Several stages for critical policy-making at school level follow directly from these ideas. I introduce these stages here, and say more about them and the research methods they entail, in Chapter 11.

1. Identifying the real problem(s)

Critical policy-making begins when people identify a regularity or an irregularity of some kind in their school. Those responsible for the change process then try to state this 'effect' clearly as a problem. Next, they allow their statement of the problem to be criticized by a wide range of participants, or by their representatives, who have an interest at stake in the problem. If this confirms that the problem is a real one for participants, the problem then becomes the starting point for policy-making.

2. Trial policies

In critical and open dialogue, participants work out a trial solution as a response to the problem, aimed at replacing the unwanted problem with a wanted policy.

3. Testing policies against the views of participants

Participants in the change process test the effectiveness of their solution. Using critical dialogue, they undertake small-scale research of several types: for example, they observe the trial policy in action and get feedback on it; or they look for alternative solutions, including devolving decision-making to some smaller unit in the school.

4. Policy adoption and implementation

The policy-making ends when the policy solution meets the needs and interests of relevant participants; or, should the policy fail to meet people's expressed needs and interests, it is modified or rejected.

Part III

Practice

Chapter 7

Higher Education in Britain: Policy and Practice 1956–92

JOHN PRATT

Until 1992, policy for higher education in England and Wales was dominated by the existence of two sectors with distinctive institutions, organizational structures, purposes, traditions and cultures. The division was most visible and deliberate from 1965 to 1992 when a 'binary policy' was explicitly operated. The division ceased, at least formally, with the 1992 Further and Higher Education Act. The Act abolished the binary divide, granting the polytechnics and leading colleges of higher education the power to award their own degrees and the right to use the title 'university', and unified funding and quality assurance arrangements. This chapter summarizes a number of studies of post-war policies, using the approach set out in Chapters 2 and 4. It offers examples of 'policy testing', the application of ideas of 'situational logic' to policy and institutions, and it concludes by suggesting some lessons for policy and policy-making.

A very brief chronology of events in the period covered by the present chapter helps to clarify some of the policy issues and the questions they raise for analysis:

- *February 1956:* A White Paper (Ministry of Education 1956) proposes the establishment of eight (later ten) colleges of advanced technology (CATs).
- *October 1963:* The Robbins Committee (Robbins 1963) proposes that the CATs be upgraded to university status. This was accomplished by 1966.
- *April 1964:* The new Labour Secretary of State enunciates his idea for a 'binary policy' in higher education, recognizing the two traditions of the universities and the technical colleges.
- *May 1966:* A White Paper (Department of Education and Science 1966) proposes the designation of 28 (later 30) polytechnics to head the 'public sector' of higher education in the binary system. These were designated between 1968 and 1973.
- *December 1972:* A White Paper (DES 1972) sets out plans for dramatic

reductions in student intake to colleges of education, and outlines ways in which the colleges might find new futures by diversification and by amalgamation with other colleges, polytechnics or universities – or closure.

- *By 1980:* A new sector of nearly 60 'colleges of higher education' has resulted from this process.
- *1989–92:* Four colleges of higher education acquire polytechnic status.
- *March 1992:* The Further and Higher Education Act enables all 34 polytechnics, a few other colleges of education (and their sister institutions in Scotland), to acquire university status as higher education is 'unified'.

It is hard to avoid concluding from this chronology that history seemed to be repeating itself. In a period of less than 40 years, three generations of specially designated institutions were established, and they then changed into something else. Those who know their history will not be surprised to learn that these are but the most recent in a longer series of similar events, stretching back into the last century. What was going on? How do we analyse, explain and understand these policies and their outcomes?

The realist approach espoused in this book, summarized in the formulation by Pawson and Tilley (1997:58) that 'outcomes follow from mechanisms acting in contexts', is helpful as a basis for analysing policy, since policy is concerned with all three elements of this schema. It is a purposive activity (Hogwood and Gunn 1984), using (usually a variety of) mechanisms intended to achieve particular outcomes. The approach is itself subject to the effect of a variety of other social mechanisms in particular contexts. There are many ways in which to analyse policies, and many grounds on which to judge them; one is to take as a basis the formal statements of policy-makers about what the problems are and what the policies are supposed to do. In the Centre for Institutional Studies (University of East London) we have developed an approach to politics, public policy and public institutions which we believe helps to bring these into the realm of rational inquiry and improvement. As Chapter 4 makes clear, we are not restricted to such official statements, and we may find that other formulations more accurately account for events as they unfold, but in terms of analysing policy one good starting point is to scrutinize what governments say they think they are doing.

THE COLLEGES OF ADVANCED TECHNOLOGY 1956–66

In the years after the Second World War, the government in Britain was much exercised by problems of higher technological education. The issue was highlighted by the Percy and Barlow reports (Ministry of Education 1945; Lord President of the Council 1946) which expressed concerns about the shortage and quality of technologists to support post-war industrial growth. The position appeared parlous. In 1943, according to the Percy Report, the annual 'national output' of civil, electrical and mechanical engineers was only about 3,000. The technical colleges produced, nearly all through National Certificates and Diplomas, more than half of these, and the universities' contribution – about 1,200 – had not changed much for decades. The Report suggested that this was the limit of desirable expansion. Put crudely, the Percy and Barlow reports accepted that the universities were not interested in responding to the demand for practically orientated technologists, but they recognized that the technical colleges traditionally had responded, and were increasingly pressing to expand this provision. Both reports thus advocated selection of a limited number of technical colleges in which new degree-level technology courses could be developed.

Although the government received the opposite advice from the Advisory Council for Scientific Policy (1949), it was eventually convinced of the need to designate the eight colleges of advanced technology in 1956 (and two more later) to provide a full range and substantial volume of work exclusively at advanced (higher education) level (Ministry of Education 1956).

In studying the development of the CATs, my colleague Tyrrell Burgess and I began by treating the events as, as it were, history, recording the changes and seeking to understand how they occurred. But we were increasingly struck by the incongruity between the stated aims of the 1956 policy and its outcome in the mid-1960s; so we examined the policy aims and compared them with the outcomes. Such an approach to policy was unusual at that time. We found that in a number of ways the outcome was a clear reversal of the stated intentions of less than a decade earlier. In 1956 the purpose had been to create a group of institutions which were distinctive from, and would serve different purposes from, the universities. By the early 1960s they were sufficiently like universities that their transformation became inevitable, and a relatively conservative Committee of Enquiry (Robbins 1963) recommended that they become universities.

The policy implied that by designating certain institutions, a number of outcomes would follow. Relatively simple tests of the policy showed the reverse was happening. Our analysis revealed a number of unintended consequences of policy. For example, although the CATs concentrated on advanced work, much of the growth of this took place elsewhere in the further education sector. The CATs had just under 20,000 advanced students in 1958 – out of a total of just under 100,000 in the FE sector – and roughly the same number in 1964 when the sector total exceeded 140,000 (Burgess and Pratt 1970:54). While the CATs had concentrated on and developed the new degree-level full-time and sandwich Diploma in Technology courses, they had dropped much of their part-time work.

In seeking to understand and explain these developments, our study suggested that deeper processes were at work. We found that the designation of the CATs reflected and reinforced an historic pattern of aspiration in further education, which itself reflected the social and economic context of the sector. One aspect of this process of aspiration was the way that further education acted as a route for students – particularly those of working-class origin or working themselves – to remedy deficiencies in, or exclusion from, other forms of education. In turn, colleges sought to extend this opportunity to degree level (and even doctoral level) by offering external university degrees (in the design and control of which they had little say). The CAT policy now granted status to institutions which had predominantly degree-level work. They excluded the lower-level courses that led to it, and were rewarded by being given university titles. In doing this, the CATs were merely following a pattern that had affected the technical colleges for the previous century. Many of the colleges founded in the nineteenth century in the technical college tradition had turned into universities, and in some cases, as in Manchester, the pattern was repeated several times (Robinson 1968). We later called this historical process 'academic drift' (Pratt and Burgess 1974).

The study of the CATs also showed how government used few, if any, of the 'instruments of policy' available to it to counter these pressures. It seemed simply to assume that if you enunciated the policy, institutions would behave accordingly. Some of the instruments of policy it had used, like financial arrangements, while encouraging expansion of advanced work, had been more effective in the other colleges than in the CATs, not least because of the increased aspiration for status that the designation 'CAT' generated in these other colleges.

After its experience with the CATs, the government was anxious to avoid making the same mistakes again. The next phase of policy was introduced explicitly to 'reverse 100 years of educational history' (Burgess and Pratt 1970:179). As the CATs acquired their university charters, an incoming Labour government announced the establishment of a 'binary' policy in higher education, and the designation of new 'polytechnics'.

POLYTECHNICS 1965–92

The binary policy was a response to, and a rebuttal of, the structural assumptions of the Robbins Report (1963) – and most of British society. Lord Robbins had seen higher education as broadly synonymous with university education. His recommendations for expansion included not only awarding the CATs university status, but a succession of upgradings of the leading technical colleges as they developed advanced work. Anthony Crosland, the Secretary of State for Education and Science in 1965, explicitly rejected this 'ladder' system in higher education (Crosland 1965) in favour of one giving due recognition to the two traditions of the universities and the technical colleges. The colleges would provide vocationally-orientated degree courses, using the new Council for National Academic Awards to do so; they would meet the needs of thousands of young people for sub-degree courses, and of 'tens of thousands' of part-time students seeking advanced courses.

This and subsequent statements by the Secretary of State, together with the 1966 White Paper (DES 1966) announcing the government's intention to create polytechnics from more than 50 colleges in the further education sector, set out a range of aims for the new policies against which the outcomes could be tested. Among other things, the polytechnics were to be 'comprehensive academic communities', under 'social [that is, local authority] control', and to offer economies of scale. With the CAT policy, Tyrrell Burgess and I had argued that policy objectives should be set out 'in terms which enable their success or failure to be measured' (Burgess and Pratt 1970:178), and had criticized the 1956 policy statements as 'declaratory only' – 'not so much a plan as a peroration' (Burgess and Pratt 1970:179). For the polytechnics, there were stated policy aims, although we later criticized the 1966 White Paper as 'a failure at all levels: educational, administrative and intellectual' (Pratt and Burgess 1974:45). But one of our concerns was that the government appeared to believe that the important thing was to designate the polytechnics first, and only then to sort out other matters – like their educational development plans. With these concerns in mind we undertook a study of the initial years of the polytechnic policy.

This study (Pratt and Burgess 1974) clearly could not test the policy in the way that the retrospective analysis of the CATs could. After all, the first polytechnics were only designated in 1968, and the last two not until 1973. The study recorded and analysed the developments in the polytechnics and their constituent colleges from the announcement of the policy until 1971. But we were able to do two things. First, we set out the grounds on which policy, even in the early years, could be tested. Central to this was the expansion of policy statements into definable aims. Policy, typically, is couched in vague generalizations – in the case of the polytechnics the term 'comprehensive academic communities' was one such statement. We asked, 'What would the policy look like if it was working?', and were thus able to formulate a series of characteristics of the polytechnics (for example, of the nature of the student body, of the staff, of the processes of governance) that might define a comprehensive academic community, and that could be examined, even at an early stage. Second, we brought to this policy the experience of the CATs study, and thus our own hypotheses about the likely developments of the polytechnics. These hypotheses (alongside those embodied in the policy) could be tested, and they guided our selection of key issues to examine.

Thus we were able to identify important developments in the polytechnics even before they were designated, to draw attention to, and, I think we can claim, to help to arrest some of the changes that were inconsistent with policy aims. A couple of examples: the polytechnic colleges began to shed part-time students within a year or so of the announcement of the policies (Pratt and Burgess 1974:73); they began to increase the proportion of students aged 18 to 21 (Pratt and Burgess 1974:79–81); proportionately fewer students were studying engineering (Pratt and Burgess 1974:77); and their proportion of working-class students appeared to be declining (Pratt and Burgess 1974:86). These developments flew in the face of the policy aim that they should be 'comprehensive academic communities' (DES 1966).

In a later study (Pratt 1997), it was possible to assess the extent to which our 1974 fears had been realized. This study examined the polytechnic policy after it too had finally achieved a *prima facie* reversal of its intentions – some 27 years on – when the polytechnics acquired university titles. The conclusion then was more equivocal. In the years since our 1974 study, the polytechnics have begun, eventually, to recover some of the lost ground. They had, for example, maintained a comprehensive range of courses, and nurtured significant educational developments. They had sustained the part-time route, after the initial decline in numbers. They had become identified as institutions for mature students and those without traditional entry qualifications. They became the larger sector in higher education, by expanding particularly rapidly (again after years of sluggish growth) in the later 1980s. I argued that they had made possible mass higher education in Britain (Pratt 1997:307).

The major failure of policy – whether or not the acquisition of a university title is regarded as a mark of success (or even reward) – was in the arrangements for their governance. Put crudely, the polytechnics and local authorities did not get on. There was a history of wrangles and dissatisfaction on both sides that eventually, in 1988, led to their removal from the local authority sector as independent statutory corporations, which made easy the changes of the 1992 Act (and thus an explicit failure of the 1960s policy aim). The problems of governance – an instrument of policy – led, as much as anything, to the abolition of the binary policy, simply because they led to the independence of the polytechnics, and thus eliminated the main administrative distinction between them and the universities.

The analysis of the mechanisms affecting the outcomes of the binary and polytechnic policies revealed significant changes in the way that the government operated. I argued that it, too, began to learn some of the lessons of history, particularly the increasing realization of the power it could exercise through various instruments of policy, specifically the control of resources (Pratt 1997:317): 'Its funding agencies exercised greater, more detailed and more directed control over the polytechnics (and the universities) than ever before.' It is possible to see developments such as these as a concomitant part of the emergence of a 'contractual state' and 'audit society' (Scott 1995), illustrating the way that particular policy outcomes in higher education are both a result of and part of wider social forces.

One of the key instruments of policy that facilitated the development of the polytechnics was the Council for National Academic Awards (CNAA). The study revealed not only the way in which this body operated in an educational context, but suggested some more general lessons for policy-making and the design of institutions as instruments of policy. There was something paradoxical in the way that the CNAA facilitated innovation in the polytechnics and colleges: institutions under central bureaucratic control were more innovative than those with the autonomy they aspired to.

The reasons for this lay in the CNAA's processes, though few in the polytechnics recognized their significance at the time. CNAA procedures required vast amounts of information and were costly. The interactions with the Council tended to the inquisitional, despite CNAA efforts to promote dialogue. It was difficult to be wholly frank about problems if the course could be closed as a consequence. There was danger of discussion centring on the satisfaction of bureaucratic rather than educational issues.

But the CNAA placed responsibility for initiative with the colleges. Institutions themselves designed the courses and argued for them. This process of argument was the key to the CNAA's success (Pratt 1997:214–15). For if proposals had to be argued before a body of people as knowledgeable as the proposers, basic assumptions were exposed and had to be justified. The CNAA's (tedious) procedures required the proposers to show how their courses were justified in economic, social and educational terms, to demonstrate their intellectual coherence and progression, and to justify teaching and assessment procedures. Often, course teams found that existing assumptions and accepted conventions did not stand up to this kind of questioning. It was, in the end, the academic conservatism of CNAA visiting parties that promoted innovation. A further element was the way in which the CNAA required the whole course team to be involved in the validation of courses. This offered junior members of staff opportunities for questioning the assumptions of their established colleagues; often, it offered opportunities for personal advance. Junior staff, too, quickly realized that the CNAA process offered them a way to outflank their conservative colleagues; a course team could gain approval for a course that was being resisted within its own institution.

The operation of the CNAA showed how institutions can have 'a life of their own' – its actions could not be predicted simply from its membership. Although often composed of academic conservatives, it promoted innovation. At the same time, its membership constrained it, and by the 1980s, as Silver (1990:201) noted, it had 'acquired many of the characteristics of a classic bureaucracy'. What the CNAA offered, at its best, was an example of a way of resolving some key dilemmas in higher education – giving national currency to locally created courses, and promoting innovation and maintaining standards, yet using existing personnel in the system to do so. The lesson has not been lost on others. In Austria, for example, a new Fachhochschulrat (Council) has been set up to undertake a similar function in a country with a considerably more conservative academic tradition. To most people's surprise, although inevitably it is composed of representatives of the existing dominant groups in the Austrian academy and wider society, it has maintained a remarkably independent line (Pratt and Hackl forthcoming).

THE COLLEGES OF HIGHER EDUCATION 1972–82

At about the same time as the polytechnics were designated in pursuance of a set of policy objectives, the government embarked on another policy in higher education on an explicitly different basis. In 1972 the government published a White Paper (DES 1972) which initiated, over the next few years, the largest and most controversial reorganization of higher education in England and Wales there had ever been. Because of a reduction in the projected need for teachers, some 200 colleges were reorganized. The college of education sector disappeared. Twenty-five colleges closed; many amalgamated with polytechnics or universities and largely lost their separate identity. The remainder, singly or after mergers, emerged as a group of nearly 60 colleges of higher education located in the largely unfamiliar environment of the further education system and, effectively, formed a second tier in the public sector; a few of these eventually attained polytechnic status, and some of these acquired university titles after the 1992 Act.

Analysing this policy presented a number of significant differences from that of the CATs or the polytechnics. By comparison with the policies for the CATs and the polytechnics, in this reorganization the government's intentions were less explicitly stated and less concerned with the educational purposes of the reorganized colleges. The 1972 White Paper did not predict, prescribe or advocate the outcome. The Secretary of State at the time, Margaret Thatcher, rejected what she called an 'architectural' approach to policy in favour of an 'organic' one (Locke *et al.* 1985:152). In the phrases of the time, colleges were left to 'sink or swim', or in another metaphor to 'wither on the vine' (Locke *et al.* 1985:1). There was no government statement about the nature of colleges of higher education (as there had been with both the CATs and the polytechnics), nor even about the desired number, type or size of colleges. Moreover, the projections of the overall student numbers in teacher education that the colleges were supposed to accommodate changed frequently and dramatically.

The government simply outlined opportunities for the futures of nearly 200 varied colleges, and made the outcome for individual colleges a matter for negotiation between the DES, local education authorities and voluntary bodies, and the colleges themselves. We found not an educational policy but logistical imperatives; the primary questions about colleges' futures were about their viability. The DES moved the colleges of education (except those which joined universities) into the further education sector and expected them to respond to its constraints and opportunities. The colleges could be seen as needing to serve a market, or to adapt to their environment. Our concern in the study was primarily with the impact of the policies on the development of the colleges.

The lack of explicit statements of policy for the reorganized colleges complicated our research task. Another of our studies had investigated how an individual institution changed under the CAT and polytechnic policies (Locke 1978). This showed that, while academic drift could be seen to be against the interests of national policy, it could be very much in the interests of a particular institution. It suggested that we should expect colleges to respond to the constraints and opportunities in which they were placed, and to seek institutional benefits – staffing, building, resources, status, etc. It would be unsurprising to find a college determining on a course of action which improved its staffing establishment, say, whether or not this corresponded to national policy. Thus, the theoretical framework that we had developed matched the approach taken by the DES in reorganizing the colleges. We further developed the theoretical framework by reference to Popper's ideas of 'situational logic' and 'situational analysis' (see Chapter 4). The theory of situational logic suggested that a college would respond to the logic of its situation, as it understood it. This paved the way for us to set out hypotheses of how we would expect colleges to develop, given our knowledge of their environment, and then to test how far they did indeed develop like this.

In planning this study we brought to bear, also, the hypotheses we had developed in earlier studies. In particular, our approach to these institutions was shaped by the theory of academic drift (Pratt and Burgess 1974). We hypothesized that the reorganized colleges would aspire to the status of the favoured institutions (polytechnics) in the sector. Thus we had two sets of hypotheses: the government's policies; and our expectations of likely developments based on knowledge from our previous studies.

This impacted in two ways on the research methodology. One led us to explore the constraints and opportunities for the colleges during the years of reorganization. The analysis of the constraints and opportunities of the colleges' situations is a 'paper test' rather than being based on, say, a survey of principals' or teachers' perceptions of the major factors, but it enabled us to identify data which might test the hypotheses it generated; for example, it suggested that different groups of colleges might respond differently. The data suggested that the proportions of initial teacher training in the colleges affected their development. It showed how the DES had failed to recognize the nature of the environment in which it placed the colleges, and that the assumptions of the 1972 White Paper were faulty. No one had planned to create a second tier of aspirant polytechnics.

LESSONS FOR POLICY

This brief summary suggests a number of lessons that can be learnt from studies of this kind, for both higher education policy in particular, and for improvement to policy-making in general. The failure of the CAT policy to develop distinctive institutions suggested the need for a more directed and comprehensive approach to policy and its implementation when the binary and polytechnic policies were launched. Although the polytechnics eventually attained university status, and might be accused of succumbing, again, to academic drift, the policy was more of a success than a failure, not least because by 1992 the universities had changed too, acquiring characteristics hitherto typical of the polytechnic tradition. The resilience and influence of the polytechnics ultimately relied, I have argued (Pratt 1997), on an educational philosophy. It would be true to say that many staff in polytechnics would have struggled to define this philosophy, and some were unsympathetic to it although it shaped their work. It was articulated by the key proponents of the polytechnics (Robinson 1968) and was manifest, for example, in the regulations and practices of the CNAA. I suggested that for any education policy to work there must be a coherent and valid *educational* philosophy behind it. One wonders to what extent some current developments in school education and teacher training meet this condition.

For the unified system of higher education in Britain, the auguries are not good. The policy documents advocating the change (DES 1991, for example) expressed a general concern to maintain 'diversity' of provision, and spoke of the need for funding arrangements related to 'the distinctive missions of individual institutions' (DES 1991:14), and of the need in particular to maintain and extend the polytechnics' and colleges' emphasis on vocational studies and widening access. The subsequent Dearing Report (National Committee of Inquiry into Higher Education 1997) offered a (very) brief vision of a 'learning society', but largely carried on as if it had not, and lapsed into immediate practical detail. To maintain diversity in a unified sector requires continuing consideration by institutions of the nature of vocational and professional education at the turn of the twenty-first century, and for an intellectual framework within which courses and curricula are designed.

The development of an educational philosophy is not, as history has shown, a sufficient condition for the maintenance of diversity in higher education. Even when a distinctive philosophy was articulated, there were many pressures towards uniformity. For the unified system, Brown's (1971:25) observation that 'In an unequal system the deprived tend to formulate their goals in terms of the favoured' remains as true now as it did for the polytechnics, or the CATs before them. As Pawson and Tilley (1997:58) note, outcomes depend on context. The lesson of history, summarized in this chapter, is that a wide range of organizational, governmental, financial and other matters need to be addressed to maintain diversity in higher education. The 1991 White Paper referred to the need for funding arrangements related to 'the distinctive missions of individual institutions' (DES 1991:14), but offered no indication of what these might be, and there were few clues as to how the polytechnic tradition might further be developed once the distinctive features of their policy environment had been removed. If one lesson is that attention to all the instruments of policy, such as these, are necessary to secure desired outcomes, then the converse also applies: if you neglect them, the outcomes are less likely to be achieved. The question now for British higher education is: Has anyone noticed?

Chapter 8

Empowering Lecturers to Improve Assessment Practice in Higher Education

JOANNA SWANN AND
KATHRYN ECCLESTONE

> You cannot construct foolproof institutions, that is to say, institutions whose functioning does not very largely depend upon persons: institutions, at best, can reduce the uncertainty of the personal element, by assisting those who work for the aims for which the institutions are designed, and on whose personal initiative and knowledge success largely depends.
>
> Karl Popper (1985c:308–9)

Assessment of student achievement in the United Kingdom higher education sector is problematic for a number of reasons. This chapter does not offer a panacea for the system's many weaknesses; rather, it offers a framework of support for teams of lecturers who wish to improve assessment practice in specific contexts. Two sets of problem-based activities have been developed. One encourages lecturers to formulate practical problems relating to assessment, create and trial solutions, and evaluate critically the outcomes of their endeavours. The other, more simply, focuses on the analysis and critical evaluation of policies initiated outwith the research or developmental process. The problem-based activities have been tested and developed in the context of action research undertaken at the University of Sunderland (Swann and Arthurs 1999; Swann and Ecclestone 1999; Ecclestone and Swann 1999).

Although the methodological activities are discussed here with reference to the problem of how to improve assessment practice in higher education, they can be adapted by professionals addressing a variety of problems in all sectors of education. The activities (supported by methodological principles and collegial ethics) can be used to create an empowerment agenda for lecturers and teachers with a broad range of concerns. This agenda fosters the desire for improvement, and encourages initiative and constructive criticism.

INCREASED CENTRALIZATION

There is a widespread assumption, particularly among policy-makers, that improvement in services provided by educational institutions will be brought about mainly by increased external regulation, target-setting and the specification of common standards. This is evident in the work of government departments and agencies, and education quangos. Policies based on this assumption lead to increased centralization, concomitant with a subtle shift from democratic to authoritarian approaches to decision-taking. These policies often have far-reaching and undesirable consequences. In particular, they tend to demotivate individuals working at lower levels in the hierarchy, and stifle initiative and creativity. The over-riding task of teachers becomes that of implementing externally determined policy to enable students to meet specified common standards. Fulfilling these externally formulated expectations can be extraordinarily time-consuming; consequently, teachers and students who wish to broaden their expectations are often inhibited from doing so.

This scenario is fully enacted in the compulsory sector of education, particularly in England, and increasingly in colleges of further education. Professionals and students are, in effect, not trusted to make judgements about their circumstances and how best to respond to them. People are discouraged from making (and learning from) their own mistakes; they are obliged to practise on the basis of mistakes made by other people (note, for example, the major flaws acknowledged by successive administrations regarding national curriculum content, and the repeated amendments to the assessment regime in General National Vocational Qualifications).

In general, a target-setting approach to planning and evaluation discourages criticality (see Chapter 5): policies are deemed to be successful insofar as they have been implemented, and their consequences are often marginalized or ignored. Thinking about learning is a casualty of increased regulation and the extensive use of targets and specified common standards. Assessed achievement (defined in terms of prescribed outcomes) and learning have been conflated, to the detriment of thinking about learning in its broadest sense.

When failure is acknowledged by the instigators of a policy, it is often attributed to people charged with policy implementation, or to a lack of clarity and detail in the policy. This reasoning leads to an increase in external regulation and greater specification of required outcomes.

Illustrations from the compulsory sector and further education are indicative of what may happen in higher education as its institutions become increasingly subject to centralized control. The work of the Quality Assurance Agency for Higher Education (QAAHE), under pressure from the funding bodies, makes the sector vulnerable to external injunctions to regulate assessment procedures (QAAHE 1998b). Although the QAAHE modified its initial plans for a 'national quality assurance system' in light of feedback on its consultation document (QAAHE 1998a), the systems and procedures being developed and introduced will have a significant and, arguably, deleterious effect on the nature of what is taught and learned (this view is shared by others; see, for example, Utley 1998). Regulation may not stop at 'threshold standards' and 'subject benchmarking'. Universities are already working with a national curriculum for initial teacher training (Department for Education and Employment 1998b). In general, there is a growing homogeneity, based on regulated systems of outcome-based assessment, between higher, further and adult education, and the compulsory sector (Ecclestone 1999).

PUBLIC DEBATE ABOUT ASSESSMENT

Against this background, public debate about assessment policy in UK higher education is currently focused on the following problems:

- How can common standards be defined and applied with regard to levels and degree classifications?
- How can assessment be made more valid and reliable in credit-based systems?
- How can assessment practices promote better student learning? (In this context, learning is usually conceived in terms of specified observable outcomes.)

In addition, there is the issue of whether traditional degree classifications should be retained (Higher Education Quality Council 1996).

Literature on teaching, learning and assessment aimed at university lecturers acknowledges the consequences for assessment practice of the increased number of students entering the sector. The more practically-orientated texts also address educational aims – specifically how to make assessment more effective in promoting learning, and fairer to students. (See for example: Brown and Knight 1994; Gibbs 1994; Knight 1995; Brown, S. *et al.* 1996; Brown, G. *et al.* 1997.)

Yet much advice about the use of formative feedback to improve student learning, or ways of streamlining lecturers' marking, is technical. Among other things it urges that more consistent use should be made of explicit learning outcomes and assessment criteria, combined with a greater emphasis on formative feedback, self- and peer-assessment, and standardized marking schemes. Authors producing this practical advice clearly wish to make assessment fairer, more transparent and rigorous. It is also apparent that their advice is informed by educational beliefs and research findings about the importance of diagnostic and formative feedback in learning. In addition, there is a pragmatic recognition that lecturers are under great pressure to provide high-quality marking and feedback despite a significant increase in the numbers of students they have to assess. These beliefs, coupled with an acknowledgement of resource pressures, are reinforced by the extension to higher education of political initiatives to base learning on explicit descriptions of levels, learning outcomes and assessment criteria (National

Committee of Inquiry into Higher Education [Dearing Report] 1997; Higher Education Quality Council 1997; QAAHE 1998a, 1998b).

Despite extensive press coverage of political initiatives (particularly in the *Times Higher Education Supplement*), and the kind of academic and professional texts described above, the complexity of assessment policy and its wider implications are rarely discussed by university lecturers. When lecturers consider assessment issues it is usually in the context of formal and semi-formal structures, such as assessment boards and departmental meetings. Changes in assessment procedures at school and departmental level tend to be *ad hoc*; they are often ill thought-out and subject to limited evaluation. Belying both the amount of time spent on the task and its significance, assessing student achievement is a low-profile activity in terms of lecturers' job descriptions and the activities for which they are given credit.

A FRAMEWORK FOR CHANGE

Although discussion about assessment within universities is limited, there are lecturers, uneasy about the processes in which they engage, who are willing to formulate and tackle assessment problems. They are often constrained, however, by the need to address other aspects of their work, the difficulties of making changes which require collaborative action (which effective changes to assessment invariably do), and a sense of powerlessness caused by recent changes in the sector.

One way of supporting lecturers who wish to be proactive in the improvement of assessment practice is to offer a framework for change which:

- raises the public profile of the policy and practice of assessment;
- acknowledges that there is considerable scope for the improvement of assessment practice (without implying that weaknesses are peculiar to particular institutions or individuals);
- provides methodological and collegial support which encourages and helps teams of lecturers to formulate and address practical problems specific to their situation.

Problem-based action research of the kind developed at the University of Sunderland provides one such methodological and collegial framework. Derived from the philosophy of Karl Popper (in particular, Popper 1979), it is based on the idea that there is a logic to all learning (see Chapters 2 and 10), and that wherever and whenever learning takes place the logic is present (even if the learner is unaware that this is so).[1] All learning begins with a problem and an attempt to solve it, which leads to the possibility of error and thus a new problem. The task of anyone who wishes to improve practice is to: formulate a pressing practical problem (which subsequently may be refined and made more specific); create and implement one or more trial solutions; test the effectiveness of the solution(s) by reference not only to the intended consequences of action but also to those which are unintended (and potentially undesirable). As discussed in Chapters 4 and 5, the unintended consequences of action are often more far-reaching than those that are intended, and many are undesirable. A policy designed to improve a situation may have a detrimental effect, despite the explicitly stated goals or targets having been achieved.

A methodological innovation to this Popperian approach to planned change is the use of 'What is stopping . . . ?' and 'What is inhibiting . . . ?' questions, such as 'What is stopping or inhibiting the improvement of assessment practice within this programme?' (see Chapter 5 for discussion). These questions focus attention on the present situation, and what needs to be done to improve it; they foster an open-ended view of what is desirable and, indeed, possible.

THE SCOPE AND SCALE OF OUR RESEARCH

In autumn 1996 a proposal for problem-based action research at the University of Sunderland was initiated by the authors of this chapter, both of whom were, at the time, lecturers in the university's School of Education. The subsequent research took place in two phases, January to July 1997 (funded by the university as part of its teaching and learning initiative), and September 1997 to July 1998. The research, involving fourteen lecturers from four of the university's schools, was designed to address the over-arching practical problem: 'How can we improve lecturers' assessment practice in higher education?' Lecturers, working in teams of two to four members, were expected to share and address broadly similar problems concerning the improvement of assessment procedures (specifically, aspects of assessment over which they have some control), develop and test a problem-based methodology (Chapter 5 provides a full account of the methodological principles and procedures), and adhere to an agreed set of ethical principles. There was scope for a wide variety of responses concerning the formulation of sub-problems, trial solutions and methods of testing. (The methodological principles have since been adopted as the basis of one of the university's staff development courses.)

Eight (sub-) problems became the focus of research by the various teams (four in phase 1 and four in phase 2, with two teams participating in both phases). The problems, and the number of students directly involved, are shown in Table 8.1. In general, these problems (and associated issues) can be located within the wider debate about assessment in higher education in the UK.

THE METHODOLOGICAL ACTIVITIES

Characteristic of our problem-based action research is a series of activities (encapsulated in headings) designed to help lecturers to adopt the problem-based methodology. The first activities are preparatory; they are undertaken – preferably in a workshop – prior to implementing new procedures or

Problem	Whether problem addressed at module or programme level	Level of study	Number of students on module or programme
How can we provide detailed descriptions of grading criteria for students and offer better written feedback through a standardized form based on the criteria?	module	2 (under-graduate)	78
How can we learn more about student responses to feedback on written assignments in order to develop future assessment procedures which will help students to improve the quality of their work?	module	1 (under-graduate)	180
How can we use formative feedback on oral presentations throughout the module to help students improve the quality of their work?	module	masters	5
How can we validate changes to assessment procedures by seeking and responding to student opinion?	module	2 (under-graduate)	103
How can we ensure that students submit their own work and are capable of working independently?	module	1 (under-graduate)	250
How can we improve assessment practice on this module?	module	2 (under-graduate)	70
How can we improve assessment practice on this module?	module	3 (under-graduate)	50
How can we encourage students to improve their work and grades by learning from diagnostic and formative assessment feedback?	programme	1, 2, 3 (under-graduate)	144

Table 8.1: The scope and scale of the research

practices. The preparatory activities were modified in light of feedback from our phase 1 colleagues. The headings used for phase 2, which address targeted modules or programmes, are shown in Table 8.2.

Having worked through the initial set of activities, lecturers attend to the business of implementing their chosen trial solution(s), mindful of the potential for unintended consequences (desirable or undesirable). That is, each adopted solution is tested. By treating implemented policies as trials, lecturers are encouraged to discard those which are failing. It is nevertheless

---

(1)   With regard to assessment practice on this module/programme:
        What do we feel is going well? and/or
        What do we think will go well?
        What do we want to defend, maintain and develop?

(2)   With regard to assessment practice on this module/programme:
        What is not going well at present? and/or
        What do we think may not go well?
        Which aspects of the state of affairs pertaining to this module/ programme do we wish to change?

(3)   What seems to be stopping or inhibiting desirable changes in assessment practice regarding this module/programme?

(4)   Impediments to change within our sphere of influence:

(5)   In light of our responses to the above, we will address the over-arching problem of how to improve assessment practice on the module/programme by addressing the practical problem(s) below.
        [Please use the 'How can we . . . ?' form for your response.]

(6)   We could address this sub-problem (these sub-problems) by . . .

(7)   Of the ideas listed under item 6, this semester/academic year we will . . .

        [Note: some teams of lecturers may wish to conflate 6 and 7.]

(8)   Our solution to the problem of how to improve assessment practice will be successful insofar as it results in . . .

(9)   Our solution to the problem of how to improve assessment practice will be a failure if it results in . . .

(10)   Success and failure will be judged, in part at least, by . . .

Table 8.2: Headings to help lecturers address the problem: 'How can we improve assessment practice on our targeted module/programme during this semester/academic year?'

important to allocate sufficient time to testing a trial solution. In particular, judgement is needed to determine what is a fair test.

The next step is to evaluate what has taken place, with reference to the questions: 'To what extent, if at all, has (have) the initial problem (or problems) been solved?' 'What unintended and unexpected consequences (desirable or undesirable) have arisen?' 'With the benefit of hindsight, might other strategies (referring both to problems and solutions) have been preferable?' If competing solutions are tested, and if, in the course of policy implementation, new ideas from other sources become available, then the empirically tested solutions can be compared and discussed alongside new material.

At the end of this process, lecturers engaged in action research (rather than merely staff and/or institutional development) are expected to write a formal account of what has taken place and, in particular, what has been learned. This is done to stimulate discussion with other interested parties.

A truncated version of the action research methodology is required in some circumstances, specifically those in which lecturers are not in a position to determine their own trial solutions, or where a trial solution has already been developed and a decision to adopt it has been taken. In these situations, a new set of methodological activities that encourages the testing of a policy – in light of the problem it was designed to solve – is offered to lecturers. The headings used for the truncated methodology are provided in Table 8.3. After an initial meeting, a team using this approach follows the same implementation and evaluation procedures as teams who adopt the full methodology.

Description of new practice:

To be completed before implementation:

(1)   The new assessment practice is designed to solve the practical problem of . . . [Please use a 'How can . . . ?' formulation.]

(2)   The new assessment practice will be successful insofar as . . .

(3)   The new assessment practice will be a failure if . . .

(4)   Success and failure will be judged, in part at least, by . . .

Table 8.3: Headings for preparatory activities when the truncated methodology is required

COLLABORATIVE ACTION RESEARCH

The authors' conception of action research is similar to that of Carr and Kemmis (1986:165):

There are two essential aims of all action research: to *improve* and to *involve*. Action research aims at improvement in three areas: firstly, the improvement of a *practice*; secondly, the improvement of the *understanding* of the practice by its practitioners; and, thirdly, the improvement of the *situation* in which the practice takes place. The aim of *involvement* stands shoulder to shoulder with the aim of *improvement*. Those involved in the practice being considered are to be involved in the action research process in all its phases of planning, acting, observing and reflecting.

Our research at Sunderland was designed to be collaborative, with all participants becoming action researchers. We saw ourselves as co-ordinators and facilitators within the project team. In practice, a fully collaborative project was an aspiration rather than a reality. We initiated the research, formulated its over-arching problem and methodology, devised workshops to lead participants through the activities, and asserted the importance of collaborative ethics (see below). This inevitably meant that our ownership of the project was greater than that of our colleagues. However, it was not our intention to control every detail: our colleagues were responsible for formulating their own sub-problems, and for creating, implementing and evaluating their trial solutions. A fully collaborative approach to action research is nonetheless an important standard at which to aim; the greater the degree of collaboration, the greater the participants' sense of involvement and responsibility.

Lecturer participation in the project was entirely voluntary, and from the outset rigorous efforts were made to ensure that individual lecturers and students could not be identified in public documents arising from the research (except, of course, where lecturers were the authors or waived their right to anonymity). Anonymity and confidentiality were very important to some of our colleagues. They recognized that there is little point in reflecting on practice if one only reflects on things that are going well; yet by acknowledging difficulties and weaknesses there is always the risk of exposing oneself to hostile criticism. It is particularly galling if disclosure of limitations in one's practice is misused by colleagues or managers whose practices would not withstand similar scrutiny.

Our research colleagues agreed to adopt the principles for collaborative action research set out in Kemmis and McTaggart (1988:106–8). These principles demand considerable attention on the part of researchers to the interests, expectations and viewpoints of those affected by research.

OUTCOMES, LIMITATIONS AND CONSTRAINTS

Reports of the outcomes of the Sunderland research have been published elsewhere (Swann and Arthurs 1999; Swann and Ecclestone 1999; Ecclestone and Swann 1999). Here we summarize the main findings with regard to methodology.

The preliminary methodological activities – both extended and truncated versions – were very well received by the participant lecturers. With regard to the extended version, our colleagues particularly valued the opportunity to express negative feelings about their professional context, while not being allowed to become overwhelmed by them. They also seized the opportunity to brainstorm strategies for improving their assessment practice.

All eight teams, in accordance with their initial plans, developed and implemented trial solutions to problems of how to improve assessment practice. Six of the teams produced a research report which showed they had reflected on and analysed their assessment practice, and were able to discuss critically the outcomes of decisions they had taken. It was also apparent that, with guidance, they were able to use the suggested evaluative questions. In addition, without prompting from us, they had considered how their research and/or developmental activities could be extended.

In general, our colleagues judged the methodology to be effective in that it encouraged them to reflect on and respond critically and creatively towards their own assessment practice. With reference to the quotation from Carr and Kemmis (1986:165), on the basis of the evidence available to us we are confident that our action research led to an increase in lecturer understanding and, as a corollary, the situations in which the research was undertaken were improved.

Other lecturers will, we hope, be interested in developing and testing a similar methodology. For this reason it is important to consider some of the methodological limitations we identified and practical difficulties we encountered.

Analysis of the outcomes of both phases of the research suggests that efforts to improve assessment practice by involving students more actively in assessment need to go beyond small-scale technical changes initiated by motivated individuals and groups. Initiatives which focus on helping students to get better grades, for example, may encourage them to adopt a predominantly instrumental attitude towards their formal education. We do not wish to denigrate the potential value of small-scale technical changes, rather we acknowledge the limitations of the initiatives that were supported by our methodology.

In addition, none of the teams was able to provide definitive evidence of an improvement in student work as a consequence of the research; but the project was not designed to generate such evidence. As an illustration, the results of research undertaken by one of the teams suggested that the introduction of a new assessment practice had been, to a significant extent, successful in encouraging students to reflect on their progress and make plans to improve their work and grades (Swann and Arthurs 1999). Nevertheless, it was not possible to establish a causal link between students' known responses to the practice, and changes in grades between one set of assignments and the next.

All participant lecturers, including ourselves, wanted demonstrable evidence of improvement, and everyone agreed that, wherever possible, the relative effectiveness of different practices should be tested. We recognize, however, that comparative testing of assessment procedures is fraught with difficulty given the range and nature of the variables involved. All research is inevitably flawed or limited in some way. Qualitative case studies of the kind generated by our project – involving self-conscious trial and error – are, however, despite their limitations, an important means of pursuing improvements in practice in specific situations, and generating ideas for public discussion (stimulating attempts to improve practice in other contexts).

While the participant lecturers valued the methodological activities, some had doubts about the merits of action research (specifically, our version of it). In particular, one team from outside our School felt that the empowerment agenda – which led us to distance ourselves from practical decisions made by the various teams – was too limited; they wanted greater emphasis on the quality of the changes being made. The team members argued that, in any extension to the project, detailed theoretical input would enable them to make better changes and/or be better able to criticize and develop their practice. Although some help of the kind they requested was provided, we were unable fully to meet their expectations due to lack of time.

In general, lecturers within the School of Education appeared to be more familiar and comfortable than lecturers in the other disciplines with open-ended, largely qualitative, non-comparative approaches to inquiry.

With regard to practical matters, finding lecturers with an interest in our project was not difficult, but most, because of other commitments, were unable to attend meetings and engage in systematic research. Outside of the School of Education, we were unable to recruit teams that included lecturers with substantial experience of teaching in higher education. Without initial funding from our university (participants in phase 1 received additional payment or teaching cover in lieu of time spent at workshops and meetings) we would have been unable to get the research under way.

EMPOWERING LECTURERS

Improvement rather than mere change in assessment practice in higher education requires the commitment of people who possess intimate day-to-day contextual knowledge of assessment, and who recognize its educational and political complexities. Thus, while the authors accept the need for some external monitoring and regulation of assessment, we warn against centralized interventions which run counter to the professional development of one of higher education's key resources – lecturers. Changes to social practice inevitably have repercussions which are difficult to foresee. Many of these repercussions go unnoticed – or, if noticed, their origins are not necessarily understood – by those with the most power and influence in the system. Lecturers, working individually and in small teams, have comparatively little power and influence, but they are often among the first to recognize the impact, for good or ill, of policy changes. They are able to respond flexibly and creatively to difficulties and opportunities which arise during, for example, their interactions with students. What is often lacking is encouragement and the opportunity to engage in professional debate and *systematic* reflection on the policy and practice of learning, teaching and assessment. In the UK, the Research Assessment Exercise has tended to discourage lecturers, apart from those in education, from engaging in pedagogical research; many lecturers have been put under pressure to focus exclusively on their subject discipline.

In the context of increasing centralized control, what role can lecturers play in the improvement of assessment practice? If they are to maintain their professionalism, upon which improvement depends, they must develop an understanding of macro- and micro-level issues pertaining to their situation, reflect critically on the policies and procedures they implement – regardless of where these ideas originate – and, as appropriate, initiate change in order to bring about improvement. In line with the quotation from Popper with which this chapter begins, our problem-based action research was designed to encourage such initiative, understanding and criticality. The research outcomes suggest that the approach adopted has significant potential and merits further testing.

NOTE

1. There are, of course, non-Popperian problem-based methodologies. See, for example, Robinson (1993).

Chapter 9

Reconsidering the Prescribed Curriculum

RONALD SWARTZ

> It has been said, only too truly, that Plato was the inventor of both our secondary schools and our universities. I do not know a better argument for an optimistic view of mankind, no better proof of their indestructible love for truth and decency, of their originality and stubbornness and health, than the fact that this devastating system of education has not utterly ruined them ...
>
> Plato ... hoped to arrest political change by the institutional control of succession in leadership. The control was to be educational, based upon an authoritarian view of learning – upon the authority of the learned expert ...
>
> Karl Popper (1966a:136, 137)

This chapter poses the questions, 'Is it time to examine the whole idea of a prescribed curriculum?' and 'Can educational programmes avoid authoritarianism?' In dealing with these questions, an interpretation of Karl Popper's views on rationality is used to suggest that a seminal United States text on science education may have unknowingly offered an account of science as an authoritarian social system. (See Chapter 10 for an account of an implemented alternative to the prescribed curriculum.)

QUESTIONING THE PRESCRIBED CURRICULUM

In 1990 the American Association for the Advancement of Science published a book called *Science for All Americans: Project 2061*, which was intended to represent 'the informed thinking of the science, mathematics, and technology communities as nearly as such a thing can be ascertained' (Rutherford and Ahlgen 1990:xxiii). The first chapter 'lays out recommendations for what knowledge of the way science works is requisite for scientific literacy' (Rutherford and Ahlgen 1990:1). We learn, in particular, the following:

> Fundamentally, the various scientific disciplines are alike in their reliance on evidence ... Sooner or later, the validity of scientific claims is settled by referring to observations of phenomena ... The essence of science is validation by observation ... challenges to new ideas are the legitimate business of science in building valid knowledge. Even the most prestigious scientists have occasionally refused to accept new theories despite there being enough accumulated evidence to convince others. (Rutherford and Ahlgen 1990:3–7)

I would like to suggest that the individuals who contributed to the views articulated in *Science for All Americans* have provided an answer to the question: 'What are the best sources of our knowledge?' Their approach mirrors that of Kant, who argued: 'education can only advance by slow degrees, and a true conception of the method of education can only arise when one generation transmits to the next its stores of experience and knowledge, each generation adding something of its own before transmitting them to the following' (Kant 1960 [1803]:11–12).This contrasts with the view of one of the twentieth century's most distinguished scientists:

> I want to oppose the idea that the school has to teach directly that special knowledge and those accomplishments which one has to use later directly in life. The demands of life are much too manifold to let such a specialized training in school appear possible ... it seems to me, moreover, objectionable to treat the individual like a dead tool ... The development of general ability for independent thinking and judgement should always be placed foremost, not the acquisition of special knowledge. (Einstein 1950:36)

Einstein raises a serious question about the value of a prescribed curriculum. My own experiences, as a disillusioned second-year undergraduate student in the autumn of 1964 (Swartz 1974, 1999), when I had discussions with Joseph Agassi about educational problems, raised similar concerns for me. I recall that I came to him with questions such as: 'Should students spend a great deal of their time learning the vast amount of information that teachers consider to be important?' 'Is it reasonable to have educational programmes that allow students to decide for themselves what is learned in school?' 'Are teachers reliable authorities who know important ideas that students need to learn?'

Later, I read Agassi's review of Michael Matthews' book, *Science Teaching: The Role of History and Philosophy of Science*, in which he notes:

> the quality of life greatly deteriorates as the result of the use of the carrot and the stick ... What we want to achieve is a system in which learning is a challenge and a pleasure ...
>
> The main question is of fact: are the carrot and the stick essential for progress? It is hard to say. It is probably easier to say that the

curriculum can hardly be imposed without them. But is the curriculum essential for progress? . . . is it time to examine the whole idea of a prescribed curriculum? It is well and good to demand exams for proficiency in any skill before qualifying for a diploma in that skill, but should we go further than that or should reformers demand the abolition of all curricula except the core curriculum and the diploma exams. (Agassi 1996:76–7)

SOURCES OF KNOWLEDGE

The answer offered by the authors of *Science for All Americans* to the question, 'What are the best sources of our knowledge?', can be summarized as follows: the sources of valid scientific knowledge are the observations of phenomena or evidence that support an hypothesis or theory suggested by scientists. Furthermore, those who contributed to the consensus view outlined in Rutherford and Ahlgen's text do not claim that any hypothesis which receives the support of the accumulation of evidence is absolutely true. In the section called 'Scientific Knowledge is Durable', we learn that

Although scientists reject the notion of attaining absolute truth and accept some uncertainty as part of nature, most scientific knowledge is durable. The modification of ideas, rather than their outright rejection, is the norm of science, as powerful constructs tend to survive and grow more precise and to become widely accepted. For example, in formulating the theory of relativity, Albert Einstein did not discard the Newtonian laws of motion but rather showed them to be only an approximation of limited application within a more general concept. (Rutherford and Ahlgen 1990:3)

The view of science articulated by Rutherford and Ahlgen is an extremely complex network of ideas, and in this brief chapter I will not be able to isolate and suggest criticisms of many of the specific assumptions made about what knowledge is requisite for scientific literacy. But the seemingly innocent question, 'What are the best sources of our knowledge?', has been viewed by Karl Popper as one of the major reasons why empiricists have often endorsed an authoritarian view of science. For Popper:

an experiment may . . . add to our knowledge, and in a most important manner. But it is not a source in any ultimate sense. It has always to be checked . . . the empiricist's questions 'How do you know? What is the source of your assertion?' are wrongly put. They are not formulated in an inexact or slovenly manner, but *they are entirely misconceived*: they are questions that beg for an authoritarian answer . . . traditional systems of epistemology may be said to result from yes-answers or no-answers to questions about the sources of our knowledge. *They never challenge these questions, or dispute their legitimacy*; the questions are

taken as perfectly natural, and nobody seems to see any harm in them
... these questions are clearly authoritarian in spirit ... *all* 'sources' are
liable to lead us into error at times. And I propose to replace, therefore,
the question of the sources of our knowledge by the entirely different
question: *'How can we hope to detect and eliminate error?'* . . . the
traditional question of the authoritative sources of knowledge is
repeated even today – and very often by positivists and by other
philosophers who believe themselves to be in revolt against authority.

The proper answer to my question 'How can we hope to detect and
eliminate error?' is, I believe, 'By *criticizing* the theories or guesses of
others and – if we can train ourselves to do so – by *criticizing* our own
theories or guesses.' (Popper 1972b:24–6)

Popper's views about some questions being authoritarian in spirit
developed over many decades. From 1945, when he first published *The Open
Society and Its Enemies*, until his death in 1994, Popper argued that most
philosophical traditions within Western intellectual thought have
unknowingly provided answers to questions which have made it difficult, if not
impossible, for people to avoid developing authoritarian ideas. Now, of course,
it may indeed be the case that Popper is mistaken in his claim that political and
epistemological theorists have unknowingly endorsed authoritarian ideas
which are answers to authoritarian questions. In my opinion, much work needs
to be done before we can begin to see the potential errors in the ideas Popper
developed over an extremely productive and long academic career. In this
chapter, I do not wish to defend or criticize Popper's highly challenging and
complex notions about authoritarianism. What I wish to suggest is that the
individuals who developed the consensus view about science articulated in
Science for All Americans may have unknowingly endorsed authoritarian
ideas, even though they 'believe themselves to be in revolt against authority'
(Popper 1972b:26). That is, as with the positivists who Popper criticized
throughout his life, the view of science articulated in *Science for All Americans*
may endorse authoritarianism in the sense that observation reports and
evidence have become the unquestioned authorities that are appealed to
when people wish to make a decision about the adequacy of a scientific theory.

The notion that experiences and observations are not the ultimate
authorities in making decisions about scientific theories may seem a bit
strange to people who are unfamiliar with the work of Popper and other well-
known philosophers and historians of science such as Imre Lakatos, Thomas
Kuhn and Paul Feyerabend. And, in order to understand that the view of
science advocated in *Science for All Americans* may perhaps be authoritarian,
one would have to spend a great deal of time studying recent and past
philosophers and historians of science.

Over time, the view of science suggested in *Science for All Americans* may
eventually be improved. And, interestingly, Matthews (1994) has suggested
that Rutherford and Ahlgen's text should not be regarded as, and was not
intended to be, a definitive statement about science. For Matthews, it is a

document that has the potential to engage people in a dialogue about the philosophical and historical foundations of science. He has suggested that

> Project 2061's image of science is clearly informed by current history, philosophy, and sociology. As the document is meant to be a curriculum framework and not an academic treatise, it does not contain detailed arguments for the theses advanced. But as the project intends that local bodies will reflect on and respond to the document, then these theses will have to be more fully developed at that level ... the document is a valuable starting point for reflection, and it clearly requires that teachers and decision makers be comfortable with philosophizing about science. (Matthews 1994:40–1)

I am a bit lost for words when I think about what Matthews has said in the above quotation. This is partly the result of not being able to believe that someone can be as optimistic as Matthews appears to be when it comes to evaluating how *Science for All Americans* might be viewed by teachers and decision-makers who represent local bodies, such as public school districts in the State of Michigan (where I live). My experience with local public school districts during the last 25 years may not be typical, but it suggests to me that teachers and decision-makers at the local level are highly unlikely to see themselves as individuals who are expected to develop, and perhaps even criticize, ideas that have been carefully chosen by a committee of distinguished scholars who represent the American Association for the Advancement of Science. Rather than develop and criticize the ideas in *Science for All Americans*, teachers and decision-makers who read this document are likely to spend time studying it as if it were some kind of gospel containing wisdom which has the potential to make a person an enlightened individual.

AUTHORITARIANISM IN EDUCATION

I do not think that the role of critic has been cultivated in our schools or society. Although those who developed the consensus view of society in *Science for All Americans* may have wanted people to challenge and perhaps even to criticize their ideas, I think it highly unlikely that a document such as *Science for All Americans* will help people to feel 'comfortable with philosophizing about science'.

How might people feel comfortable with philosophizing about such matters as science, science education and education in general? Since my early days of teaching undergraduate and graduate students, I have tried to help them to understand why some of the questions asked by philosophers of education are worthy of attention. I think it worthwhile to suggest to future teachers that there is some value in discussing questions such as, 'Can educational programmes avoid authoritarianism?'

In my efforts to help students to be comfortable with philosophizing about education, I have tried to explain the value of asking questions about the educational enterprise. Moreover, I often offer the question about authoritarianism suggested at the end of the previous paragraph. When a student asks me why I am interested in seeing if educational programmes can be designed to avoid authoritarianism, I say something like: 'This is important partly because authoritarianism in all its forms can be viewed as one of the great threats to human freedom and the development of human potential.'

What I am saying about authoritarianism may seem rather vague, and perhaps it appears more romantic than I would like it to be. Nevertheless, I suggest that learning to become comfortable with philosophizing about education is far more likely to happen when we encourage people to ask questions, rather than read books such as *Science for All Americans*. Also, I suggest that most people who come into contact with Rutherford and Ahlgen's text are unlikely to view it as the starting point for a philosophical dialogue.

In this chapter I have attempted to explain how modern educators may endorse ideas that are authoritarian, even though they may think they are avoiding authoritarianism. Moreover, when it came to educational matters, Popper saw the need to suggest that some form of authoritarianism may be necessary. That is, although Popper regarded himself as a critic and enemy of authoritarianism, when it came to educating children he thought that at least 'one element' of authoritarianism was reasonable. For Popper, the model for the good teacher is Socrates (as he is portrayed in Plato's *Apology*). Popper has claimed that Socratic teaching at its best is as follows:

> The uneducated seems thus to be in need of an authority to wake him up, since he cannot be expected to be self-critical. But this one element of authoritarianism was wonderfully balanced in Socrates' teaching by the emphasis that the authority must not claim more than that. The true teacher can prove himself only by exhibiting that self-criticism which the uneducated lacks. 'Whatever authority I may have rests solely upon my knowing how little I know': this is the way in which Socrates might have justified his mission to stir up the people from their dogmatic slumber. (Popper 1966a:129–30)

Do uneducated people need an authority to wake them from their dogmatic slumber? Must self-criticism be taught by having an educational authority impose this idea on uneducated people? Can we confront people with the choice of being dogmatic or self-critical in non-authoritarian educational situations? Questions such as these need to be considered when we are trying to answer a question such as 'Can educational programmes avoid authoritarianism?' Furthermore, in order to understand how to avoid authoritarianism in educational programmes, it is worthwhile making some kind of an attempt to criticize Popper's views on how Socratic teaching needs to be authoritarian. In other words, it would be a mistake to view Popper (or anyone else) as having the last word in the dialogue about authority in educational programmes.

DEMOCRATIC SCHOOLS

For many years, as a student and young adult, I struggled with what a number of my elders regarded as 'an authority problem'. I have come to realize that in a number of ways my youthful zeal to disagree with those in authority was a manifestation of an inarticulate desire to join a liberal democratic self-governing educational community. In other words, following a somewhat unconventional combination of ideas – developed in works such as John Stuart Mill's *On Liberty* (1989 [1859]) and A. S. Neill's *Summerhill* (1968) – I have come to think it highly reasonable to have schools and educational programmes that are liberal democratic self-governing learning situations in which all individuals, students included, are free to think for themselves and perhaps even disagree with anyone who happens to be a social or political authority.

Similarly, Agassi has suggested that Popper's one element of authoritarianism is not needed in schools where authority is democratically controlled. For Agassi

> [Popper's] opinion always was that children are authoritarian by nature and they have to be charmed by their teachers and educated in an authoritarian manner – in order to have them grow out of their authoritarianism, need one say. I do not agree: A major argument in his *The Open Society and Its Enemies* is, after all, that we do not know what human nature is (though we may refute some views about it if they are not defended apologetically). Moreover, his view is refuted by democratic schools where authority is democratically controlled and pupils learn no worse than in authoritarian schools. (The fate of democratic schools, as far as longitudinal studies show, is not different from that of other schools in similar situations: some fail, some do not; those who do not fail constitute the refutation of the tradition or at least the hope for improvement.) (Agassi 1993:59)

When Agassi speaks of democratic schools, he has in mind educational programmes such as Homer Lane's Little Commonwealth, Janusz Korczak's Orphans' Home, A. S. Neill's Summerhill, and Daniel Greenberg's Sudbury Valley School (Agassi 1977, 1993). These educational situations are quite different in many ways, but what unites them is some kind of twentieth-century reform movement; they have attempted in one way or another to make a school a liberal democratic self-governing learning community. In democratic schools, a major feature of the prescribed curriculum is that students are expected to develop the general ability for independent thought and judgement (Einstein 1950:36). Of course, people of varying ages will be more or less independent given the choices they are capable of making and the desire they have to develop their independence. Thus, learning in a democratic school involves many opportunities to practise making decisions about what one should do with one's time in school.

In a sense, it is correct to say that democratic schools do not really provide students with a standardized academic curriculum. Academic learning in a democratic school becomes optional. In order to stay in a democratic school, all a person has to do is live and act according to the laws and social conventions which govern one's school. Stated differently, the prescribed academic curriculum in a democratic school is based on the idea that specialized training in school is not desirable, partly because the 'demands of life are much too manifold' (Einstein 1950:36). Yet in democratic schools science might be chosen as one of the areas for study if the members of the school (both students and teachers) can learn to view scientific learning in such a way that the study of science is seen as a worthwhile 'challenge and a pleasure' (Agassi 1996:76–7). How can science education become a part of the curriculum in democratic schools where academic learning is merely an option? Will students who attend democratic schools be able to learn about life-threatening issues such as AIDS? Can democratic schools require the learning of specialized knowledge without becoming authoritarian? Questions such as these appear to me to be an outgrowth of Popper's philosophy, and Agassi's challenge to examine the whole idea of a prescribed curriculum.

NOTE

An earlier version of this paper was published in *Toward Scientific Literacy: The History and Philosophy of Science and Science Teaching – Proceedings of the Fourth International Conference*, by the Faculty of Education, University of Calgary, Canada, 1999 (reprinted here with permission).

Chapter 10

The Logic-of-Learning Approach to Teaching: A Testable Theory

JOANNA SWANN

> I dreamt of one day founding a school in which young people could learn without boredom, and would be stimulated to pose problems and discuss them; a school in which no unwanted answers to unasked questions would have to be listened to; in which one did not study for the sake of passing examinations.
>
> Karl Popper (1992:40)

In 1978 I began to research the practical problem, 'Children in classrooms could be learning more: how can this state of affairs be brought about?' Working with Karl Popper's theory of learning and the growth of knowledge, and the educational theory of Tyrrell Burgess, I set out to develop theory directly relevant to the improvement of practice. The method I adopted, consistent with the logic of learning, was to seek to remove error rather than define objectives, and the question then asked was, 'What is stopping children from learning in classrooms?' On the basis of philosophical argument, the answer chosen was, 'Children in classrooms are inhibited from learning because the theory implicit in teacher and student practice neglects the logic of learning.' The next step was to identify and describe the logic of learning (phrase attributable to Burgess 1977; see also Burgess 1979), the educational practices consistent with it, what is logically invalid as an account of learning, and the widely accepted ideas that assume an invalid account.

The new and empirically testable theory arising from this research is presented in my PhD thesis (Swann 1988). The thesis is concerned with factors common to all human learning, using specific examples from action research carried out in my teaching of primary schoolchildren (see also Swann 1983). It presents an argument for the adoption of independent study methods, whereby students are encouraged and helped to (a) initiate and plan processes which promote learning, and (b) implement these plans and assess outcomes (within the constraints of the given situation, and with the support of institutional procedures for accreditation and validation).

The chapter draws on this and subsequent research (see Chapters 2 and 5, and Swann 1998a, 1999) to outline: the logic of learning, the theory of classroom practice based on this, and the means by which the theory may be tested.

An implicit understanding of aspects of the logic of learning, and their implications for the conduct of education, is evident in the practice of many teachers and the writings of many theorists. Few educationists have, however, made reference to Popper's logical analysis of learning and the growth of knowledge. Fewer still have attempted to use this analysis as a basis for developing an educational theory. Those who have include Tyrrell Burgess, Ronald Swartz and Richard Bailey – all of whom have chapters in this book – and Henry J. Perkinson (1971, 1980, 1984, 1993).

THE LOGIC OF LEARNING

Two commonsense ideas about learning

In Chapter 2 it was explained that Popper's discovery of an asymmetry between verification and falsification led him to develop not only an important new theory of the growth of knowledge, but also a theory of what happens when an individual learns.

Popper's (non-inductivist) theory of learning can be better understood by making reference to two commonsense ideas. Both regard learning as a consequence of experience (they are empiricist), but they differ in the way experience is considered to impinge on the individual. One of these ideas is that learning takes place through the abstraction or absorption of ideas from experience; the other is that learning takes place through a modification (or rejection) of pre-existing ideas which the learner brings to bear on experience – learning from one's mistakes. Observation is important in both accounts, but the role attributed to observation is different. With the first idea, observation entails some form of theory-free data gathering; in the second it is regarded as inevitably theory-laden, with what we see being dependent (though not wholly) on the ideas (including expectations) brought to the act of observation. In simple terms, the first idea carries with it the notion of *having* an observation, an essentially passive experience, while the second attributes a more active role to the would-be learner, with an observation being *made*.

The first idea about learning is clearly compatible with inductivism, and when elaborated into a slightly more substantial theory it becomes what Popper has disparagingly called the bucket theory of the mind (1979:Chapter 2, Appendix 1; 1985a). According to the bucket theory, learning begins with the mind as an essentially passive receptacle for sense data. Someone who wishes to learn first allows herself to be open to or become aware of inputs of information via the senses. Knowledge consists of 'things' that are in some sense true and certain, and the mind of the learner acquires these elements of knowledge by observation (which is, by implication, theory-free). Following Popper, it can be argued that the first commonsense idea and the bucket theory of the mind are deeply flawed, not least because of their implied acceptance of theory-free observation, the passive role attributed to the learner, and the simplistic view of the relationship between external stimuli and learner response (Swann 1998a, 1998b). Popper's theory of learning is an elaboration of the second commonsense idea – that we learn from our mistakes.

Learning and survival

The discovery of mistaken, limited and inadequate ideas leads to problems that the individual attempts to solve: 'Every organism and every species is faced constantly by the threat of extinction . . . this threat takes the form of concrete problems which it has to solve' (Popper 1992:177). The response to problems for many species is determined by genetic inheritance and random factors; others, however, are capable of learning. An ability to learn constitutes a specific form of adaptability, and the ability to adapt gives a species, or individual members of a species, an evolutionary advantage.

How does learning aid survival? An animal will react when it encounters a life-threatening situation. If it reacts 'appropriately' it is far more likely to survive. For many animals, survival depends primarily on inherent dispositions (laden with expectations), and where these are mistaken or inadequate, death is often consequent. However, the inborn expectations of many other animals are modified significantly during interactions with their environment. A minimal level of learning may take place when an animal encounters an unforeseen situation and reacts in a way which is not purely the result of prior expectations; in other words, when an expectation fails, the animal responds by creating, under environmental pressure, a new expectation. Alternatively, an animal may react according to prior expectations, and if the initial reaction is problematic but not a total failure (that is, if death is not consequent) it may, in a comparable situation, be inclined to try something different. In short, learning is a way of improving upon inborn expectations and potentialities.

Of all animals, humans possess the greatest facility for learning, a facility that is highly dependent on the descriptive and argumentative functions of language. These functions have enabled us to develop a world of public knowledge in which our ideas exist independent of us; unlike other animals, we often let our hypotheses die in our stead (Popper 1979:244).

What happens when learning takes place?

It is argued, on the basis of the preceding discussion, that learning takes place when a human or other animal has a problem, attempts to solve it and survives, creating changes in the world and in the learner (Swann 1999). As discussed in Chapter 2, the elements characteristic of any incidence of learning, and their inter-relationship, have been highlighted by Popper in the simplified schema of conjecture and refutation (Popper 1979:243):

$$P_1 \rightarrow TS \rightarrow EE \rightarrow P_2$$

Learning begins with a problem (P_1). A problem occurs when an individual experiences or anticipates a mismatch between expectation and experience that she desires to resolve. A trial solution (TS) is then applied to the problem. Put another way, experience (actual and anticipated) reveals errors and inadequacies in an individual's implicit assumptions and explicit theories. A discovery of error or inadequacy is often (but not always) problematized by the individual, who then attempts to regain equilibrium by creating (or selecting) and applying a trial solution. (As noted in Chapter 2, most learning is haphazard, accidental and implicit in situations; it requires only a minimal level of consciousness, and even for human beings most learning is unself-conscious.)

A solution – any solution – is a trial: it is laden with expectations and, as with the disappointed expectation which led to the initial problem, provides further scope for the discovery and elimination of error (EE) or inadequacy. Thus the attempt to solve a problem (P_1) often leads to a new problem (P_2).

Popper's schematic answer to the question of what happens when learning takes place is useful because it helps us to focus on features of learning that are present whenever and wherever there is learning. In short, while many diverse processes can be characterized as learning, there is an identifiable process common to any incidence of learning, whether it is the learning of a young child, a world-famous physicist, or someone's pet dog.

Popper's theory is not compatible with Pavlovian conditioning theory and all crude stimulus-response theories of learning which imply induction. Nor is it compatible with Skinner's idea of operant behaviour because, while Skinner regards learning as a process of trial and error, the trials are thought to be random and not dependent upon conjecture (James 1980:Chapter 6). Although Popper's theory is incompatible with radical constructivism (Swann 1995), it is compatible with the basic constructivist idea that 'Learning outcomes depend not only on the learning environment but on the prior knowledge, attitudes and goals of the learner' (Scott 1987:7).

While people often accept that Popper's account is applicable to some learning, specifically that described as 'problem-solving', they tend to balk at the idea that it is applicable to all forms of learning, including imitation and rote. But we do not have to reflect on learning in order for the logic to be present; when we do, the fact that the logic may be hard to identify does not mean that it does not pertain. Rote learning can facilitate the memorization of ideas through encapsulation, pattern-making and repetition, but the underlying process is nonetheless organic rather than mechanistic, active rather than passive – each apparent repetition is a modification of a previous trial.

Implicit in the logic of learning is the idea that activity is a necessary feature. This activity is autonomous: learning is a process in which the individual is always active and, in essence, responsible. Thus there is no such thing as passive learning. Learning always involves trial and error, whether or not teachers or students (or educational policy-makers) are aware that this is so. It would be foolish to deny that learning takes place in situations where the policy and practice of teaching assume passivity on the part of the learner – people can learn despite being taught in this way, though what they learn is often not what the teacher intends. Assuming that a process is passive does not make it so.

The idea that there is no such thing as passive learning is sometimes rejected by people who confuse passive learning with unconscious learning; but a lack of conscious awareness does not mean the process is passive.

TEACHING AND THE LOGIC OF LEARNING

General principles for good teaching

Popper's logical analysis of learning provides the basis for a logically coherent educational theory; it can be used to support teachers and other educationists who wish to defend and promote logically sound practices that are under threat as a consequence of increasingly centralized control of education. Whether educational practices which derive from the logic of learning are more effective than those which are not is, however, an empirical rather than a logical matter, and, to date, rigorous comparative tests have not been carried out. But it is better not to practise on the basis of ideas that have been shown to be logically invalid – specifically those which assume the theory of induction – when logically defensible alternatives are available.

In light of the logic of learning, the teacher's main task is to help students to discover and eliminate their mistaken and inadequate ideas. This is essentially an affirmative process in which the learner is liberated from ignorance and incapacity. There is, however, no secure knowledge of what is mistaken, just as there is no secure knowledge of what is true. As secure knowledge is a myth, there is no absolute authority we can call upon to decide what is worth learning and what is right or good, true or valid. We can take advice – and to disregard what appears to be sound evidence and persuasive argument would be foolish – but as teachers and/or learners we should be wary of being overly dependent on people whose judgements, like our own, may be mistaken or misguided. This is an important reason why teachers should encourage students (including young children) to embrace the process of discovering and working with error and inadequacy.

In broad terms, the teacher's role is to foster student self-confidence, provide access to appropriate resources in the world of public knowledge, and encourage students to be constructively critical of their own thoughts and actions, as well as those of others (see Burgess 1977).

Constructive criticism facilitates the discovery of error and inadequacy; it is central to the business of teaching. The teacher should strive to create situations in which her students' assumptions about themselves, the world and their place in it, are challenged. Although most people encounter a great deal of criticism during the course of their education, it often fails to address assumptions which underpin their comprehension of the world. Where there is a pre-specified curriculum of knowledge and skills to be taught, much of the criticism experienced by students focuses on their interactions (or lack of interaction) with it. A national or regional curriculum may thus encourage a disregard for the wide range of ideas that students bring to the classroom; these ideas, by being ignored, are allowed to continue unchallenged.

It is also important to recognize that learning is not inevitably synonymous with improvement. Not all learning is good learning: what we learn may be misleading, false, invalid, even dangerous (for example, learning to smoke). Students may learn to behave badly; and they may learn things that are, at best, trivial. The learning we should strive for in the short term is that which leads to greater learning in the longer term. We should, as far as possible, avoid creating situations in which students discover mismatches between expectations and reality only to adjust their expectations in ways that discourage future learning.

For example, a child may go to school thinking she can make mistakes without being penalized, only to discover that being seen to make a mistake results in some form of rebuke or sanction; she may thus learn to associate the discovery of error with an unpleasant experience. She may also judge that further unpleasant experiences can be avoided by not making (or by not being seen to make) mistakes, and she may decide (probably unself-consciously) that one of the best ways to avoid penalties is to do as little as possible, because the more one does the greater the risk of discovering error. Clearly this may become a serious inhibition to learning.

How teachers and schools set out to challenge students' assumptions is problematic. If a student anticipates that discovering an error or inadequacy may result in some form of sanction or punishment, she may be reluctant to engage fully in learning. Thus the teacher must strive to provide a safe place in which to learn, where the discovery of error or inadequacy is not penalized *per se*. This has implications for, among other things, the use of summative assessment and behaviour management practices. With regard to the latter, while rules, rewards and sanctions may be necessary to discourage and prevent behaviours which are undesirable because, for example, they inhibit the learning of other students, the purpose of any sanction should be to maintain the efficacy of the learning environment rather than to punish the student.

An important psychological factor in the discovery of error and inadequacy is the self-confidence of the student. The pursuit of learning involves risk-taking – the risk of being wrong in a discussion or of making a practical mistake. As Burgess (1977:160) points out, fear of failure is a major inhibition to learning: 'The world is unhappily full of people who fear to fail, and thus fail to learn. Students must be confident enough to fail, to face failure and to use it.' It follows that teachers will often need to respond positively to the work of their students before they judge it; the discovery of error and inadequacy is not best promoted by offering criticisms without taking account of the student's current level of confidence. This principle is already known to many parents, teachers and educationists.

The logic of learning is not antithetical to teaching specific ideas from the world of public knowledge. However, when we decide to teach something to someone, we should bear in mind that any learning which takes place will stem from the learner's prior expectations (including values and desires) and involve a process of trial and error. In a sense, each of us has to 'reinvent the wheel'. Our circumstances differ from those of our distant ancestors in that we are able to interact with an extensive world of public knowledge (including artefacts, theories and arguments), and by engaging with this world we are able to invent and reinvent ideas more quickly. Our engagement is necessarily active and involves us in a creative process of conjecture, refutation and modification.

Impediments to learning

The logical analysis of learning generates methodological principles and procedures that we can adopt self-consciously to accelerate our own learning, and apply as teachers and educational policy-makers in order to advance the learning of students of all ages. These methodological procedures include the use of 'What is stopping . . . ?' and 'What is inhibiting . . . ?' questions (see Chapter 5).

A basic question which should be addressed by any teacher, educational policy-maker or indeed anyone who is concerned with the practical problem of how to promote better learning is, 'What is stopping or inhibiting learning?' in the particular problem situation – be it 'in this education service', 'in this school', 'in this classroom', 'for this student' or 'for me'.

Innumerable inhibitions or impediments to learning may apply in any situation. However, as indicated in the chapter's introduction, philosophical analysis has led to the identification of an over-arching impediment of particular significance to formal education: failure to acknowledge the logic of learning.

The investigation of this over-arching impediment, in the context of course development (Burgess 1977) and empirical research (Swann 1988), has led to the identification of a series of subsidiary impediments, each with practical significance in a variety of situations. These include: restricting autonomous activity; discouraging confidence and desire; inappropriate and/or inadequate criticism; penalizing the discovery of error; offering 'unwanted answers to unasked questions'; the myths of secure knowledge and 'the subject'; failure to promote argumentative language; inadequate attention to problem formulation; objectives-based planning (in contrast to problem-based planning); adherence to authoritarian ideologies of educating (in relation to the last point see Chapter 9, and, for a useful sociological analysis, Meighan and Siraj-Blatchford 1997). In general, the assumption that learning can be the outcome of a passive process is associated with many of the impediments listed above. (For further discussion of these and other impediments to learning, see Burgess and Swann forthcoming.)

Some very significant impediments are embedded in the institutional organization of teaching. Teachers committed to the promotion of student learning must attempt to mitigate the damaging effects of these impediments.

Student-initiated curricula

Taken to its logical conclusion, acknowledgement of the logic of learning in teaching leads to a radical departure from orthodoxy: the extensive use of student-initiated curricula largely replaces curricula initiated by governments and their appointees, examination boards, educational institutions and teachers. The formalized and institutionalized use of student-initiated curricula is the principal means by which schools and teachers can avoid generating unnecessary impediments to learning.

A formal process for developing (and accrediting) student-initiated curricula was developed at the School for Independent Study (1974–91) at what is now the University of East London (Burgess 1977; Stephenson 1980, 1981). In my action research with children, I adapted key features of the School for Independent Study approach, and formulated a seven-stage procedure applicable to the development of student-initiated curricula in a range of contexts. The procedure has been designed for teachers working with a group or class, but the basic ideas are applicable to all teacher–student relationships.

First, the teacher sets out to help students formulate their learning problems (not to be confused with learning difficulties); that is, to give an account of changes they wish to make in what they know, understand and can do, or, to put it another way, the personal mismatches they wish to resolve. (Learning problems are practical problems – see Chapter 5.) By addressing these issues, the teacher discovers what her students wish to learn. There will be problems for which students already have (conjecturally) satisfactory strategies, but the primary focus is on problems for which solutions are not immediately forthcoming. ('What is stopping ... ?' and 'What is inhibiting ... ?' questions are useful at this stage.)

Initially, students tend to focus on what they think will be permitted; they may not flex their imagination or be aware of how they might utilize available resources and expertise. Helping students to formulate and develop learning problems is rarely a straightforward or easy task (see Chapter 14 for further discussion).

At the second stage, the teacher identifies which of these learning problems can be addressed within the specific learning environment by the teacher, other teachers and students, using existing resources, or by involving individuals and agencies outwith the learning environment. Students may formulate learning problems for which the teacher/school can be of little or no help; but some ideas which at first seem impractical or even impossible may be addressed in a modified form. For instance, an 11-year-old girl in one of my research classes wanted to become a book publisher. She learned a great deal from designing and publishing a school magazine.

Third, the implications of learning aspirations which seem to be unacceptable or incapable of being addressed by the teacher(s) and the institution should be considered. A student may wish to pursue learning that is morally unacceptable or not feasible in terms of resources. When a student's learning proposal is rejected, the arguments underlying this decision should be made explicit.

Fourth, the teacher's task is then to help students plan their learning, paying attention to: their successes, skills, talents and achievements; available resources and expertise; their learning problems; time available; critical evaluation (by helping students to state what would count as a failure of their educational plans). Explicit attention to what happens when learning takes place (the logic of learning) may form part of the discussion. (At the School for Independent Study the learning plans of undergraduate students were subject to formal validation.)

Fifth, the teacher supports students in the fulfilment of their plans, offering, where appropriate, encouragement, additional resources (when available) and critical discussion.

Sixth, the teacher critically discusses with students the scope of their learning problems and proposed solutions after they have been worked on, considering to what extent the choice of problems has been valid, whether better problems could have been formulated, and which factors (if any) can be identified to improve future problem formulation. In my experience, this is the most difficult step to apply satisfactorily; it may best be left until after the following stage in order to allow sufficient time for reflection.

Seventh, the teacher helps students to compile a record of their learning, including statements of successes, skills and attainments. The record will include a statement of the initial learning problems; it will show where trial solutions were found to be successful, and where they failed and what was learned from the experience. It will also include an outline of learning problems that have developed from the work undertaken. (At the School for Independent Study, student attainment was formally examined and accredited at this stage.)

This is, of course, only an outline of a logic-of-learning approach to teaching. Difficulties in applying these ideas with children, and how these difficulties can be overcome, have been discussed elsewhere (Swann 1988).

Note: a Popperian approach to teaching, as conceived by Burgess and Swann, is neither subject-centred, nor is it student- or child-centred; rather it focuses on the *learning problems* of the student. The approach is more structured, and requires greater challenge and criticality than much of what is commonly referred to as progressive education.

A TESTABLE THEORY OF CLASSROOM PRACTICE

An explanatory theory

The outcomes of formal education are disappointing. After eleven years (in the United Kingdom) of compulsory full-time schooling, many young people are still woefully ignorant; they demonstrate only limited levels of competence with regard to the skills which enhance life beyond educational institutions; and, worse, they lack confidence in their ability to transform their lives through learning. Tyrrell Burgess and I offer the following explanation for this phenomenon: failure to acknowledge the logic of learning in the conduct and organization of teaching (see, for example, Burgess and Swann forthcoming). We predict that more and better learning on the part of students will ensue if the policies and practices of education are changed to acknowledge the logic of learning.

This explanatory theory is potentially testable. (See Chapter 2 for an account of scientific explanation, prediction and prohibitive hypotheses.) Although the broader argument is not confined to a particular age range of student or size of class, the following prohibitive hypothesis – based on my empirical research with seven- to nine-year-olds, taught in classes of 25 or less – was developed:

> Given that Class L is a class of between 20 and 25 children, taught for two years from the age of seven to nine by a teacher who acknowledges the logic of learning (as per the principles, methodology, practices and skills set out in Swann 1988), and Class N is a comparable class taught by a teacher who does not acknowledge the logic of learning, then there does not exist a situation in which the learning of children in Class L will be less successful or merely equivalent to that of the learning of children in Class N.

Note: if measurable effects are to have time to develop, the logic-of-learning approach must be adopted consistently for a period of at least two years.

To make the hypothesis testable, elaboration is required. Successful learning involves changes in competences, knowledge, understanding and attitudes which have a bearing on the individual's long-term potential. Learning is an open-ended process, not subject to definition by a limited number of pre-specified and observable outcomes. Though it is possible to demonstrate that individuals have learned by focusing on short-term changes, it is not possible to account for all learning in this way. The assertion that the logic-of-learning approach has greater long-term benefits than other approaches is important, but there are considerable practical difficulties in empirically testing for long-term effects (there would, for example, be many uncontrollable variables). Predictions of measurable short-term benefits are, however, more readily testable. The prohibitive hypothesis has thus been reformulated so that the logic-of-learning approach can be tested with reference to specified changes in attitude and competence that are measurable in the short term:

> Given that Class L is a class of between 20 and 25 children, taught for two years from the age of seven to nine by a teacher who acknowledges the logic of learning (as per the principles, methodology, practices and skills set out in Swann 1988), and Class N is a comparable class taught

by a teacher who does not acknowledge the logic of learning, then there does not exist a situation in which the progress of children (with regard to demonstrable improvements in self-confidence, social skills, attitudes to learning, literacy and the use of oral language) in Class L will be less than or merely equivalent to that of children in Class N.

The range of specifiable improvements included in the hypothesis is, of course, value-laden and rooted in the philosophy which has generated the logic-of-learning approach. To test the logic-of-learning approach in terms of, for example, England's national curriculum attainment targets and related standardized tests is not being proposed. The detail of the specified improvements would also be value-laden; for example, literacy would be assessed in terms of the ability to use language effectively rather than to analyse its structure.

The nature of Class N teaching is not specified in the hypothesis, but it is conceivable that research designed to test the logic-of-learning approach would also provide an opportunity to test the efficacy of objectives-based teaching: a Class N teacher could use the tests by which student improvement will be assessed (with regard to self-confidence, social skills, etc.) to formulate intended learning outcomes. It is a feature of my theory that Class L children who had not been taught 'to the test' would do better at the tests than Class N children who had.

In any specific context in which the hypothesis is tested, thought would need to be given to potential unintended and undesirable consequences, and how such consequences might be identified. For example, at the end of the two-year period, Class L children's numeracy skills should not compare unfavourably with those of the children in Class N.

Setting up medium- to large-scale research to test the hypothesis would be both complicated and financially expensive, not least because of the difficulties in constructing a valid test and the need to involve a number of specimen Class Ls and Class Ns. The practical experiment would require not only the involvement of comparable classes (taking into account, for example, socio-economic factors), but also prime Class L and Class N exponents of the art of teaching. However, pairs of teachers working in schools with parallel classes could, on their own initiative, undertake small-scale research.

In England, for example, a pair of teachers could compare the logic-of-learning approach with one that adheres to central government policy (incorporating national curriculum programmes of study and attainment targets, the literacy and numeracy hours, etc.). Such research in state-maintained schools would, however, require permission from the Secretary of State for Education and Employment to suspend the national curriculum for all subjects in the 'logic of learning' classroom.

The future?

In England and Wales, following the Education Reform Act 1988 and the subsequent introduction of a national curriculum, the extensive use of child-initiated curricula became, to all intents and purposes, unlawful in state-maintained schools. The development of the logic-of-learning approach to teaching was curtailed, not because it was found to be educationally flawed but because of ideological and political changes at national level.

In light of renewed demands for educational research with direct implications for classroom practice, this is an opportune moment to promote the idea that theories of classroom practice can be tested as part of a new science of education (see Chapter 2), and that the logic-of-learning approach to teaching outlined in this chapter can be formulated as a testable theory. It remains to be seen whether there is the political will to permit (or even encourage) researchers to engage in 'imaginative criticism' (Popper 1979:148), to challenge current practice (including that which is consistent with government policy), and strive to create ways and means by which it may be improved.

Chapter 11

Using Critical Realism in Policy-making at School Level

DAVID CORSON

Many contemporary research methods have emerged from the same post-positivist environment that produced Bhaskar's theorizing. A partial list of these research methods includes:

- the various approaches to discourse and content analysis practised across the social sciences;
- classical ethnography;
- historical analysis;
- prosopography;
- participant observation;
- conversational analysis;
- ethnography of communication;
- ideology critique;
- critical ethnography;
- critical discourse analysis;
- documentary analysis, etc.;

and the triangulation of all these methods. In some limited way, each method tries to uncover the reality of the accounts and the reasons that portray social structures at work in research activities. When these methods are used as multiple approaches in the study of the same phenomenon, they provide compelling evidence for uncovering and explaining that reality. They offer a form of 'depth hermeneutics' that both interprets and explains human phenomena (Thompson 1990).

These methods offer ready tools for those engaged in policy-making at school level (see Corson 1998). In Chapter 6, I introduced the stages of critical policy-making aimed at putting these methods to work. Here, I elaborate on those stages (see Corson 1999) and discuss school reforms that tentatively respond to real problems identified by teacher practitioners, administrators, and their school communities.

CRITICAL POLICY-MAKING

Identifying the real problem(s)

The problem situation

The interests, attitudes, values and wishes of people with a stake in the policy area provide the basic evidence for critical policy-makers. To get access to that evidence, the circle of decision-makers in a school widens to include people fully in touch with all these things. In this way, the actual influence of the 'outsiders' is strengthened. The school taps the expertise of these people, using it to broaden their understanding of the problem situation and add insights about the range of possible solutions. This means consultation to identify the needs and interests of relevant teachers, students, parents, community members, and policy-makers working in the wider system.

The role of expert knowledge

Evidence from studies of expertise confirms the value in solving a problem of being 'an expert' (Glaser and Chi 1988). Clearly experts and novices contrast with one another in their problem-solving ability. The greater success that experts have comes from their coherent understanding of what counts as relevant knowledge. This contrasts with the fragmented grasp that novices have. But in a school trying to serve diverse communities, the professionals are often the novices. The expertise needed extends well beyond the professional knowledge that teachers and administrators acquire as part of their regular work. It requires the depth of insight into the local community and its cultures that experts in those cultures possess.

Skills relating that local knowledge to the work of teachers and administrators can come in other ways too. Study in fields like anthropology, applied ethics, and sociolinguistics is a valuable form of professional development. Sometimes it is mandated, as happened in a celebrated legal challenge in the United States (Labov 1982). However, when parents and others are brought into a school to provide local knowledge, they are often ready to accept the authority of the professionals on face value alone. In this situation, teachers and administrators working with parents have more demands than usual placed on their expertise. They try to become as expert as possible, or at least make it their business to know where to find real expertise.

The problem(s)

Having developed expertise in the field of the problem, a group assembles a set of key points from their study of the problem situation. Each point represents a fact of some kind, or an informed assumption, or even an important community or staff attitude relevant to the problem situation. From discussion around these points, key problems start to emerge. However, different people see similar problems in different ways, and they want to state the problems in their own way. When this happens, it is important to treat these as different problems, at least until the group reaches consensus about the way they are stated. If there is no consensus, then the problems are probably different and need to be treated differently.

The language in which a problem is framed is central. Again, if people cannot agree on the framing of a problem in simple language, there is probably more than just one problem to address. Different people often see different interests at stake in a problem situation, and so have different perspectives on it. So it is important that the statement of any problem is unambiguous, because if it means different things to different members of the policy group, then it will have no consistent meaning for other people trying to understand the policy.

A decision-making group often prioritizes to some degree the problems that it deals with. Again, conflict is likely, because people from diverse backgrounds often have trouble achieving unanimity when ranking complex problems. But a critical approach to policy-making invites this kind of disagreement, because conflict is the essence of the approach. People rarely solve conflicts by trying to adjudicate between alternative value systems that produce very different conceptions of a problem or its solution. Different group interests are not rival claims; they are incompatible claims that need some sort of compromise, which comes about when people of goodwill negotiate on the basis of an agreed norm. This suggests two types of problem: compatible and incompatible.

Incompatible problems are met through an informed consensus, where the decision-makers compromise in pursuit of their greater goals by agreeing to solve one another's incompatible problems as best they can. Often there are fewer incompatible problems in formal decision-making settings than people expect. Decision-makers of goodwill, who are concerned about social justice, can become skilled in adopting other people's problems as their own. They do this by trying to see the world from the different points of view of these others. However, when people from very different cultures are involved, it is a mistake to think that we can fully understand other people's points of view (Corson 1997). In other words, it is not helpful to see compatibility where it does not exist, just for the sake of 'consensus'.

Compatible problems provide the material for drawing up norms that can be referred to again and again when dealing with new problems. The over-arching problem of 'providing the best education possible for all children in the school' is the most important source of policy norms. A policy group identifies the things needed to address that over-arching problem, and these things become norms for referring to when making other decisions. Critical policy-makers build a context for discussion where everyone can participate in deciding norms without the intrusion of unreasonable power factors. To make this work, teachers and administrators adopt a very different leadership role, which I introduce elsewhere: emancipatory leadership (Corson 1998).

Trial policies: the views of stakeholders

Policy guidelines

Policy guidelines are solutions to policy problems. Sometimes each guideline offers a single solution to a problem; but more often, it takes many different guidelines to solve a complex problem. Sometimes too, a set of guidelines helps to solve a range of problems.

The value of these tentative guidelines depends on how readily they can be tested as solutions against the real world of the school's problems. This means that they are stated very clearly, like the statement of the initial problems themselves. In other words, the language used in the guidelines is not vague, high-sounding but empty, or overly restricted in meaning to some privileged group. The guidelines can only be put through the tests of the next stage if they are understood in much the same way by everyone who meets them. People with a stake in the policy area put the guidelines through a critical inspection, to make them sensible, and to ensure they replace unwanted with wanted forms of policy determination.

Controllable change: stages in policy guidelines

Guidelines for change often move forward too fast. When reform activities move quickly towards a major restructuring of a school, it is important that the organization is not permanently damaged by hasty implementation. To avoid this, policy-makers evaluate the implementation process, in some way, at every suitable stage. For dealing with complex problems, solutions can be in the form of guidelines set out in linked stages. Each of these stages is then tested in some way against the reasons and accounts of all those likely to be affected by the policy.

Some stages need small-scale research to be carried out before later stages can be reached, or even before they can be identified. I have listed above some of the methods available for this purpose, and I elaborate on them elsewhere (Corson 1999). The policy guidelines set out both the nature of this research and its purpose, because this activity is also part of the solution to the school's problems.

Testing policies against the views of participants

Testing policies by trial applications

The critical responses of people to the trials are the key to this stage. If the trials are carefully conducted, perhaps within a single department or age-level of the school, this allows small adjustments that improve the policy. Alternatively, the trials might lead to wholesale rejection of the policy guidelines, sending policy-makers back to reconsider their problem. They might modify the guidelines, or devolve the solving of the problem to a unit that is more relevant to it, such as a school department, an individual grade, or a single class. But this is not the same as shelving the problem.

Firmly constructive action of some kind needs to follow, otherwise the use of 'trial applications' might be mistakenly seen as an administrative device to stall the reform. For example, pilot programmes often delay genuine change while creating an impression of reform. But if decision-makers can assure people that they are really searching for solutions to critical problems, and if they continually bring people up to date, then there should be less room for doubting that real reform is on the way.

Testing policies by research

Small-scale and large-scale research methods are useful for supplementing trial applications of policy guidelines. However, as methods they too are subject to critical error elimination, because they may not reveal what policy-makers think they reveal or all that policy-makers need to know. For example, a survey of community opinion based on questionnaires can be an unreliable guide in deciding an important policy point. The survey's results could be overturned by later evidence that might come, perhaps, from focus groups taken as samples from the same community. In complex settings of cultural and linguistic diversity where much is at stake, decision-makers accept research findings in the same way as courts accept the verdict of a jury: that verdict can be quashed or revised in light of later evidence. Like a jury's verdict, a policy is always open to further criticism.

Policy implementation and evaluation

The final stage in policy research is the statement of the 'official' policy. Yet even this policy will still be tentative because in every school the social context is dynamic. Problems come and go as the sociocultural and political setting of the school changes; and the solutions offered to one set of problems cannot be applied logically to new problems that arise from a changed context. Also the priority of various parts of the policy will change, perhaps as a result of critical challenges by people who find they do have an interest in the problem field after all. These changes in perception and context are aspects of organizational conflict that critical policy-makers welcome and build into their planning.

What the above describes, in outline, is really an evolutionary approach to planning that allows teachers and administrators to work closely with community members. This seems to work best in schools with complex sociocultural problems, especially schools in inner-urban settings or remote communities. These schools can experience rapid changes in many areas of operation. A policy responsive to the school's dynamic, social, cultural, and political context should partly 'self-destruct' about once a year. This happens in response to changes in staffing, funding, community involvement, first and second language needs, horizontal and vertical policy changes from within the wider system, and new knowledge arising from relevant research.

CRITICAL POLICY-MAKING IN SETTINGS OF DIVERSITY

Elsewhere I set out in detail a range of school policies from North America and Australasia, all developed for real schools in response to carefully identified problems. Each policy is based on dialogue, attending to the reasons and accounts of participants (Corson 1999). Here, I discuss first a policy aimed at beginning that process of consultation; then, I describe a school that reformed itself in response to its own processes of 'critical policy-making'.

1. A policy for community fact-gathering and staff development

'Huron' Elementary School began its language policy work by reviewing the commonsense knowledge that teachers had about their students and their families (Webster 1995). Although this knowledge was, like all commonsense knowledge, affected by error and bias, the teachers' everyday insights into the school community had a number of features that seemed unique to it:

- Many immigrant families left the community for extended periods during the school year and travelled to their homelands taking students with them.
- Many families consisted of grandparents and the families of their sons, all living in one house where the adults shared in disciplining the students.
- Many other students lived with more distant relatives, rather than with their parents.
- Many parents, in their homelands, experienced a rote-learning educational system, taught by teachers whose authority was unquestioned and often brutal.
- Many parents seemed confused about the way English was taught in the school and became defensive whenever teachers tried to advise them on language practices for use in the home and family.

The fact-gathering policy introduced below is designed to bridge the gap between the teachers' rather scanty knowledge about the highly pluralist community that the school serves, and the real cultural world of that community. It uses questionnaires and discussions aimed at correcting the many stereotypes that staff have about the community, so that school–community relations can move forward on a well-informed basis; and so parents and others can begin to see the school as more organic to its local community.

The full policy (see Corson 1999) is not shown here for reasons of space and because these things are specific to individual schools. Figure 11.1 shows the first section, a statement of the problems the policy aims to address, and then the headings of later sections which offer solutions to those problems, based on small-scale research. Like most small-scale working policies in schools, this has teacher professional development as its focus. Although it is just the beginning of a long-term process of engagement with the school's real problems, it is an action plan that has immediate application.

1. **Identified or Perceived Language Problems**

    a.   Staff have inadequate or inaccurate information about community.
    b.   There is inconsistency of knowledge among staff regarding current research related to language issues.
    c.   Previous attempts to involve the community have been unsuccessful.
    d.   There is a mismatch between parents' and teachers' understandings of educational methods.
    e.   A wide need exists for second language instruction.
    f.   There is a trend towards first language loss among students.
    g.   Many students have academic difficulties after they have received the maximum level of ESL [English as a Second Language] support.
    h.   A lack of reading skills is reported by junior level staff.

2. **A 'Language in the Curriculum' Committee**

3. **Staff Development**
    3.1 Objective
            Plan of Action
    3.2 Objective
            Plan of Action
    3.3 Objective
            Plan of Action
    3.4 Objective
            Plan of Action

4. **Fact Gathering**
    4.1 Goals of Research
            Plan of Action

5. **School and Community**
    5.1 Objective
            Plan of Action
    5.2 Objective
            Plan of Action
    5.3 Objective
            Plan of Action
    5.4 Objective
            Plan of Action

6. **Curriculum**
    6.1 Objective
            Plan of Action
    6.2 Objective
            Plan of Action

Figure 11.1: A policy for community fact-gathering for 'Huron' Public School

2. Critical policy-making in practice

This is an abridged version of a description of Richmond Road School in Corson (1998). The key policy issue was how to provide an organization integrating a curriculum, pedagogy, and evaluation system that recognized the different cultural values of its highly pluralist local community. To increase the alternatives available to children from diverse backgrounds, the school tried to celebrate group collective identities and to lay constant stress on fairness for everyone, especially for those of little power. Because this school provides a model for schooling of this type, it has already been the focus of international attention.

By the early 1990s, Richmond Road School already had a well-functioning pluralist curriculum and organizational structure. Dating back many years, a Maori educational leader had been able to communicate to the staff his vision of what a multi-ethnic school for students and teachers should be. He was helped in this by a strong sense of his own Polynesian identity which gave him the provisional authority of having more authentic knowledge in this key area. The process he adopted closely resembles the approach to critical policy-making outlined above. It is clear from the account of May (1994) that the principal's restructuring of the school, from his earliest efforts, drew on his skills as a person committed to critical and emancipatory reform. He based his reforms on problem identification, and on the negotiation, consultation, and error elimination needed to find workable policy solutions.

The restructuring process in outline

In 1990, Richmond Road School had 270 students, of whom 21 per cent were Samoan, 20 per cent were European New Zealanders, 18 per cent were Maori, 34 per cent were the children of other Polynesian immigrant peoples, and 7 per cent were Fijian Indian and others. In providing for this diverse student body, the key to the principal's reform was to establish new and very different organizational structures. Cazden (1989) describes organizational structures and patterns of interaction among staff, children and the community which were clearly effective in meeting the values of the cultural majority, as well as the range of cultural communities from which the school draws its pupils. Cazden describes how:

> In contrast to the isolation of teachers in single-cell classroom schools, Richmond Road teachers work in a setting of intense collectivity. Children and staff interact in complex organizational 'systems', as they are always referred to: vertical/family groupings of children; non-hierarchical relationships among the staff; curriculum materials that are created by teacher teams at the school and rotate around the school for use by all; and monitoring systems for continuous updating of information on children's progress. (1989:150)

For his vertical grouping system, the principal borrowed from the example of non-graded country schools. Six ropu (vertical groups) operated in shared or separate spaces: there was a Samoan bilingual group, a Maori bilingual group, a Cook Island Maori bilingual group, and the ESL language unit for non-English speaking newcomers to New Zealand; the fifth and sixth ropu were English-speaking only.

Each ropu included children from the entire age range, from 5-year-old new entrants to 11-year-olds. Children stayed in the same ropu for their entire time in the school, working with one home-group teacher in frequently changing vertical home groups of 16 to 20 pupils. Also attached to the school were Maori, Samoan, and Cook Island immersion culture/language pre-schools. The school's three dual-immersion bilingual units received the graduates from these pre-school language nests, if parents agreed. During half of each morning and every other afternoon, the teachers in these units spoke only Maori, Samoan, or Cook Island Maori, and they encouraged the children to do the same.

Paired teaching and peer instruction were common. The provisional authority of the principal, coming from his specialist cultural and administrative knowledge, was a model for provisional authority among the school community. In other words 'whoever has knowledge teaches'. As a result, the official hierarchy had much less meaning among the school's people. For example, the school's language leaders or language assistants had no formal professional training, yet they worked as full teachers because of their expertise and the valuable on-the-job training they had received. Also, the school's caretaker was involved in educational work as a valued colleague, supporting children and staff, respected by parents, and a friend to all the children. Parents too contributed their special knowledge, and 'the front door was always open'. The school became organic to its cultural community.

The stress on communal activity for the students was extended in other directions: bonds were forged at various levels. The vertical grouping of the ropu allowed co-operative curriculum and resource development by the teachers. Working in five curriculum groups that cut across the ropu teaching teams, teachers collaborated in making 'focus resources' for school-wide topics. These topics followed a multi-year plan, so that all the different cultural groups were assured of exposure to each topic. Each team made materials at ten reading levels, for use in four learning modes; each teacher was responsible for making a number of different items. When ready, teachers presented their materials to colleagues during staff meetings. The materials were rotated throughout the school, staying in each ropu for fixed periods. Clearly, as well as collaboration, there was efficiency and effectiveness. Like the school itself, curriculum materials matched the community that the school served, and they targeted the needs of the students.

Richmond Road was also a learning community for adults: they learned about teaching, about other cultures, and about themselves. Community-based education became a practical reality. Professional development moved forward as well. The principal encouraged staff to share and explore their own and each other's cultural and class backgrounds, which were as diverse as the children's. He stressed teacher workshops and conferences, contact with up-to-date theory, worthwhile staff-meeting discussions, and critical policy development. By working together, teachers learned about collaborative ways of learning, and this offered a sound model for the students.

Clearly, the competitive nature of regular schooling was missing from this more collectivist environment. The school put the self-esteem of the pupils ahead of their academic performance, while expecting to improve that performance as a result. This stressed the students' growing sense of cultural pride, their sense of who they were, and their sense of involvement in a worthwhile school community. Academic development did not suffer as a result. May (1994) offers extensive data confirming that the children's academic progress was as good or better than comparable students elsewhere.

May's critical ethnography shows that the principal's success came from several things: his ability to cultivate enthusiasm for his restructuring; his democratic approach to deciding the course of change; and his willingness to give people all the time they needed to change. I see his approach to school administration as a form of emancipatory leadership. This is still rare in schools today, but it was even less common in the 1970s and 1980s when reforms of this type began. May also confirms that the principal's plans for change were gradual and carefully managed. He brought about key structural changes over eight to nine years.

Coming from an oppressed community himself, the principal knew that traditional forms of schooling act in a hegemonic way. They maintain inequalities for children from diverse backgrounds by making them conform to the dominant culture; this they tend to do by not allowing much room for protest inside the school's controlling structures. He wanted to reduce these pressures to conform, and used this idea to develop his policy-making strategy. May sets out the principal's strategy. Some of the detail is recounted below to illustrate similarities between the critical policy-making process recommended in this chapter and the actual practices followed in Richmond Road's development.

Identifying the real problems

The social conditions of community deterioration and dislocation that surrounded the school prompted the reforms. But the principal himself was the catalyst for change, by showing his willingness to build the knowledge and ideas of others into his own thinking. Through his own critical openness, he freed the staff to look for issues in the school's problem context. He asked them to raise problems, and to take the lead in discussing them in formal meetings. He consistently asked staff to look for critical alternatives in their practices, to break away from the constraints of monocultural or dominant ways of doing things. While promoting a strong sense of teacher ownership over the curriculum, he also made sure that everything was decided according to what was best for the children, both as individuals and as members of different cultural groups. This became the school's over-riding normative principle. He also encouraged teachers who were unsympathetic to his vision to leave, and he waited for this to happen before pushing forward with radical change.

Richmond Road raised expert knowledge to a level that is rare in schools. In one sense this meant capitalizing on external professional expertise by letting it work in the school's interests. But in a more important sense, it meant recognizing the value of the expertise of the staff and the community. To foster staff expertise, the principal used staff development as his key strategy, encouraging staff to see the school's problems from different theoretical perspectives. The staff library had many subscriptions to high quality, cross-disciplinary journals; these were read by all the staff. The journals were often used as the starting point for the professional development programme, which was built directly into the structure and timetable of the school.

Participation in this programme was part of a teacher's duty. Full attendance was expected and sessions often lasted three to four hours. Once a relevant problem was identified in a meeting, the staff targeted the field of the problem through a stimulus paper read by one or more staff members, or through the distribution of readings on the topic. In-depth discussion was often followed by a week's break. This allowed wider reading by all staff. It also stimulated new ideas and interest-group discussions. Finally, in another full meeting, policy action was proposed, and implementation followed. Through this process, the staff became used to adopting a theorized approach to their practice. They developed collaborative expertise at the same time, and worked always to keep lines of communication open between themselves.

The school also gave priority to keeping communication lines open with other people who had an interest in its development. Early in the reforms, the staff created an 'open door policy' for its community. They worked to reduce the usual gap that stands between parents and teachers by giving parents a sense of their own status and efficacy. They welcomed them into the school and asked them to say what they liked and disliked. To build a sense of community involvement, the school regularly held open-house events that celebrated new developments. Staff incorporated the ceremonies and customs of the communities into these events. The school also held regular cultural ceremonies to which community members flocked. As a result, parents felt drawn to contribute to the teaching and other activities.

In their interactions with community members, staff worked hard to develop inclusive and reciprocal relations with all parents, especially with people from non-dominant backgrounds. Through their behaviour, disposition, and speech they tried to show intense respect for human and cultural difference. This atmosphere led to a natural growth in community involvement in policy-making. A good example of this was the creation and organization of each of the three language and culture immersion pre-schools on the premises. These changes were community driven. The later development of a fourth pre-school was also in response to community suggestion and advocacy. In the pre-schools, the buildings were controlled by the school's Board of Trustees (school council), but the parents controlled their own finances and sorted out their rules. Matching the principal's objective of elevating those with little power, these practices freed the parents to do it all themselves.

For more than a decade, the school involved influential members of the community in matters of governance and gave them real power to direct the school in the community's interests. As a matter of policy, the school encouraged these leaders to mediate in difficulties that arose for children from diverse backgrounds or among community members. This policy included appointing professional and ancillary staff drawn from the local communities, giving them status in the school, and involving them directly in school governance. Later, with these structures in place, it was easy to consult the interests of parents and community members, and to relate them to the interests of students and staff.

To achieve all this, the principal built commitment to the changes through constant dialogue with participants. He helped people to see that conflict and criticism are inevitable and productive. He fostered a sense of self-worth among staff. This encouraged them to withstand the inevitable pressures that radical reforms like these create, even when gradual. The principal's policy of having staff, pupils and parents formally choose to be in the school, after learning of its differences, also built a sense of commitment and loyalty. This policy extended to choices about enrolling in the different units within the school. For example, the school always counselled parents on the role and purpose of the bilingual units, and then gave them the choice of enrolling children there, or in the English-only units. This choice extended to the children as well, who had the option of using either of their two languages at any given time in bilingual classroom programmes.

Finally, the school showed a critical realist approach to power relations within the wider system. To advance the interests of the school, the staff kept in touch with those power relations and adopted a stance of guarded scepticism towards them. This meant collaborative resistance, as a school, to unwanted outside pressures. At the same time, it meant provoking or anticipating change where necessary. Most usefully, it meant taking strategic advantage of rule changes in the wider system to solve school problems and to further the process of reform. For example, in 1985 the school introduced New Zealand's first inner-city Maori bilingual unit, as soon as a change in the government's rules allowed.

In ranking its problems, the school also adopted a critical realist approach to internal power arrangements and decision-making. The decision-making groups used conflict constructively in their problem search. To achieve this, they compromised where necessary by agreeing to solve each group's incompatible problems as best they could. For example, although the larger Samoan community was the first to ask for its own pre-school and bilingual unit, the Board of Trustees, under the chairmanship of a Samoan parent, acknowledged the right of the smaller Maori community, who are the ancestral people of the country, to have the first pre-school and bilingual unit. But with that development firmly in place, unanimous support for the Samoan developments followed quickly.

Trial policies: the views of stakeholders

The principal moved in careful stages when addressing more complex problems. Even after involving the staff and the community in the decision-making process, he made only small changes and did so gradually. He underlined the fact that there are no quick answers to complex policy problems, but took pains to convince the community that the school was engaging in genuine reform. He achieved this by carefully demonstrating to the community the success of each stage in his reconstruction, and then by consulting them again, modifying the process, and moving on to the next stage.

To provide opportunities for staff to consider the more professional aspects of the reforms, he organized the school so that formal curriculum teams could consider curriculum problems. Individual teachers were released from class-time on different mornings to take part in these sessions where problems were identified and tested against the knowledge and interests of teachers. In these cycles of error elimination, the problem area was crossed and re-crossed; the theories of participants were continually tested against the evidence available, including that most important form of evidence, the views and wishes of stakeholders themselves.

In its long history of reform, Richmond Road developed a tradition of using trial applications of its policies, and of evaluating the critical responses of people to the trials. Over several years, for example, senior teachers trialled and then modelled for others the new family grouping structure, using the features of the ideal family as a model for inclusive and extended relations. Applying emancipatory leadership, the principal gave these senior colleagues full discretion in trialling, adopting, and discarding different arrangements. At the same time, he and the teachers promoted free communication with all parents of the students involved.

When the school found a successful family grouping model, the innovators slowly encouraged interest in their ideas among other staff. They then established similar units, without the principal's direct involvement. The school eventually followed the model preferred by the trial group, but it still allowed teacher discretion over structural details within individual units, such as timetabling, teacher turn-around in responsibilities, etc. This whole process took five to six years, and, as an expected outcome of the reforms, the school allowed the structural changes to flow through into pedagogical changes.

In summary, addressing the school's problems deliberately, in an ingenious and imaginative way, the principal reorganized the school's grouping system through community negotiation and professional education. He created a flat and more egalitarian management system. By negotiation, he lessened undesirable structural constraints, like those that prevented staff from diverse backgrounds from being hired, or community members from having a strong voice in governance. The school's critical approach to policy development was underpinned by its commitment to a culturally pluralist, integrative, and process approach to education.

Chapter 12

Equal Opportunities in Secondary Education: A Case Study

JOHN PRATT

The Sex Discrimination Act 1975 made sex discrimination in education (with certain exceptions) unlawful in the United Kingdom. At the time the Act was passed, differentiation in subject choice between pupils of different sex had long been a feature of secondary education in the UK. A national survey (Department of Education and Science 1975) found that differences appeared even in the curriculum in primary schools, but by the time of 'option choice' in the fourth and fifth years of secondary school, there were striking differences in the subjects studied by boys and girls. This kind of differentiation now became a matter of law, as Section 22 of the Act made it unlawful for an educational establishment to discriminate against a woman (or a man) 'in the way it affords her access to any benefits, facilities or services, or by refusing or deliberately omitting to afford her access to them'. This chapter reports on the first national study of the impact of the Act in the process of choice of option subjects in secondary schools. The research was commissioned by the Equal Opportunities Commission (EOC), and published as Pratt *et al.* (1984). It offers an example of the kind of policy-testing advocated in Chapter 4 of this book.

The study took place before the major curricular reforms introduced by the 1988 Education Reform Act, which restricted the option choice available to pupils by introducing a national curriculum in England and Wales. At the time of the study, pupils at the end of their third year of secondary school generally selected about seven option subjects in addition to English and mathematics. I briefly note some of the implications of the study for the 1988 reforms later in this chapter.

THE STUDY

The EOC required the research to examine the extent to which the Sex Discrimination Act was being implemented, both in letter and spirit, and its effects on a wide range of secondary schools. The study was designed to identify and assess the practical problems which could preclude a free choice of curricular options by both sexes, and to examine possible solutions.

First we attempted to establish the national picture of subjects taken by boys and girls after option choice, the extent of differences between them, and the changes, if any, since the Act. This we did by a survey of subjects taken by pupils in a sample of secondary schools, and by the examination of specially commissioned tabulations of examination entries from DES statistics. This information was supported by detailed statistics on subject choices from selected case study schools. We also gathered information from schools, careers offices and DES statistics on the future educational or career destinations or aspirations of pupils, enabling us to examine the issue of the relationship between educational opportunity and future careers.

This aspect of the study could be seen to be concerned with the 'outcomes' of the education process. In Pawson and Tilley's (1997:71) summary of a realist explanation, they constitute a 'regularity'. We posited that these outcomes resulted from a number of factors, including the policies and practices of schools, and other factors in what Pawson and Tilley refer to as the 'context', such as the prejudices and preferences of pupils, parents, employers and teachers.

The second aspect of our study, therefore, was concerned with the educational process. We attempted to determine the extent of good or bad practice, and to investigate whether practice was associated with outcome. We based our understanding of good practice on the EOC's published guidance about the 1975 Act and education (EOC 1979), augmented by a wide literature search. This aspect of the study involved detailed investigation in case study schools. There were several candidates for the most important influence on pupils' choice of options and variations in the extent to which schools were behaving in accordance with the Act. We gathered evidence from survey schools about how option subjects were presented to pupils and parents in school literature, and various other potential influences were examined. These included: staffing patterns in schools; differences in punishments; and ways in which subjects were presented either to encourage or discourage the non-traditional sex to opt for them.

Some progress towards estimating the extent to which pupils were influenced by various factors could be made by seeing whether variations in an influencing factor were associated with variation in subject take-up. Thus, we tried to ascertain whether different ways of grouping subjects for option schemes were associated with differences in take-up, whether the overall stress that a school placed on equal opportunities as a policy (as measured by various items on the survey questionnaire and combined into a score) was associated with variation in subject take-up. Variation in teacher attitudes from school to school was compared with subject take-up in the schools.

The study also collected information about extra-school factors. Pupils were interviewed about the extent to which teachers, their peers or parents influenced their choice. Visits to careers offices and interviews with careers teachers provided information about the expectations of local employers.

Four main approaches were thus employed in the study (in line with Tooley's strictures about triangulation in Chapter 15): a postal survey; case studies of selected schools; analysis of national statistics; attitude surveys. The postal survey involved sending questionnaires to two samples of secondary schools. The questionnaire asked for basic information about the school (age range, catchment area, etc.), and about organization and practices concerned with equal opportunities (for example, whether a member of staff had special responsibility for this issue), derived from the EOC guidance (EOC 1979). We were testing the hypothesis that if the equal opportunities policy was working, then these features of good practice would be found. A general principle embodied in the questionnaire was that information should be, as far as possible, gained from existing school records or from the various enclosures (such as prospectuses) that were asked for. This, too, reflected the 'If – then' approach, since routine documents would be one place where policy should be evident, though we also wished to minimize demands on schools for special information. The first, *nominated* sample, consisted of 139 schools in 63 local education authorities in England and Wales. All Chief Education Officers in England and Wales were asked to nominate one or more schools in their authority that, in their view, were examples of good practice in the area of equal opportunities. The second, *cluster* sample, consisted of the 216 secondary schools of six local education authorities, including one from Scotland.

The purpose of choosing these two samples was to compare what it was hoped were examples (the nominated sample) of good practice with a sample more representative of the state of affairs in the UK (the cluster sample). The samples represented seven per cent of secondary schools in England, Wales and Scotland.

Fourteen schools were selected for detailed three-day case study visits. A guiding factor in the selection of schools was that some should exemplify good practice and others bad. We also chose one from each of the cluster authorities. In terms of age range, geographical location and type of school, we aimed to choose a cross-section; two single-sex schools were included.

We commissioned special tabulations from the DES of statistics from the 1980 school-leaver survey. These showed the numbers of pupils entering and passing school-leaving examinations in selected subjects and groups of subjects, and their post-school destinations.

We undertook studies of the attitudes of teachers and pupils towards equal opportunities. Our teacher sample consisted of 850 teachers in 50 schools in England and Wales. The pupil sample consisted of nearly 1,000 pupils in the fourth or fifth year of secondary school.

THE FINDINGS

Despite the passing of the Sex Discrimination Act, by 1980–81 boys and girls still differed in the subjects they chose at the age of 13+. More boys than girls took physical sciences and technical subjects, while more girls chose biological and vocational subjects and languages. The pattern of choice had changed little since the passing of the Act: there were few differences of subject choice in nine major academic areas between our survey results and those from an HMI survey conducted in 1973 (DES 1975). On leaving school, pupils similarly exhibited differences in destinations according to sex. More boys than girls aspired to and achieved apprenticeships; more girls than boys aspired to and achieved secretarial jobs. The patterns were reflected in post-school education: secretarial, para-medical and teaching courses attracted more girls than boys; engineering and scientific courses attracted more boys. Our analysis showed that if pupils did take subjects non-traditional for their sex at school, they were more likely to take up a non-traditional post-school course, but the sex of a pupil was a factor more statistically important in destination than the subjects studied. Thus, a girl taking sciences at school was more likely than other girls to follow a post-school science course, but less likely to do so than a boy who had not studied science.

Local authorities and schools appeared to wish to be seen as taking equal opportunities seriously, at least in their written responses to us. Most schools in our survey had discussed the issue in staff meetings, a large minority had considered it at meetings of governors and parent–teacher associations, though fewer than a sixth had given members of staff special responsibility or set up working parties on the issue. Very few made explicit reference to their policy in prospectuses.

In terms of school organization, over a third of schools claimed to balance numbers of each sex in streams (which practice the EOC regarded as unlawful), and most kept registers that listed boys and girls separately. A few schools still restricted some subjects to one sex in defiance of the Sex Discrimination Act, but a high proportion offered all subjects to both and taught most subjects – including physical education, games and sex education – in mixed groups, though in some schools some craft subjects were offered in single-sex groups to encourage and respond to non-traditional choice. Ninety per cent of schools offered a rotational craft system, many as a response to the Act; but few offered compensatory courses for pupils taking subjects non-traditional for their sex.

Overall, it appeared that perhaps 75 per cent of schools conformed to the letter of the Act, though they did not go much beyond this. Some 10 per cent had strong equal opportunities policies, and some 15 per cent exhibited a number of features of 'bad practice'.

This picture of overall school policies was a cause for both encouragement and concern. We could say that most schools survived the test of policy, at least in its milder 'letter of the law' form. It was encouraging that only a few schools actively discriminated on grounds of sex, and the great majority showed features of good practice. But the existence of the minority who did discriminate, and the apparently widespread belief that equal opportunities was simply a matter of not breaking the law, suggested that much more needed to be done to encourage schools to pass the more severe 'spirit of the Act' test.

School policy and organization are not the only consideration. Did they have any effect? The study enabled us to test some of the implicit hypotheses in the 1975 policy. The policy of which the Act was an embodiment implied that if good practice were implemented, sex discrimination would diminish. Our study showed that there was little overall association between good practice (as assessed by our measures) and non-traditional subject take-up in the major academic subjects. There was some indication that rotational craft timetables encouraged non-traditional choices, but the feature most associated with non-traditional take-up was single-sex schools, reflecting other research findings (for example, Dale 1974).

We examined some of the features of school practice that may have contributed to these findings. We looked at the combinations of subjects that option systems permitted or prevented in a sample of 130 schools. This showed that in most schools the structure of the option system neither encouraged nor prevented sex-biased choice, though some schools had a system which encouraged traditional patterns of take-up, and few made non-traditional combinations difficult. A large minority permitted no science to be taken. When we compared the schemes with take-up we found that 'good' schemes were not associated with non-traditional take-up overall, though some subjects appeared to be affected to some extent. So the marked differences in take-up could not be explained solely by reference to formal rigidities of option choice systems.

We looked, therefore, at the influences within schools and their option systems which might have affected pupils' choice of subjects. First, we found that teachers frequently intervened in option choice, advising on 'acceptable' or 'suitable' combinations of subjects. Second, some option schemes linked subjects in ways which were discriminatory, in that girls might have found it more difficult to meet the conditions for acceptance – such as a craft subject with a physics link. Third, many schools introduced, for lower ability groups, para-science courses (such as engineering science or health education) which were effectively sex-stereotyped. Fourth, rotational craft schemes were often badly implemented, being offered in an abbreviated form, and so offering an inadequate experience base for pupils to make a serious choice. Last, we found that option choice forms themselves were often in practice restrictive on choice because of the way they were structured and applied. Many listed subjects in multi-disciplinary blocks reflecting the school timetable, thus fitting pupils to timetable rather than timetable to pupils' choices. Some were so complicated as to be almost incomprehensible.

Another major factor that might have influenced subject take-up was the way in which subjects were presented to pupils at option choice time, and subsequently the ways in which they were taught. In formal literature, such as option booklets, over half the schools made it clear that both boys and girls were welcome in some subjects, but only one in nine stated that all subjects were open to all pupils. Some craft subjects were presented as for one sex (for example, 'Girls' Needlework'); science descriptions often demonstrated a hierarchy of difficulty, though some schools specifically encouraged girls to choose physical science.

Perhaps the main evidence from the case studies was of the contrast between teachers who were attempting to reduce disparities in take-up and improve teaching practices, and those who said it could not be done. Thus, in the physical sciences we were offered more explanations of problems than solutions. Many teachers ascribed the failure to follow physical sciences to the pupils and influences on them, but many also believed there was no career relevance in the subjects for girls. In other schools we came across examples of ways of tackling the problem – including creating girls' physics classes, and revision of syllabuses. The school most successful in getting a majority of girls to study a physical science to 16 had a core curriculum science programme, and seemed to surmount the problems which most teachers expressed about core curriculum science. Similarly, in craft subjects we found a disturbing reluctance by teachers to encourage non-traditional choice, more among (male) technical craft than (female) home economics teachers. The introduction of design and technology courses, rather than traditional crafts, in some case study schools allowed a widening of opportunities for both sexes, but this was often greeted with hostility by some members of staff.

Conflicting views of teachers were also a feature in careers teaching. This was an important factor in option choice, as most schools suggested that pupils consider possible careers when choosing their subjects at 13+. Our survey revealed that a large number of schools had considered equal opportunities in relation to careers teaching, had made use (with mixed results) of equal opportunities-orientated literature, and introduced features such as speakers who exemplified non-traditional role models. Some schools incorporated topics on sex roles and equality in core subjects such as English or social studies. However, only four out of fourteen case study schools provided careers advice before option choice, and most took a passive attitude to post-option advice. Only two employed positive equal opportunities features. Many teachers expressed the view that schools should remain 'neutral' in this area, as in curriculum choice. And we found that some schools, and in particular one careers office, colluded with employers to channel pupils into jobs, or work experience, of a traditional nature.

The idea of 'neutrality' emerged again in our study of teacher attitudes. Most teachers were committed to equal opportunities in principle, though they showed decreasing enthusiasm for practical implementation of the principles. Their views were to an extent associated with their sex, but more strongly with subject, with teachers of traditionally stereotyped subjects – such as physical sciences and crafts – often holding strong stereotyped views; this was also true of some in the core subject of mathematics. The minority opposed to equal opportunities commented that schools should not positively intervene in the process of choice by pupils – they should supply 'neutral' information and let the pupils decide. In our view, this stance denied the existence and importance of the factors promoting stereotyping, and it also failed to take account of the attitude of pupils.

Our attitude study of pupils suggested that the problems of achieving equal opportunities in education also derived from them. Pupils were even less likely to agree with equal opportunities principles than teachers, and boys were less likely than girls. But there were striking contrasts in pupils' attitudes. Most agreed that schools should set an example in reducing sex discrimination, yet fewer than half the pupils believed that boys and girls could be equally good at all subjects. Pupils identified many jobs, careers, personal qualities and activities in the home with one sex; again, boys more consistently than girls. We concluded that, if pupils were to have equal opportunities, these presuppositions would have to be confronted.

MANAGING POLICY

Given our findings, it was clear that, if the policy embodied in the Sex Discrimination Act is regarded as a tentative solution to the problem of how to reduce inequality, by the early 1980s it had achieved only limited success. But its failure to achieve more arose as much from the failure to implement it as from its inadequacy. The study suggested that, although this was a national policy which required implementation at all levels in the education service, the management of schools was crucial in achieving change.

The study had shown that most of the objections to implementing an equal opportunities policy were invalid. The main objections to practice were that 'it can't be done' for administrative, economic, educational or discipline reasons. Yet for every objection we found, some other school had managed to cope with the problem. So while good practice may have been difficult, it was not impossible.

It was clear that some schools still had to consider the issue of equal opportunities, and most schools had failed to make policy explicit in their literature. We suggested that all schools should, at meetings of governors, staff and parent–teacher associations, consider – and from time to time reconsider and appraise – their policy towards equal opportunities. This would involve recognition and analysis of the differences in the subjects studied by pupils, the pressures towards sex stereotyping and the school's attitude to confronting them, and the steps the school intended to take to deal with them. We recommended that the policy should be set out in the prospectus and other school literature, especially option booklets.

The study revealed the importance of day-to-day detail in implementing policy. We noted that the ethos of a school was manifested through such features. The administrative and organization structures of a school enforced a hidden curriculum as much as the hidden values and assumptions of the teachers and the system. We recommended that a senior teacher or working group should be responsible for ensuring that school documents were consistent with school policy. We found that administrative arrangements could affect subject choice and must be consistent with the aims of policy. The organization and administration of option schemes was a crucial component of school policy on equal opportunities. We advised on the need for clarity and simplicity, and the importance of designing the timetable to fit option choices rather than fitting choices to the timetable. It seemed to us self-evident (yet surprisingly overlooked in some schools) that some careers advice should precede option choice.

Administrative and procedural reforms of this kind would not, of course, eliminate stereotyping on their own. The study showed that schools and their staffs needed to reassess their attitudes, educational practices and educational philosophies. We suggested that teachers needed to ask, subject by subject, whether their approaches and practices offered pupils of either sex a worthwhile educational experience. In many cases, we believed, this would have been a new experience for the teachers. We were struck by the inability of many teachers we talked with to offer any account of what it was that their subject offered to pupils that other subjects did not. This process would lead, we believed, to some searching reappraisal of classroom practices and attitudes, and also to redevelopment of existing syllabuses. The subject areas in which such reform seemed most needed included not only the more obvious sciences, crafts and technical subjects, but also some core subjects like English and the humanities. Our case studies had shown that progress towards equal opportunities often arose from curricular reforms which sought to avoid excessive subject specialization, like the creation of integrated science courses and the emergence of design and CDT (craft, design and technology) courses.

We noted, too, the apparent importance of 'protecting' small numbers of pupils of one sex in a class predominantly composed of the other. There seemed to be a 'threshold' – of about four or five pupils – below which minority pupils were prone to give up an option; but if this was surmounted, others tended to be encouraged to follow. For example, most schools kept small numbers of girls in physics classes together, rather than splitting them between different classes. Similarly, some schools made successful use of single-sex classes – for a limited period – for non-traditional subjects.

We emphasized that one particular area of the school curriculum required attention. This was careers teaching, which was important not least because of obvious breaches of the law. Since so much hinged on a pupil's choice of subjects at 13+, it seemed to us incumbent upon schools to offer pupils some positive assistance with that choice. It was no great discovery that careers guidance was a 'Cinderella' of education. But by the time pupils reached the age of 13, they had perhaps been exposed to inadvertent and subtle pressures and stereotyping for at least eight years. Radical reforms of school timetables were required to combat this – a couple of hours a week would hardly be sufficient. Since pupils were to be obliged to make far-reaching decisions, they needed:

- help to develop decision-making skills;
- experience in considering arguments and the consequences of alternative courses of action;
- help in evaluating evidence;
- assistance in researching and examining their self-images and the pressures upon them.

Few, if any, schools offered this kind of experience. We also suggested that schools should examine carefully the benefits of work experience programmes, which often forced schools into making sex-biased placements.

Our findings suggested that the head teacher had a crucial role in the management of policy. The study showed that in many schools there was a need to ensure the commitment of staff to equal opportunities as to any other policy. Conflict between departments or individuals was a disconcertingly frequent feature in our case studies. Where policy was widely implemented, as in one case study school, this had been achieved by the head's use of a wide range of management devices to 'carry' the staff with her. Instead of imposing an equal opportunities policy by fiat, she had initiated curriculum development groups which, with the help of sympathetic teachers, had devised new curricular policies consistent with equal opportunities. The effect was to make staff, who were initially unsympathetic, committed to the new ideas because they had themselves been a part of them. Teachers responded to the logic of their environment.

The study showed that teachers played a key role in option choice. Yet they displayed (in the case studies and in the attitude surveys) considerable disparities of view about equal opportunities. Many teachers felt there was an apparent contradiction between good educational practice and good equal opportunity practice. The need to gain examination passes was cited as grounds for selecting the pupils traditionally most likely to succeed – and in many subjects this involved a preference for those of one sex. There were, however, helpful findings from our study. Though their views were often contradictory, most teachers were in principle against discrimination or disadvantage on grounds of sex. They recognized that children brought stereotypes with them into schools, and that teachers sometimes supported and even encouraged these stereotypes, even if they believed them inappropriate. Our abiding impression was that teachers were looking for a clear lead on the topic of equal opportunities. They were unhappy about the dissonance between their beliefs and their practices.

We saw these problems as part of a general dichotomy between the views that teachers hold about the purposes of education and the practices that actually follow. This dichotomy has been documented by Raven (1977), who found that when asked what they thought the objectives of education ought to be, teachers, pupils and parents were in broad agreement; but when asked what aims were implied by their actual teaching, teachers reported that they implemented quite different ones.

It was clear to us that the resolution of this discrepancy lay in curricular reform. The study suggested that schools and policy-makers ought to think in terms not just of importing equal opportunities into existing curricula, but rather of creating courses afresh that started from the needs and interests of both boys and girls, not from the 'demands of the subject' or the predictions and presumptions of teachers about pupils' needs. Good equal opportunities practice, we concluded, followed from – indeed, was identical with – good educational practice. For stereotyping is essentially treating pupils not as individuals but as members of a group. Where we found good practice, it involved considering the needs of pupils as individuals rather than as members of one sex or the other, and considering what pupils might need to equip them for the vicissitudes of life.

Thus we felt that reforming the curriculum for equal opportunities involved a fundamental reassessment of schools' educational philosophies. Indeed, we found ourselves questioning the idea that education should consist of discrete academic subjects (mirroring Swartz's concerns about a prescribed curriculum, as described in Chapter 9). In a sense, sex stereotyping in education arose because of the existence of separate subjects. If there was no 'physics', boys and girls could not choose whether or not to study it. This is not entirely trivial. Subjects reflect a structuring of knowledge, and they impose structures on schools which encourage stereotyped choice because of their associations and implications for pupils of either sex.

We suggested, therefore, an approach based on the development of qualities and general competences in pupils to help them cope with and control their own lives in the world after school. We pointed to the work of Raven (1977, 1982), who argued that secondary schools should be concerned with developing 'the whole person'. Specifically, this involved fostering such qualities as the willingness and the ability to exercise initiative in introducing change in their society, independence, the ability to make their own observations and learn without instruction, the ability to apply facts and techniques to new problems, to develop their characters and personality, and to ensure that they leave school intent on controlling their destinies. These qualities offer a basis for developing a *general* educational approach, which is particularly pertinent for equal opportunities as it involves the recognition by pupils and teachers of the pressures and prejudices that pupils face. It is thus part of this process for girls or boys to recognize and confront the disparities in culture and circumstances that face them because of their sex, and to devise programmes of education to challenge, accept or avoid them. Raven (1977) showed how his ideas could be developed within subjects as they were currently organized, and itemized ways in which specific subjects could be presented to pupils to encourage the development of competences, using a variety of different inputs geared to different objectives.

This, of course, suggests that individual needs can only be met by individual educational programmes. It also suggests that pupils themselves should be involved in formulating their problems and their programmes. Programmes of independent study are already established and working at post-school level in the UK and elsewhere. Swann (Chapter 10) argues for an approach to education based on a similar 'logic of learning', and Burgess and Adams (1980) showed how such programmes for the last two years of compulsory education could be devised.

THE NEW 'SOLUTION'

As noted earlier, the 1988 Education Reform Act has made significant changes to school curricula and practices. In particular, it has restricted the opportunity for sex-stereotyped subject choice by pupils. The prescribed core curriculum now involves science for all pupils. It could be said to be a solution to the differentiation in subject choice that was of such concern in our study. Yet the searching reappraisal of classroom practice and curriculum that we advocated, and the proposals for individually-based programmes, are not now possible under law. The importance of examination passes has increased with the publication of school league tables. We have a new solution that facilitates the fulfilment of the letter of the law; but embracing the spirit of the 1975 policy, in the way indicated by our study, may be further away than ever. The 'problems of the solution' (see Chapter 4) may, in the long run, turn out to be as bad as the original problem of differentiation in subject choice.

Chapter 13

Exploring Informal Practitioner Theory in Adult Basic Education

YVONNE HILLIER

Much has been written about informal theories used by professionals (Argyris and Schön 1974; Usher and Bryant 1989; Bright 1996). Informal theory as described by Argyris and Schön refers to the many informal propositions, beliefs, views and attitudes we have about the world. Unlike academic theory which is subject to extensive analysis, criticism and testing, informal theory remains private, implicit and not rigorously tested. This chapter describes how informal theory was elicited from a group of practitioners in the specialized field of adult basic education using Kelly's repertory grid, an in-depth interview technique based on his theory of personal constructs. Making explicit the main tenets of informal practitioner theory brings the tacit into the public domain and provides an opportunity to test assumptions.

PERSONAL CONSTRUCT THEORY

Personal construct theory is based on a view of 'man [sic] the scientist' (Kelly 1969:66). Kelly was trained initially as a physicist, and his theory reflects a scientific approach to analysing the world. His view of science, though different from that of Karl Popper, accords with the idea developed by Popper that there is a reality behind the world of appearances (see Chapter 2).

An inquiry is an attempt to unpeel the layers of reality in pursuit of developing knowledge about that reality. People develop hypotheses which make claims about events, processes and behaviours in the world as experienced by individuals operating in it. According to Popper, scientists test their hypotheses through observations of particular events. Theories are tentative conjectures which, having been proposed, can be 'rigorously and ruthlessly tested by observation and experiment' (Chalmers 1982:38). Popper was primarily concerned with the way that scientific knowledge is developed through the process of making bold conjectures and refuting them (Popper 1972b). Experience can 'resist a theory by running counter to its predictions'

(Doyal and Harris 1986:13), and Popper proposed that experience provides the authority by which scientific knowledge can be refuted.

Popper's theory, that experience is a necessary component of the way in which theories are tested, is consistent with Kelly's personal construct theory which is based upon the meanings given to events as individuals experience them. Kelly was concerned primarily with the way that people make sense of their environment. Like Popper, he argued that people go along with the best 'theories' they have about events, and will only change their way of construing these events when their expectations are challenged. Kelly (1955a, 1955b, 1970) argued that people invent and re-invent an implicit theoretical framework, a personal construct system, affecting all aspects of their lives. They construct theories about their reality, and subject them to a process of continuous testing. Kelly suggested that we comprehend events through a variety of constructions. Events are given individual meanings through the way we make sense of them in our personal construct system. The events themselves do not possess any inherent meaning; we construe this.

Kelly asserted that our constructs are bipolar in nature and systematically organized. For example, the construct 'warm' could have a number of bipolar opposites including 'cold' and 'unfriendly'. 'Warm' is defined, at least partly, in terms of what it is not. This bipolarity was referred to by Kelly as constructive alternativism. If someone construes someone as being 'kind', she must be aware of the concept 'unkind'. The bipolar opposite could, of course, differ in different situations. People 'prove' or 'disprove' what their construct systems allow them to see in terms of possible alternatives.

Sometimes we construe a situation tightly, in other words we have a very definite way of looking at an event. At other times events are construed loosely, when we are less definite and more willing to accommodate different perspectives. It is at this stage that we are able to change our views about the world. As events place changing demands on our construct system, we may move from construing tightly to loosely, and then tightly again, as new events are accommodated into our existing construct system. Constructs direct a person's outlook, and ultimately control her behaviour. For example, it is not the events of the past *per se* which create the primary basis for predicting the future, rather it is how the past is construed: 'we say that a person is not the victim of his biography but that he may be enslaved by his interpretation of it' (Kelly, quoted in Bannister and Mair 1968:41).

A construct system is, Kelly argued, hierarchical, with core and peripheral constructs. Core constructs, which are deep-seated and long established, direct the way in which other constructs are organized. It is extremely difficult for core ways of construing to change without some degree of trauma to the person's psychological system. This explains why, for example, people can accept an individual with a characteristic they are prejudiced against; they may accept wholeheartedly a member of a racial group, but continue to make racist comments about that group. Core constructs apply across a range of contexts and direct the way people view the world. They affect an individual's professional practice, as well as personal relationships.

Personal construct theory provides, therefore, a model of analysis that can be applied to professional practice, in particular to the tacit, implicit and idiosyncratic ways in which individuals, such as those in adult basic education, approach their own practice.

FORMAL AND INFORMAL THEORY IN ADULT BASIC EDUCATION

There has been considerable debate in recent years about the extent to which adult educators' teaching skills should be underpinned by knowledge and understanding (Chown and Last 1993; Hyland 1993). It has been argued that adult educators are not necessarily aware of formal theories about adult education, and even if they are they may not find them helpful (Bright 1989; Usher and Bryant 1989; Brookfield 1993).

Adult basic education in the United Kingdom encompasses a range of activities including literacy, numeracy, and language development. A recurring theme for basic education practitioners is that of 'good practice', although it has proved difficult to find clear definitions of what this may mean (Hillier 1994). Adult basic education practices and culture have developed within the wider field of adult education. Professional development for adult basic education draws on the theoretical models used in adult education theory.

There is a rich but confusing literature on adult education practice. Theories of adult education practice have various purposes: they address adult learning styles; they attempt to identify purposes and delivery; they explain adult education as social policy, and as a means of empowerment and self-fulfilment. Educational theory in general is drawn from a variety of disciplines including psychology, sociology and philosophy. The variety of theoretical perspectives for adult education has resulted in literature which is either superficial or grossly over-simplifies complex theories and perspectives (Bright 1989:3). A newcomer to teaching in adult education, and adult basic education in particular, is likely to be bewildered and frustrated by the confusing application of source disciplines to the study of educating adults.

It is not only newcomers who are likely to be confused by theory. Brookfield (1993) and Usher and Bryant (1989) suggest that experienced practitioners have not accessed in any systematic way the theory behind their practice. It is not even clear what adult education is, given the emphasis on lifelong learning and inclusive education that pervades formal and informal adult learning. As Brookfield (1988:298) suggests, 'There is much less of a consensus, or a clearly discernible espoused theory, about what comprises adult education.'

Where can practitioners learn about and examine the theory of their practice? Staff development and training should provide a means by which the theoretical underpinning of good practice may be examined. But not all practitioners are able to undertake staff development and training, and those that are not are less likely to be influenced by theory. (It is also important to note that formal theories in books are not always easily understood or applied by practitioners.) However, practice itself contains much tacit and implicit knowledge (Eraut 1994). This knowledge is defined as practical theory by Carr and Kemmis (1986), and informal theory by Usher and Bryant who argue that informal theory enables practitioners to relate their activities to what is both desirable and possible within the situations in which they work (Usher and Bryant 1989:80). It forms their practice and enables them to make sense of what they are doing. Usher and Bryant (1989:82) suggest that the focus on practitioner knowledge derived from problem-solving in everyday practice means that theory can be 'socially-located, very often complex and problematic, and consciously and intentionally carried out.'

According to Griffiths and Tann (1992), there are public and personal theories; the former have been privileged over the latter which, they argue, should also be valued. Griffiths and Tann argue that personal theories have a powerful influence on practice. Practitioners should be encouraged to make explicit their personal theory so that it can be used to create public theories derived from their practice. Furthermore, if ideas are drawn from practitioners who are continually developing and refining their practical knowledge, then formal theories could be tested and refined more effectively. Thus, although adult education practitioners experience difficulty with formal theory, they do not operate in an atheoretical way (Gibson 1986). Examining their informal practice could, therefore, inform and refine formal theoretical analyses of educational practice.

Griffiths and Tann (1992) suggest that public theories of education in the education of teachers, and the personal theories embedded in their practice, are of equal importance. However, analysing formal theory is relatively easy compared to the analysis of tacit, implicit informal practitioner theory because the former has been made public and is available for scrutiny and debate. Part of the task of educational theory, according to Usher and Bryant (1989:91), is to 'make *explicit* what is largely *implicit* in informal practitioner theory.' Yet how is it possible to articulate what is implicit?

One possibility is to use the processes of critical reflection to analyse the 'taken for granted' aspects of everyday practice. The importance of reflecting on and critically examining practice (Schön 1983, 1987) is widely acknowledged by professional groups and debated in their professional journals (Eraut 1994; Webb 1995; Bright 1996). Given that practitioners use informal theory, reflective practice should increase their awareness of their 'hidden knowledge' and enable them to assess its quality, status and role within the design of action. But as Brookfield (1995) argues, encouraging practitioners to reflect critically is not easy. Not only do they need to identify deeply-held and implicit assumptions about their practice, they must be able to analyse it in ways which are meaningful not just to themselves but to others. Otherwise, practice will continue to operate in the superficially analysed way highlighted in Argyris and Schön's (1974) model I – potentially blocking the development of good practice.

Thomas (1998:151) criticizes educational research for its search for theory in every aspect of professional practice, to the extent that 'personal knowledge

... can be cleansed, burnished and theorised via the tools of academia and emerge as a shining epistemological sword.' Yet without testing implicit assumptions, educational practice cannot be developed into informed practice based upon *phronesis* ('rightness of action').

How, then, can tacit, implicit and possibly unexamined informal practitioner theory be elicited, so that it may be publicly espoused, critically reflected upon, and subsequently used to inform formal theory? A methodology is required that enables us to identify hidden meanings, unexpressed ideas and ways of looking at the world, which may not easily be articulated. Such meanings form the basis of informal theory and can be described as, to use Kelly's term, personal constructs. In this context they form an individualized conception of professional practice.

REPERTORY GRID TECHNIQUE

Kelly developed the repertory grid to make explicit the implicit way that people construe their experience (1955a, 1955b). The repertory grid technique was developed in a clinical setting in which the clinician and the client were considered to be involved in a co-operative enterprise. Fundamental to the technique is the expectation that the researcher and her subject are together trying to explore and understand the way in which the subject makes sense of her world. The researcher aims 'to stand in others' shoes, to see their world as they see it, to understand their situation, their concerns' (Fransella and Bannister 1977:5). The use of the repertory grid is thus intended to enable a researcher to gain access to private worlds. This makes it a particularly suitable method for eliciting and examining informal practitioner theory.

The repertory grid technique comprises an in-depth interview in three parts: elicitation of elements, elicitation of constructs and the rating of constructs for 'fit' against the elements. This complex process results in a series of factors statistically derived from the rating-grid which can be described as analyses of the individual's construct system. It is this outcome which can provide the basis for developing an explicit statement of informal practitioner theory.

Elements represent the area to be investigated. They might comprise people known to the respondent, tasks in an occupation, or products used in market research.

In order to elicit constructs, the elements are given to the respondent in threes (triads). The respondent is asked to identify in what way two of the elements are similar and different from the third. For an adult basic education practitioner, a triad of activities could consist of 'training tutors', 'assessing potential students', and 'acting as a computer technician'. A possible combination selected by the respondent could be 'training tutors' and 'assessing potential students', with 'computer technician' as the 'odd one out'. If asked in what way the first two are similar and different from the third, the respondent might say that the first two are to do with what is important, and the third is an important but less enjoyable activity. Additional probing might establish that the first two are linked because they relate to working with people, the third with machines. In this circumstance, all three would be important to the respondent, but what defines the difference is the person-centred aspect. This triad could be further explored through elicitation until the respondent becomes unable to express any further differences. This way of describing difference ultimately produces a bipolar construct, entirely formulated in the respondent's own words.

After the constructs are obtained, each with two poles or 'opposites', respondents are asked to rate how much each construct applies to each of the elements. The rating exercise results in a numerical grid with scores for each element and construct. Thus, a bipolar construct 'unpredictable – predictable' would have a rating of 5 for unpredictable and 1 for predictable. The element 'staffing requirements' might be given a score of 4 because of the unpredictability of working with part-time staff, whereas the element 'training administration staff' might have a rating of 2, having been construed as a tried-and-tested activity.

This grid of scores for constructs against all the elements is analysed to establish similarities between constructs and elements, normally using either principal components or cluster analysis. This information is then interpreted to provide a focus for discussion with the respondent. The interpretation of the factors is a significant aspect of the technique. Identifying the ways of construing for the range of elements, and then establishing key underlying factors, offers an ideal opportunity to discuss whether this has meaning for the respondent; it provides an additional probe into the respondent's tacit and implicit ways of thinking about the context under discussion.

USING THE REPERTORY GRID WITH ADULT BASIC EDUCATION PRACTITIONERS

The repertory grid technique was used to elicit the informal theory of a sample of 30 tutors and organizers of adult basic education drawn from the North East London region (Hillier 1994). The tutors were involved in five areas of basic skills work: literacy, numeracy, special needs, government training schemes, and open learning. All tutors and organizers had a minimum of one year's experience in their role. They were interviewed twice, once to elicit the repertory grid and once to discuss the resulting factors.

Practitioners were asked to identify a range of tasks they undertook in their roles, including those they might perform infrequently but consider to be important. These tasks formed the elements in the repertory grid. They were given to the interviewees in triads, and the interviewees were asked to state in what way any two of them were similar and different from the third. This elicited the constructs which were finally scored in the repertory grid against the elements on a five-point scale. The grids were analysed using SPSS (Statistical Package for Social Sciences) principal components analysis. Each grid contained a minimum of nine constructs. There were usually three to four factors resulting from the factor analysis, although in some cases only two factors emerged. Each factor was then examined for constructs or elements which best exemplified it. A two-dimensional graph with the first two factors as axes was used to depict the results for each person's grid.

A modification of the standard repertory grid technique was used in the follow-up interviews. Normally, the researcher interprets the statistical information and identifies suitable labels for the principal factors which emerge. In this study, however, respondents were asked to suggest suitable labels. Some found it useful to employ diagrams to demonstrate their analysis of the statistical information. This proved to be a particularly fruitful process by means of which they were able to articulate more fully their understanding of their practice and reframe it in light of the repertory grid findings.

The factors arising from the constructs and elements, although described idiosyncratically by each respondent, provided the basis for an analysis of common themes. The search for commonality in the factors was intended to test for any coherence in basic education theory that may be held informally by its practitioners; it tested the existence of an 'ethos' of basic skills practice, usually described as 'good practice' by basic education practitioners. The full analysis of constructs and elements can be found in Hillier (1994).

A common theme for all respondents was 'student-centredness'. For 26 of the 30 respondents, this emerged in the first factor. Only one respondent did not have this theme in any of her factors. Given the wide-ranging backgrounds of the tutors and organizers, the different boroughs in which they worked, and their level of experience, it is remarkable that they appeared to be in such close agreement about how they construed their practice. When, during the feedback interviews, respondents were asked to label their factors, they often expressed relief that the student-centred factor had appeared and 'confirmed' their own perceptions of what they, as good tutors or organizers, should be doing.

The second and subsequent factors were more variable. They can be categorized in four ways: tension between student-centredness and institutional demands, ethos of basic skills, reflection on practice and practical considerations. Factor labels of 'bureaucracy/accountability' and 'adhering to requirements' indicated the tensions between student-centredness and institutional demands. They reflected the wider issues of working in basic skills. The ethos of basic skills was suggested by the labels 'strong belief' and 'seeing the way forward'. Reflection on practice was implied by such factor labels as 'ideas' and 'talking-thinking'. Practical considerations could be identified in labels including 'planning and preparing' and 'course delivery'.

The analysis of the factors suggests that practitioners' constructs about their work were pyramidal in structure, with a range of fourth and third factors at the base, rising to student-centredness at the apex. In the research reported here, student-centredness was superordinately construed, and it directed practitioners' informal theory about their practice. The subsequent factors related to tensions in this practice through:

- institutional or organizational demands that impinged on the ideal practice;
- issues of responsibility and purpose;
- the vision that basic skills teaching requires.

Identification with the ethos – in other words, 'following the party line' – in part reflects the strong sense of identity that practitioners have with their work. From a fairly wide range of constructs obtained during the first interviews, the grid analysis provided a closely-structured view of basic skills work.

INFORMAL THEORY IN PRACTICE

The research data indicated two significant sets of constructs for practitioners: their core beliefs, which appear to have been held prior to any involvement in basic skills teaching, and an ethos of basic education which is adhered to and is resistant to change.

In the teaching of literacy, numeracy, special needs and employment training, tutors and organizers in various London boroughs held a consistent interpretation of what basic education practice ought to be. It was a highly prescriptive view. The homogeneity of the first factors identified by the analysis is particularly significant given that personal construct theory argues that people have idiosyncratic ways of making sense of their environment, and therefore one would expect to discover a variety of factors.

The clear adherence to student-centredness is an example of a sacrosanct system. Throughout the interviews, practitioners referred to student-centredness as the most fundamental aspect of their practice, implying a deeply-held belief about what basic skills practice ought to be.

Practitioners' ways of construing practice do not, however, necessarily constitute a coherent theory. This construing might be described as an amorphous magma of belief, value premises and propositions. How can this be used to provide a theoretical framework?

Theory, even though informally expressed, was implicit in the practical knowledge used by respondents in this research. They were concerned with messy everyday situations. The notion of theory used here is in the original sense of *theoria* – that is, 'directed to things that happen "always or for the most part"' (McCarthy 1984:2). The formulation of theory is an important stage in refining practical knowledge. Theory uses propositions which help to describe, explain and predict. Propositions allow for critical scrutiny. Defining propositions represents a first step in the development of hypotheses which predict the occurrence of phenomena. These hypotheses can subsequently be tested to inform formally held theories. In this way, both informal practitioner theory and formal theory can be improved.

The research identified five themes of informal practitioner theory:

1. a student-centred philosophy;
2. resistance to any change in practice which threatens student-centredness;
3. the ethos of basic skills practice;
4. reflection on practical aspects of basic skills;
5. the development of philosophy and practice through experience.

Propositions were derived from each theme, a full description of which can be found in Hillier (1994). Example propositions are as follows:

- Students encounter many problems from not having a sufficient level of basic skills.
- These problems may be identified as needs.
- Students learn best if their needs are met.

These propositions are widely identified as the 'needs-meeting' rationale (Griffin 1987; Keddie 1980; Usher and Bryant 1989; Paterson 1989). The interview material contained numerous examples of needs-meeting statements although very few respondents had read any of the formal literature. These elicited propositions of informal practitioner theory have sociological, pedagogical and philosophical bases. They are located in a sociological model which identifies inequalities in society and relates them to a variety of power relations. People who lack basic skills are seen to have needs which stem partly from this unequal share of power; they do not have access to jobs, wealth and ways to develop because of their limited basic skills. The informal theory also relates to a view of learning that treats students as active participants in the learning process. It expects students to know what they want to learn, and how they should acquire the desired skills and knowledge. Philosophically, the informal theory is rooted in an ethical theory. It is normative, requiring practitioners to facilitate the personal development of their students. This relates also to the sociological model where students' basic skills needs are viewed as 'presenting problems' which may mask their 'real' problems. The students are the focus of the action, not the students' competence in basic skills.

INFORMED PRACTICE

The research discussed in this chapter suggests that adult basic education tutors practise in ways described by formal theory. They are not, however, necessarily aware of the formal theories which account for their practice. In order to improve practice, practitioners need to examine critically their informal theory and, wherever possible, identify how it relates to formal theoretical frameworks. Similarly, formal theory should be reviewed in light of informal practitioner theory. Kelly's repertory grid is an appropriate tool for eliciting informal theory of this kind. The interview technique is a particularly effective tool for reflecting on practice; it provides focus without imposing structures determined by the interviewer, and its use generates a rich source of interpretative data that can be explored collaboratively with the respondents. By analysing informal theory in this way, the theories which underpin practice can be explored, tested and developed. Without critical analysis, practical knowledge and informal theory risk 'remaining at the level of anecdotal, idiosyncratic reminiscence' (Brookfield 1993:74).

Chapter 14

Inquiry for 'Taught' Masters

TYRRELL BURGESS

It has become normal in postgraduate study to distinguish 'taught' from 'research' degrees. The distinction is signalled in the United Kingdom by the award of MA or MSc for the former and MPhil for the latter. The unstated, even unconscious, assumption seems to be that the MA or MSc recognizes postgraduate achievement in the sense that the master now knows more, or knows more deeply, than the bachelor; the MPhil, by contrast, signals a 'pre-doctoral' achievement. The MPhil student has had some training in 'research', may have made a small but noticeable contribution to knowledge and is now capable of making a bigger one, which a PhD would confirm.

The distinction between the two awards is useful if it serves to make clear to students what is expected of them and offers a ground for judging what they produce. MA and MSc reflect increased mastery of knowledge; MPhil requires some extension of it. The distinction can be dangerous, however, if it is held to imply a disjunction between 'taught' and 'research' programmes of study. Such a disjunction could have serious institutional consequences. If it were real, the interdependence of teaching and research, which is critical to most academics' view of higher education, would be harder to defend. Fortunately it is not real. It seems to arise only through the widespread habit of discussing education in terms of teachers and teaching rather than of learners and learning. Once it is accepted that the business of higher education is learning, the phantom disjunction disappears. Students learn on their courses and programmes at all levels; academics learn too, from their students, their research and consultancy. Most importantly, the logic of learning (described in Chapters 2 and 10) is the same throughout, at the beginning of undergraduate study and at the frontiers of knowledge.

A TAUGHT MASTERS

The logic of learning inspired the creation in 1993 of a 'taught' MA programme, Professional Practice in Education, at the University of East

London. The programme is part of a larger programme offered jointly by the Centre for Institutional Studies and the Department for Education and Community Studies and fits the larger programme's overall framework, which must now be briefly described.

Its structure is modular, the modules contributing to distinct 'pathways' (if the word can be forgiven) of which Professional Practice in Education (PPE) is one. Each module attracts 20 credits and implies 150 hours of study. There is a choice, for final assessment, of a major or minor project, of 50 credits (375 hours) or 30 credits (225 hours) respectively.

One criticism of modular programmes is that their flexibility leads to incoherence, that students may sample smatterings of subjects and fail to get an education. To counter this, the programme requires each student to follow a central module (10 credits, 75 hours) which runs alongside the others. Called the planning, development and synoptic module (PDAS), it is the vehicle for the student's programme planning, leading to a learning contract, study profile, self-appraisal and professional development tutorials. After completing three content modules a student may opt for a postgraduate diploma by claiming 60 credits and completing an assignment which shows how the student has integrated the learning in the content modules, in accordance with the learning agreement, and understands the extent of postgraduate achievement (see below). Students going on for MA or MSc complete the PDAS module by preparing a project proposal for either the major or the minor project – the latter being accompanied by a further content module.

The importance of the PDAS module is that students are required to plan their progress along their chosen pathway, be conscious of the contribution each module makes to their own development, and be aware at the end of the effect of the learning that has taken place. They are, in particular, asked to judge these things in the light of common characteristics of postgraduate achievement set out in the course document (University of East London 1993). These comprise:

- enhanced specialist knowledge;
- critical analysis and synthesis or arguments;
- high-level critical reflection on the inter-relationship between theory and practice;
- self-evaluation of skills of analysis, investigation and planning;
- communication at a sophisticated level;
- critical reflection on own learning.

All pathways require students to achieve these characteristics. In individual pathways students may display these characteristics in many ways. For example: in the comprehensive overview of a specialist field; high-level performance or competence in a specialism; placing the specialism in a wider context; theoretical analysis; reflexivity about professional behaviour; critical evaluation of practice; systematic gathering and use of data for decision;

planning of professional action; taking and implementing decisions after analysis and investigation; contributing to knowledge and practice; and facilitating the learning of other professionals.

The programme places significant responsibility on the learner through the learning agreement and student profile. As the course document puts it: 'The student will be expected to show progress towards master's level autonomy and independence of judgement'.

This, then, is the framework within which the PPE pathway is offered. The pathway is designed for professional educators. Participants are expected to have qualified teacher status or to have had experience in teaching or administration in colleges, universities, the Inspectorate, educational organizations or training institutions. Most are in post and thus follow a two-year part-time programme, taking three modules in Year 1, followed in Year 2 by either the major project or a further related module and minor project. They also follow the PDAS module.

DEVELOPING PROFESSIONAL EDUCATION

The object of the pathway is to develop the qualities of professional educators and to enhance their understanding of themselves as a professional group. It derives from a view of the characteristics of the professional task, both in general and in relation to education. It is assumed that in relation to students a professional educator acts so that the interests of the students are paramount. This implies an approach in which a teacher, for example:

- respects the individuality of students and does not distinguish them by race, religion, class, sex or cultural group;
- refrains from any acts that might cause them harm;
- takes no advantage of a position of authority with a pupil or student for personal, political or other purposes;
- treats all students impartially and accepts no gifts to show favours;
- maintains confidentiality of information about individual students;
- has regard to the wishes of parents of pupils of compulsory school age;
- does all in the teacher's power to secure the fullest development of the individual.

A professional educator is also assumed to act in relation to the profession in such a way as to maintain the highest standards of personal and professional conduct. In particular an educator is expected to:

- respect the knowledge and skills gained in education and training and the experience of professional work;
- develop the knowledge, skills and attitudes of self-management;
- accept responsibility for own quality, examining strengths and weaknesses and seeking improvement;
- keep knowledge and skills up-to-date and develop capability;

- place knowledge, skill and experience at the service of students;
- accept co-operative responsibility for the effective performance of an institution and the well-being of the individuals within it;
- exercise individual judgement in the solution of educational problems;
- maintain capability in the organization and management of learning, of individuals and in groups.

To this end, and amplifying the general characteristics listed earlier, students successfully completing this programme are expected to demonstrate:

- critical understanding or professionalism in education;
- commitment to capability in educational institutions;
- reflexivity about professional behaviour;
- critical evaluation of professional practice;
- planning of professional action;
- a contribution to knowledge or practice;
- enhanced inter-personal skills;
- functional management;
- the facilitation of other professionals' learning;
- improved decisions through analysis and investigation.

Initially, eight modules were designed specifically for this pathway, on accountability, the organization of learning, the ethics of education, the development of the individual, the logic of learning, planning professional development, educational policy and management, the law of education. Others have been added later, and students may also choose modules from the rest of the programme. Students are expected to select a minimum of two of the pathway modules among their first three content modules.

Masters students are required to design and undertake a project which will directly improve their professional quality. They attend a method workshop (shared with students on other pathways) to assist in the design phase, and are supported by a programme of tutorial guidance and tutored and peer seminars (shared with students on other pathways, when appropriate). A variety of forms of project are permissible, but students are required to show that their own projects relate to their professional circumstances and are capable of changing them. The changes may be personal, organizational, inter-personal, pedagogic, philosophical, epistemological or practical.

Assessment is of two kinds: diagnostic and 'final'. For diagnostic assessment, students are required, during each module, to make oral or written presentations at the tutor's discretion. For 'final' assessment, students are required to make a written presentation, related to each module, except the PDAS module. No final award of MA is made unless the presentation for each module has been judged satisfactory against the general and specific characteristics of the pathway.

The PDAS module is satisfactorily completed on the production either of synoptic study for PGDip or an acceptable project proposal for MA.

The project is assessed against the programme and pathway characteristics. It is not required that the changes planned in the project have been accomplished within the time-span of the pathway.

It may be helpful to take two examples of the modules, to show the reasons for their inclusion in the programme, the general content they might be expected to cover and the methods by which they are pursued. All these are related to the characteristics both of postgraduate study and of professionalism described above.

ILLUSTRATIVE MODULES

The organization of learning is central to professional practice in education. If this is wrong, little is right. There are three main elements. The first is the organization of the learning of individuals and comprises the art and techniques of tutorial supervision, including the management of private study, the use of tests and examinations, the recognition of achievements not measurable by tests and the use of student records of achievement. The second is the organization of learning in groups, in school classrooms, lectures, seminars, workshops and the like. This includes issues of planning, differentiation, management and discipline, intellectual coherence of materials and of the student experience and modes of work (that is, whole class, small groups and individual). The third element is the organization of learning in a whole institution, covering such issues as academic organization, the relation of instruction to private study, the balance of responsibilities and accountability. Understanding of all three is fundamental to improved practice.

The module on individual development takes it as given that education is a personal service. It succeeds, if at all, with individuals, not with systems. A professional must thus have a secure grasp of individual growth and development as a foundation of good practice. This is of even greater importance in an age when statutory curricula, tests and examinations are rigidly age-bound. The content of the module covers the course and principles of physical growth, the concept of developmental age and the relation between physiological and mental maturity. It includes the organization of the growth process, including growth gradients and sensitive periods, what is known about the development of the brain and arguments about intelligence. It encompasses the interaction between heredity and environment in influencing growth. It requires students to consider the implications of all this for educational theory, practice and policy.

The central method of all the modules is the professional seminar. All participants are required to read an agreed text – a book, document, statute or research or other report. At the seminar one or two students make a presentation of the materials which is then open to critical discussion. Students are encouraged to reflect on relevant experience of their own and relate the material to problems they are formulating. At the end of the seminar there is a formal occasion for the students to note for their own records the main outcome of the seminar for themselves and make proposals for follow-up or further study or inquiry.

Access to the module content is offered through introductory lectures and guided reading. All students are required to undertake substantial private study. All prepare an assignment of 5,000 words for assessment.

In the organization of the learning module, the professional seminar may become the occasion for students to organize learning – the learning of the group as a whole. A seminar might be planned by a student to practise tutorial and group techniques and to present proposals for institutional arrangements which might best support these.

As indicated earlier, the culmination of the pathway is the project, major or minor. The student will have been considering and planning for this through the PDAS module, and the production of an acceptable project proposal is a requirement for completing PDAS and proceeding to the project itself. There is typically considerable interaction between the early modules and plans for the project. What is more, the module assignments are prepared on the same basis as the project report: they are both the evidence on which credit is given for each module and, as it were, practice in tackling the larger project.

ACKNOWLEDGING THE LOGIC OF LEARNING

In preparing the project (and modules) students are asked first to formulate a problem. The word 'problem' is used here in the Popperian sense of what arises when our knowledge bumps up against our ignorance and we determine to do something about it. We may find we have a disappointed expectation or a frustrated attempt to change a state of affairs. In these circumstances we typically seek to resolve our difficulty by a process of more or less conscious trial and error.

No initial restriction is placed on students as to the kind of problem they may take up. It could be a problem of what is the case, of how to get from one state of affairs to another, of a formal system (like mathematics), of morals or of aesthetics (see Chapter 5). It may be a general problem in education of learning, organization, method, policy or ethics; or it may be a problem rooted in a student's own circumstances. It must, however, be consistent with the characteristics of postgraduate study and apt to contribute to the development of professional capability.

In the event, most students have formulated problems of their own professional circumstances and most of these have been addressed in their own institutions. They have nevertheless been very varied. The literacy co-ordinator of a primary school wished to find ways to improve achievement in reading by changing the school's practice. The new head of a special needs unit sought a form of staff organization which made collaboration more likely. The head of education in a women's prison needed to create a programme in response to official concerns about drug abuse.

The formulation of a problem is no light matter. It takes place over time. It demands tutorial discussion to be sure that the problem proposed is significant, practicable in all the circumstances and likely to be fruitful in the outcome. Tactful negotiation may be required if the work is to be acceptable, even welcome, in the student's own institution. Nor are students encouraged to think only of local circumstances. They are asked to inquire of each other, of other institutions and through wide reading, as to whether their problem is idiosyncratic or general and whether it might be better formulated. For example, one of the tasks the literacy co-ordinator undertook was to familiarize herself with inspection reports both of individual schools and of vulnerable local authorities. This helped her to clarify and focus the formulation of the problem in her own school.

The student's next step is to begin the search for a solution. Many students quickly produce ideas for this, but it is important to discourage an early dash to a solution, before the problem has been satisfactorily formulated and before they are aware of solutions that may already exist. They need to know the nature and applicability of existing solutions and the extent to which their formulated problems have already been solved. They embark, in other words, on a literature search, and their project report has to include a critical account and appraisal of this. The ground covered in the literature search can be extensive. For example, the project on reading encompassed not only child development, learning theory and teaching method, but the legal framework of the curriculum, school organization and personnel management.

There are typically two possible outcomes of this inquiry. The first is that a student recognizes that a solution to the formulated problem does indeed exist, or that one can readily be adapted from existing practice. In this case the project involves proposals for implementing the (adapted) solution. The second is that the student finds that existing solutions are unsatisfactory: they may not be locally apt, for example, or their 'success' rate may be unconvincing. In this event the student's project would be to propose a new solution and the means to apply it. In both cases the proposal has to include clear grounds for determining the extent to which the solution had succeeded or failed. When the solution has been worked through, the students and their colleagues are aware of how far the problem situation has changed, and are ready, and better able, to propose new solutions.

This procedure – of formulating a problem, proposing a solution and testing it – is consistent with the logic of learning and discovery (see Chapters 2 and 10), whether or not the preferred solution is original. In practice there is an element of originality in all solutions, and even the most original stands on the work of others. All students experience a growth both of knowledge and capability.

It must be obvious that effective solutions to significant problems are unlikely to be carried through within the time-scale of a postgraduate project. Nor can the award of a degree be made to depend upon the success of a particular solution. The criteria for the award are those characteristics which have been described earlier, and assessment includes a judgement as to whether the project report offers evidence of enhanced professional capability. So far, however, there has been no case of a project which did not have a significant impact, not only on the student, but upon the institution concerned.

This suggests a final claim that may be made for the pathway and the programme as a whole. It is frequently said of 'in-service training' and post-experience courses that however attractive they may be at the time, their impact is fleeting and, even where influential for the individual, hard to relate to daily circumstance. The students who follow the PPE pathway are typically pursuing a master's degree while persisting in onerous jobs. It was a priority of the pathway design that they should not waste their time, or come to feel that they had done so. The claim is that by following the logic of learning it has been possible to create a programme that is apt for them, fruitful and free from inconsequence.

Part IV

Evaluation

Chapter 15

The Popperian Approach to Raising Standards in Educational Research

JAMES TOOLEY

What is wrong with educational research? My own modest contribution to this debate was the report, *Educational Research: A Critique* (Tooley with Darby 1998), which, according to Pratt and Swann (Chapter 1 of this volume), has been partly responsible for the current debate in the United Kingdom. In part, of course, this is because the report was published by the Office for Standards in Education (Ofsted), with a Foreword in which the controversial Chris Woodhead, Her Majesty's Chief Inspector of Schools, summarized the report thus: 'Educational research is not making the contribution it should. Much that is published is, on this analysis, at best no more than an irrelevance and distraction' (Woodhead 1998:1). When someone so close to the centre of government makes such a judgement, then others are obliged to take note. In this chapter, I explore some connections between the issues raised in the report and the Popperian approach to educational research.

THE OFSTED REPORT

My research for Ofsted was prompted by Professor David Hargreaves' comments in his 1996 Teacher Training Agency lecture that there is a considerable amount of 'frankly second-rate educational research' (Hargreaves 1996:7). But much of the debate that followed his lecture was, as Professor Donald McIntyre pointed out in his 1996 Presidential Address to the British Educational Research Association (BERA), 'conducted on the basis of very limited and inadequate information' (McIntyre 1997:129). My work was a small contribution to 'improve the quality of the evidence on which these debates depend' (McIntyre 1997:129).

Four important academic educational research journals were selected – the top three British 'generic' education journals in the Social Science Citation Index journal impact list (*British Journal of Sociology of Education, British Journal of Educational Studies* and *Oxford Review of Education*), together with BERA's *British Educational Research Journal.* Thirty research questions were crafted in an attempt to scrutinize each research article in terms of its contribution to fundamental theory or knowledge, its relevance to policy practice, and whether or not it was co-ordinated with preceding or follow-up research.

The 264 articles of British origin within these journals were analysed against the background of a core set of these questions – focusing on issues such as the topic of the research, the use of triangulation, sample size, and the reporting of these. A sub-sample of 41 articles, selected using a 'counting method', was chosen to reflect categories of topics in approximate proportion to the way they occurred within each journal. This sub-sample was then analysed under the scrutiny of the full range of the 30 questions.

The selection of the four case study journals was 'at a distance' from the researchers, so that accusations of selection bias could not be brought in here. That is, the four journals were not chosen in a partisan way to illustrate partisan points concerning educational research (there were certainly other journals that could have been selected had this been my intention!). Hence one can be reasonably confident that these journals represent *an important strand* of academic educational research. Also, a transparent method for selection of the sub-sample of articles within these case study journals was used for more detailed analysis and reporting, again to distance the researchers from the selection process.

From the analysis of the articles, the conclusion reached was that there were rather worrying tendencies in a *majority* of the articles surveyed in the sub-sample, and that we can be reasonably confident that these tendencies will be found throughout this important strand of educational research. So Woodhead's comments in the Foreword (noted above) were well supported.

These 'worrying tendencies' were reported under four headings:

- The partisan researcher
- Problems of methodology
- Non-empirical educational research
- The focus of educational research

Below, I illustrate the first three of these themes in the context of a Popperian critique of educational research. Before doing that, I point to some resonances between a Popperian approach and the Ofsted critique of educational research.

A POPPERIAN APPROACH TO EDUCATIONAL RESEARCH

Swann and Pratt have gathered together the papers in this volume with the intention of presenting realist approaches to educational research, which

emphasize rigour in the analysis of physical, social or education phenomena ... are concerned with the logic and validity of the methods employed, and with the development of a rational basis for preferring some knowledge statements to others. This in turn enables knowledge to be developed that can be used with an understanding of its validity and limitations. (Chapter 1:8)

They note the key idea in Popper's philosophy which helps to develop this 'rational basis' is 'that learning and the growth of knowledge necessarily involve the discovery of error and inadequacy in existing theories or expectations' (Chapter 1:8). In seeking a Popperian approach to educational research, Swann encourages researchers

> to develop bold theories of what is the case about classroom practice; to formulate these theories in such a way that they can be tested (by the search for refuting evidence); and to devise situations in which these theories can be put to the test. (Chapter 2:29)

Are there connections between this Popperian method and the concerns about the content and quality of educational research raised in the Ofsted report? The key dimension of the Popperian method is that researchers should seek to expose their ideas and hypotheses to the test. They should seek to do this in the *conduct* of their research, and they should be seeking in the *presentation* of their work to enable others to continue with this process of rigorous and critical testing. What would be the minimal requirements of such a Popperian approach? The following list is not meant to be exhaustive, but it touches on some of the issues with which any Popperian would be concerned.

Conduct of research

In terms of the *conduct* of research, researchers would use methods which have the potential to expose any flaws in their reasoning and/or conclusions, and which have the potential to put their hypotheses to a rigorous test.

First, this would involve triangulation. This is a way of cross-validating research. It uses methods of comparison, to help assess the validity and reliability of the data collected. It can use several data sources or several data collection procedures, or a combination of these. If the data collected in this way disagree, then there is a dilemma about which the researcher is to believe – but this should then be a matter for making explicit that there is this disagreement within the data.

Second, the selection of the sample for any research is critical. For a Popperian to seek to test any hypothesis, it would be of great importance to be sure that the sample chosen was selected by a process which enabled the researcher to make assumptions about its representativeness of a wider population. If not, the Popperian would not be able to have confidence that he or she was rigorously testing an hypothesis if, for example, the sample was selected opportunistically.

Third, the Popperian researcher would be aware that his or her emotional or political commitments can cloud judgements in terms of the conduct of the research – in the choice of methods and interpretation of results. The Popperian would use triangulation and avoid sampling bias to help mitigate these biases.

Fourth, it would be anathema to a Popperian researcher to take part in uncritical 'adulation' of the ideas of other 'great' thinkers. For sure, such a researcher may well want to spend time on exegesis of a great thinker's ideas and theories. But the primary purpose of so doing would be to set about rigorously testing these ideas and theories, to explore their weaknesses and see if they could be improved, or even whether they should be discarded.

Presentation of research

In terms of the *presentation* of their research, Popperian researchers would seek to present their methods, results and conclusions in such a way that other researchers would be able to review what had been accomplished, and to continue the process of rigorously testing the hypotheses and theories given. The Popperian researcher would be concerned that all the details of sampling method, sample size, and so on were reported adequately, so that it was abundantly clear how the research was conducted, to assist others in severely 'putting it to the test'. Similarly, researchers would strive to avoid clouding their conclusions with their own biases and predilections, but would strive to report their findings in such a way as to facilitate others in being clear about the conduct and findings of the research. In other words, as in the conduct of his or her research, a Popperian researcher would be anxious to avoid partisanship.

Underlying all of these issues, of course, is the concern for criticism and scepticism about any hypothesis or theory. Hypotheses can be – indeed, should be – bold and challenging, but at all times they are only useful to the enterprise of creating a body of knowledge about education if they can be subject to criticism. The Popperian researcher would always be on the look-out to ensure such criticisms could be made.

If we turn to the Ofsted report, we see that it was precisely parallel concerns which formed the basis for the 30 questions under which the research articles were analysed (Tooley with Darby 1998:Chapter 2). Above all, it was important that the research findings could be open to critical scrutiny, and that the conduct and presentation of research should not be clouded by the researcher's own prejudices. In this way, the criticisms in the Ofsted report can be seen very much as criticisms in a Popperian vein.

Judged by these Popperian standards, much of the research investigated for the Ofsted report fell short. The next section gives some examples to illustrate these shortcomings. It must be stressed that a small selection is being used which most pertinently illustrates some of the problems of a non-Popperian approach, and that there were articles in the sample – albeit in a minority – which did not exhibit these types of shortcomings.

POPPERIAN STANDARDS AND THE OFSTED REPORT

Partisanship

A Popperian would eschew partisanship, both in the conduct and presentation of his or her research. Partisanship in the conduct of research would militate against the forming of critical judgements about the findings and conclusions. Partisanship in the presentation of research would undermine the likelihood that others could critically examine and test the hypotheses and theories developed.

However, partisanship seemed rife within the academic educational research analysed for the Ofsted report. There was partisanship in the *conduct* of research (for example, in interpreting data to support the view that the nature of choice in education is class-bound, when the data would seem to undermine that claim); in the *presentation* of research (for example, by putting research findings into the context of contentious and unsupported remarks about political reform); and in the *argument* of non-empirical research (for example, by subjecting one government's reforms to critical scrutiny while at the same time accepting at face value previous educational reforms). On one occasion, too, we noted apparent partisanship in the *focus* of research (when focusing on gender, the researcher simply ignored boys' concerns), although in general this was not an issue of concern.

Some of the areas which exhibited the most dramatic evidence of partisanship were research in gender and sexuality, and race and ethnicity. Many researchers seemed unable to tackle these issues in a manner which enabled one to be sure that they had engaged critically with their evidence, or that their conclusions were based upon what was really occurring in the classrooms examined.

I give one example from the report to illustrate some of these difficulties. The issue of racism in schools is of course of great concern – and as I write this, the Chairman of the Commission for Racial Equality is arguing that schools are 'institutionally racist' (*Times Educational Supplement*, 19 February 1999). How important it is, then, to establish a firm evidence base for the extent to which there is racism in schools, and to develop and explore hypotheses about the most effective ways of tackling racism should it exist. The approach of Connolly (1995), however, one of the sub-sample of articles in the Ofsted report, falls short of what would be demanded from a Popperian researcher.

Connolly (1995), to illuminate the presence of racism, looks at the schooling experiences of black students in one primary school. He quotes from the school report comments of a primary schoolteacher, Mrs Scott. In order to avoid misrepresenting the author, I quote in full from Connolly's paper, so *these are full records as in the article*, with passages omitted only as in the article. He tells us that 'the influence of racist discourses is more evident when Mrs Scott explains the origins of *Paul's* "disobedient" behaviour' (Connolly 1995:78, emphasis added):

Paul [...] is progressing well but needs to be guided [...] His mother is very keen that he should do well. I have had to guide his behaviour in the last few months, quite a lot, and explain to him the differences between right and wrong [...] He tends to 'follow' instead of being an independent boy. This is a shame as he has a good brain of his own and should have his own ideas in future. Good at sport. (Connolly 1995:78)

Again, an outside observer may puzzle long and hard as to how this passage shows any evidence of 'racist discourse'. Trying to read between the lines as much as possible, all I can ascertain is that Paul is an intelligent boy, who sometimes goes astray and needs parental or teacher guidance. And he is good at sport – perhaps this is where the racism lies? Indeed, Connolly thinks so:

Paul is also, according to Mrs Scott's report, 'good at sport'. This sporting and athletic image is, again, a common theme running through the teacher's views of African/Caribbean boys ... (Connolly 1995:79)

But perhaps it is simply true – Paul *is* good at sport – rather than being evidence of 'racist discourse'? Connolly does not seem to countenance such a possibility. However, a Popperian would have been keen to explore this possibility and others, seeking ways of challenging whatever partisanship one has. This brings us to the second major theme of the report, methodological concerns.

Problems of methodology

A Popperian would be concerned with research methods such as triangulation and avoiding sampling bias, in order critically to test his or her hypotheses, and to give others confidence that they have been tested. Indeed, there is an intimate connection between these methodological concerns and the issue of partisanship – for if a researcher wished for a particular partisan position to come across, then he or she would be well advised to steer clear of triangulation and not worry about sampling bias! In the case of the 'racist' primary school (Connolly 1995), one problem in the reading of the research is indeed the apparent lack of triangulation of the researcher's judgements. For example, when the researcher suggests that there is racism underlying the fact that a teacher perceives a particular black child to be 'good at sport', it would have helped if he had examined whether or not the child really was good at sport – by consulting other teachers, their parents, make-up of sporting teams in the school, or whatever. Similarly, when casting doubt on the teacher's judgement regarding African/Caribbean boys' behaviour, it would have helped matters if the researcher had provided some evidence to show that the teacher's perception of this was a matter of her racism, and not anything to do with their actual behavioural problems.

The problem of a lack of triangulation looms large in several other articles discussed in the Ofsted report. For example, Paechter (1995) relates concerns about sexism in schools. She tells us how in one school, the (female) head of the old Home Economics department was not awarded the job of head of the new Design and Technology department, which instead went to the (male) head of the old Craft and Design Technology department. The researcher's tone in describing this makes us realize we are to believe that this is an injustice, although we are told nothing about the respective qualifications for the job of the two candidates. Moreover, the woman in question says she is unhappy because there are 'particular problems' caused by the fact that the new head 'did not understand the way her department's finances worked' (Paechter 1995:80). However, we are not told whether the new head concurs with this or not. We are given the impression that her gripes are well founded, to support the case of injustice.

The point is, again, that we are totally dependent on the researcher's views of what happened; there is no triangulation, and so absolutely no way of knowing how well founded are these claims. What would a Popperian researcher have tried to do, to test the hypothesis of sexism in the school? The researcher would not have relied only on the female teacher's viewpoint, but would have sought to triangulate this by, for example, interviewing the headteacher, the male teacher, and members of the promotion panel to ascertain their reasons for the decision (that is, using several data sources); and/or investigating both teachers' *curriculum vitae* (that is, using several data collection procedures). Only in this way could the Popperian researcher have confidence that he or she had rigorously tested the hypothesis.

The issue of sampling bias is more subtle, because it all depends on what the researcher wishes to do with the research findings. A Popperian researcher may be conducting research initially to generate hypotheses, and so would not necessarily be worried about how the sample was selected. In which case, 'anything goes'. However, as soon as the researcher wishes to test particular hypotheses, then the issue of sample selection becomes of paramount importance.

In the Ofsted survey, several examples were found of researchers who wished to generalize findings, but who were nonetheless apparently happy with an 'anything goes' approach to sampling. For example, Sparkes (1994) explores the life experiences of Jessica, *one* 'white, able bodied, middle class, lesbian PE teacher in her late twenties' (Sparkes 1994:94). The paper sets out to show moments in Jessica's life to illustrate the homophobia under which she supposedly lives. If the researcher had simply wanted to describe her experiences, and not make any generalizations, then the problem of sampling bias would not have arisen. But Sparkes wishes to do more than this, it seems. He points out that the motivation for his work is to present 'the struggles Jessica faces on a daily basis to construct her life, and maintain her sense of self, in the public spaces that the school provides' (Sparkes 1994:95). His intention is 'to provide insights into how schools, as patriarchal institutions that are ideologically and culturally heterosexual, create and maintain a set of inequitable circumstances that exercise a level of control over the "private" lives of lesbian teachers' (Sparkes 1994:95).

From these and similar comments it would seem that Sparkes' intention is to *generalize* his findings. But his sampling method completely militates against this possibility. He does not tell us how his sample of one is in any way representative of the wider population of homosexual teachers – indeed, the more one reads of the account, the more unlikely this seems. Given his desire to generalize, he thus shows sampling bias. How would a Popperian researcher have approached these issues? He or she would have attempted to test the hypothesis that there was homophobia in schools by seeking a much larger non-opportunistically selected sample, in order rigorously to challenge and explore the hypothesis. It seems as though Sparkes simply wishes to confirm the hypothesis of homophobia in schools; his mind is already made up. This approach is not one a Popperian researcher could accept.

These examples illustrate Popperian concerns about the *conduct* of educational research. But parallel concerns are raised in the Ofsted report about the *presentation* of research. As noted above, Popperian researchers would be anxious to ensure that their work was open to critical engagement by other researchers. To this end, they would be sure to give sufficient information so that a critical review was possible, and to enable others to replicate the research. It was indicative of the cavalier approach of many researchers in the Ofsted sample that even simple factual details such as the sample size and how it was selected were often considered to be irrelevant to the reader. For example, in both the *Oxford Review of Education* and the *British Journal of Sociology of Education*, of all those articles reporting empirical research, almost a third did not give details of the sample size. In both journals, too, about a third of the relevant articles gave no details at all as to how the sample was selected. The picture for the *British Educational Research Journal* was slightly better, but still not good: about 10 per cent of articles reporting empirical research did not give the sample size; roughly a fifth gave no details of how the sample was selected; and about 40 per cent gave some, although inadequate, information about this.

Non-empirical educational research

In the Ofsted report, probably the most dramatic examples of research under this heading which would conflict with a Popperian approach were those dubbed in the report 'adulation of great thinkers'. A Popperian would not be willing to take uncritically the theories and ideas of a particularly noted thinker, but would seek to explore – to test – their viability and applicability, and perhaps seek to modify or reject the ideas if appropriate. This type of approach was sorely lacking from much of the research examined.

For example, one of the articles – which seemed to be typical of a genre of academic educational research – focused on linking Bourdieu's theories with education. The researcher, Reay (1995), set out to define what Bourdieu meant by the concept 'habitus'. However, she soon realizes that Bourdieu's concept of 'habitus' is rather slippery: Bourdieu is quoted as saying, 'I do not like definitions much' (Reay 1995:357), and the concept of habitus is pointed out as not intended to be 'precise or unambiguous' (Reay 1995:357). 'This results in problems of indeterminacy and changing notions of habitus within Bourdieu's writing' (Reay 1995:357). This much is helpful. She then goes on to say that

> Paradoxically, the conceptual looseness of habitus also constitutes a potential strength. It makes possible adaptation rather than the more constricting straightforward adoption of the concept within empirical work. There is also a 'messiness' about the concept that fits in well with the complex messiness of the real world. (Reay 1995:357)

An outside observer may wonder whether such a 'messy' concept could be of much use in analysing and clarifying issues in the classroom. Why refer to habitus at all? The researcher seems to be aware of this objection, because she gives us plenty of examples to show why she thinks it worthwhile. For example:

> Female habitus can be surmised as a complex interlacing of the dispositions, which are the consequences of gender oppression, with those that are the product of varying levels of social privilege. Similarly, a recognition of racial oppression would inform understandings of racialised habitus. Prejudices and racial stereotypes ingrained in the habitus of members of dominant groups can affect the life chances of any group who are clearly different in some way. (Reay 1995:360)

Would this explanation be any different without the concept 'habitus'? In the first part of this paragraph she is talking about what it is to be female. In the second, she is talking about the habits, prejudices and predilections of a dominant group – perhaps habitus could be a shorthand for that? But then it cannot mean everything, and already she has given us other definitions such as:

> habitus can be viewed as a complex internalised core from which everyday experiences emanate. It is the source of day to day practices. (Reay 1995:357)

> Habitus is primarily a method for analysing the dominance of dominant groups in society and the domination of subordinate groups. (Reay 1995:359)

A Popperian would probably have stopped there, aware that, with such a slippery concept, there was not much chance of testing its applicability to the classroom situation. By attempting critically to examine Bourdieu's ideas, a Popperian may well have arrived at a position of questioning their efficacy. However, in a fashion typical of this genre, Reay then sets out to show the 'extent to which the habitus of the classroom reflected the habitus of the home' (Reay 1995:353), by looking at pupil interactions in a 'largely white and middle-class' primary classroom alongside that of a 'predominantly working-class . . . multi-ethnic' primary classroom. She also set out to 'expand understandings of habitus to include the influences of "race" and gender alongside those of social class' (Reay 1995:353). This is so, even though she has not been able to discover what Bourdieu meant by the term in the first place. Not surprisingly, as she attempts to link classroom practice with the concept, the results are at best anodyne, at worst offensive.

Her first example concerns the finding that, in the 'middle-class' classroom, some girls are using a computer program and take on the role of the mistress, rather than the servant girl, although the converse had been true in the working-class classroom. This is fitted into the previously elaborated discussion on Bourdieu as follows: 'Bourdieu writes in terms of habitus as "the internalisation of the probabilities of access to goods, services and powers" (Bourdieu, 1992, p. 60)' (Reay 1995:362). Hence the responses of the children in the two schools to the computer program illustrated very different relationships to 'goods, services and powers'.

This is *the extent* to which Bourdieu's habitus is used to 'illuminate' the behaviour of the children in the two schools – I am quoting in full. An outside observer may wonder whether it is all worth the candle – and of course, wonder too, how representative the particular behaviour observed that day was, how 'working class' and 'middle class' have been defined, and how particular children have been fitted into these categories, and so on.

Reay's second example concerns the difference in 'tidying up' behaviour in the two classrooms. The 'working-class' girls get on with it, while the 'middle-class' girls thought that this was a job for the cleaners, hence the title of the paper, 'They employ cleaners to do that'. Again, Bourdieu is used to interpret these findings:

> Tidying up and helping generally were activities working-class girls in Milner [the working-class school] felt 'at home with' (Bourdieu, 1981, p. 308). In Oak Park [the middle-class school] such activities were both actively and passively resisted not only by the boys but by many of the girls as well. What we learn . . . is that the process of cultural capital production generated by habitus is not only a process of generating educational attainment. It is also one of producing social distinction . . . They were working on their social status in the classroom alongside, and even in the process of attending to the school curriculum. They were constructing themselves as the kind of people who are different to either 'Bess' [the computer program servant] or the cleaners. (Reay 1995:363–4)

Again, one wonders whether this complicated machinery of habitus has actually been at all illuminating. Moreover, one is struck, as noted above, by how the researcher is not seeking to explore *whether or not* the concept applies to the situation, but simply to show that *it does* fit. Such an uncritical approach would be unacceptable to a Popperian.

MOVING FORWARD

Swann and Pratt (this volume) argue that a Popperian approach would improve the quality of educational research. In this chapter, I have attempted to link a Popperian critique of some of the practices in educational research in the UK with the kinds of criticisms which emerged in the Ofsted critique of educational research (Tooley with Darby 1998).

I outlined some of the parameters by which a Popperian might judge educational research. All of the techniques discussed would assist in the creation of a testable body of knowledge about the enterprise of education; they would be necessary, although not sufficient conditions, to this end. I also showed that the criticisms contained in the Ofsted report about the quality and content of educational research seemed compatible with Popperian methodological criticisms. Select examples from the report were specifically chosen to illustrate some problems inherent in non-Popperian approaches.

The upshot of the argument is that some of the serious shortcomings highlighted in the Ofsted critique of educational research were shortcomings that would also be exposed by a Popperian critique. Swann and Pratt's suggestion that the quality of educational research could be improved by adopting Popperian methods would seem to be supported.

To round off this discussion, I wish to make two brief remarks which indicate future directions for research, but which cannot be taken any further here. The first is to distance my own work for Ofsted from the conclusions of the related Department for Education and Employment report on educational research (Hillage *et al.* 1998) – for in public meetings there has been a temptation for people to group our conclusions together. Hillage *et al.* suggested that the way to overcome some of the problems of poor quality in educational research was to create a National Forum for Educational Research, centralizing control over the content and methods of research. Pratt and Swann argue against this type of approach from a Popperian perspective: 'It is often impossible to judge in advance what will or will not be relevant to practice . . . Good research requires diversity – of people, opportunities, approaches, funding – to generate new ideas' (Chapter 1:10).

Elsewhere, I have completely concurred with these sentiments. For example, when criticizing Michael Barber's influential *The Learning Game* (1996, see Tooley 1999a), I have puzzled over his worry that there is no current strategy within the educational research community to answer questions such as:

where are the frontiers of our knowledge about education? Where would we like to push out across them into the unknown? What do we need to know most? What do we need to know first? . . . There is absolutely no sense of consensus about answers to them and little evidence of an attempt to seek one. (Barber 1996:220)

And his solution is that there should be some form of central control to ensure that answers to these questions are found. But why *should* there be a consensus? Surely, just as in other scientific research, progress depends on researchers moving forward on what *they perceive* to be the frontiers, being daring and entrepreneurial – as in the Popperian approach. There is a 'knowledge' or 'epistemic' problem which will thwart any attempt by government to decide on which are the optimum frontiers to be pursued (see Tooley 1996).

However, this then raises the issue of accountability: if government is funding education, then surely it is entitled to push the research agenda in ways it deems desirable? It would seem to me that it should be allowed to do so, that 'he who pays the piper' *should* be allowed 'to call the tune'. The way around this apparent paradox – that of desiring autonomous research from a Popperian perspective, while agreeing that government should be able to direct research it funds – is to question why we need government funding of research, and indeed, whether government funding is part of the problem of poor quality educational research. In my international research on private education, for example, I found examples of private education companies willing to substantially fund basic research on education – without any strings attached for its immediate relevance (Tooley 1999b).

But could private funding be found for, say, the kind of work on Bourdieu, Lyotard and Foucault which received criticism in my Ofsted report (Tooley with Darby 1998:56–62), and which would seem rather far removed from the concerns of teachers and pupils? I am always rather impressed that Charles Saatchi finances Damien Hirst's 'art'; there seems to be no reason why a Charles Saatchi-equivalent could not be found to fund the educational research equivalent of Hirst's pickled cows. And, of course, much of the theoretical and philosophical work which may not easily find funders does not need large amounts of money to be undertaken. Such research can always be conducted by the committed amateur, writing about whatever he or she wants to write about, in his or her own time, without funding from anyone. I would have thought that such an approach to the funding and regulation of educational research would fit very neatly into a Popperian framework.

The second brief remark, in conclusion, concerns Popper's philosophy itself. This chapter has shown the relevance of a Popperian approach to raising the quality of educational research. However, I do not think Popper has the final word to say on this issue, and I would not call myself a Popperian. Without abandoning what is best in Popper – and, in particular, the critical rigour of his approach outlined in this chapter – I believe one can move on from Popper, just as Corson in this volume also argues (Chapter 6). My preferred approach is to 'move on' by 'going back' to the philosopher David Hume, overlaying this with a more thoroughly worked-out evolutionary theory than Popper himself apparently countenanced – but nonetheless fitting in with Popper's acceptance of the relevance of evolutionary theory to the development of scientific methodology (Popper 1979). There are two major problems with Popper's views, as developed in this volume, which such an approach would overcome. First, there is the issue of *why* we should be realists. Pratt and Swann (Chapter 1) note that:

> We cannot be sure whether our constructions accurately describe reality... Our observations are inevitably theory-laden... But in realist philosophies the relationship between knowledge and its object is crucial; and relativism – the idea that all points of view are equally valid – is not only frivolous and dangerous in reality (in an aircraft you ignore the theory of gravity at your peril) but fallacious, since there are some explanations that are more successful than others (as the previous parenthesis illustrates). (Chapter 1:7–8)

Swann (Chapter 2) also gives an account of Popper's realism, noting that 'like Popper, most people believe in the existence of a shared external reality; they are commonsense realists. Commonsense realism can neither be demonstrated nor disproved.' But if it cannot be demonstrated or proved, then why would we accept it, and how can it become such an important buttress against relativists and postmodernists, as Swann and Pratt would wish? Swann argues that 'there are strong *arguments* which support the commonsense realist view.' She adapts Popper (1979), to give the following:

> there is no good reason to reject commonsense realism, therefore we should be cautious about relinquishing it; denying the existence of an external reality means that the individual is necessarily the creator of her universe, which amounts to megalomania; most science and all descriptive human language imply an independently existing world, and if we abandon commonsense realism we must, if we wish to be rational, give an alternative (and convincing) account of the nature of human language and the practices of science. (Chapter 2:17)

But surely the last approach – that of formulating 'an alternative (and convincing) account' – is precisely what many of the opponents of commonsense realism are attempting to do? (See, for example, Rorty 1980.) I believe that a more thorough exploration of evolutionary theory could give us more compelling reasons why we would want to reject relativism. As the evolutionary epistemologist Michael Ruse writes:

> Why is my world also your world? Why do we not get a fragmentation of realities? For the Darwinian, the required universality follows on the unity of humankind. Those humans who believed that 2 + 2 = 5, or that fire causes orgasms rather than pain, or ignored the virtues of consiliences, got wiped out in the struggle for existence. (Ruse 1986:189)

Our scientific method, on this approach, is built into our genes, and this is why it works and is shared by all humanity.

A second unsatisfactory part of the Popperian story is the issue of induction. Swann notes that 'Popper, following Hume, accepted that the theory of induction is logically invalid but, unlike Hume, he denied that induction ever takes place, psychologically or otherwise' (Chapter 2:22). But this seems counter-intuitive because, surely, induction *does* take place, certainly psychologically – I really do believe that the sun will rise tomorrow, strictly on the basis of the evidence that it has risen every other day of my life – and it would seem to have its place in science too. But a more thoroughly-grounded evolutionary approach would seem to get around this problem too. Quine (1969), for example, puts his finger on the problem and points to an evolutionary-based solution:

> why does our innate subjective spacing of qualities accord so well with the functionally relevant groupings in nature as to make our inductions tend to come out right? Why should our subjective spacing of qualities have a special purchase on nature and a lien on the future?

> There is some encouragement in Darwin. If people's innate spacing of qualities is a gene-linked trait, then the spacing that has made for the most successful inductions will have tended to predominate through natural selection. Creatures inveterately wrong in their inductions have a pathetic but praise-worthy tendency to die before reproducing their kind. (Quine 1969:126)

With an evolutionary epistemology, thoroughly grounded both in Hume's scepticism and in the latest ideas about the evolution of human culture, I suggest that a theory of knowledge can be developed which keeps the best of Popper and more firmly supports his realism and anti-relativism, but which does not fall foul of his strictures against inductivism.

References

Advisory Council for Scientific Policy (1949) *Scientific Policy, 1948–49: Second Annual Report of the Advisory Council.* London: Her Majesty's Stationery Office, Cmnd 7755.

Agassi, J. (1977) *Towards a Rational Philosophical Anthropology.* The Hague, The Netherlands: Martinus Nijhoff.

Agassi, J. (1993) *A Philosopher's Apprentice: In Karl Popper's Workshop.* Atlanta, GA: Rodopi.

Agassi, J. (1996) Review of Michael R. Matthews' science teaching: the role of history and philosophy of science. *Science and Education*, 5 (1), 69–77.

Allison, G. T. (1971) *Essence of Decision: Explaining the Cuban Missile Crisis.* Boston, MA: Little, Brown.

Argyris, C. and Schön, D. A. (1974) *Theory in Practice: Increasing Professional Effectiveness.* San Francisco, CA: Jossey-Bass.

Ball, S. J. (1987) *The Micro-Politics of the School: Towards a Theory of School Organisation.* London: Methuen.

Bannister, D. and Mair, J. M. M. (1968) *The Evaluation of Personal Constructs.* London: Academic Press.

Barber, M. (1996) *The Learning Game: Arguments for an Education Revolution.* London: Victor Gollancz.

Barrett, S. and Fudge, C. (1981) Examining the policy–action relationship. In Barrett, S. and Fudge, C. (eds) *Policy and Action: Essays on the Implementation of Public Policy.* London: Methuen.

Bartley, W. W., III (1974) Theory of language and philosophy of science as instruments of educational reform: Wittgenstein and Popper as Austrian schoolteachers. In R. S. Cohen and M. W. Wartofsky (eds) *Methodological and Historical Essays in the Natural and Social Sciences.* Dordrecht, Holland: D. Reidel Publishing Company.

Bassey, M. (1998) Fuzzy generalisation: an approach to building educational theory. Paper presented at the annual conference of the British Educational Research Association, The Queen's University of Belfast, 27–30 August.

Bhaskar, R. (1978) *A Realist Theory of Science.* Brighton: Harvester Press.

Bhaskar, R. (1979) *The Possibility of Naturalism: A Philosophical Critique of the Contemporary Human Sciences.* Brighton: Harvester Press.

Bhaskar, R. (1986) *Scientific Realism and Human Emancipation.* London: Verso.

Bhaskar, R. (1989) *Reclaiming Reality: A Critical Introduction to Contemporary Philosophy.* London: Verso.

Bhaskar, R. (1993) Afterword. In J. Shotter *Conversational Realities: Constructing Life through Language.* London: Sage Publications.

Billig, M. and Simons, H. W. (1994) Introduction. In H. W. Simons and M. Billig (eds) *After Postmodernism: Reconstructing Ideology Critique*. London: Sage Publications.

Blase, J. and Anderson, G. L. (1995) *The Micropolitics of Educational Leadership: From Control to Empowerment*. London: Cassell.

Blenkin, G. M. and Kelly, A. V. (1987) *The Primary Curriculum: A Process Approach to Curriculum Planning*. London: Paul Chapman Publishing.

Bloom, A. (1987) *The Closing of the American Mind: How Higher Education has Failed Democracy and Impoverished the Souls of Today's Students*. New York: Simon and Schuster.

Bloom, B. S. (ed.) (1956) *Taxonomy of Educational Objectives – The Classification of Educational Goals: Book 1 – Cognitive Domain*. New York: David McKay.

Boudon, R. (1973) *Education, Opportunity, and Social Inequality: Changing Prospects in Western Society*. New York: John Wiley and Sons.

Bourdieu, P. (1982) *Ce Que Parler Veut Dire: L'Économie des Échanges Linguistiques*. Paris: Fayard.

Bourdieu, P. (1984) *Distinction: A Social Critique of the Judgement of Taste*. Cambridge, MA: Harvard University Press (translated by R. Nice) (first French edition 1979).

Bright, B. (ed.) (1989) *Theory and Practice in the Study of Adult Education: The Epistemological Debate*. London: Routledge.

Bright, B. (1996) Reflecting on 'reflective practice'. *Studies in the Education of Adults*, 28 (2), 162–84.

British Educational Research Association (1998) Editorial. *Research Intelligence*, 66, 1.

Brookfield, S. D. (1988) *Training Educators of Adults: The Theory and Practice of Graduate Adult Education*. London: Routledge.

Brookfield, S. D. (1993) Breaking the code: engaging practitioners in critical analysis of adult educational literature. *Studies in the Education of Adults*, 25 (1), 64–91.

Brookfield, S. D. (1995) *Becoming a Critically Reflective Teacher*. San Francisco, CA: Jossey-Bass.

Brown, G., Bull, J. and Pendlebury, M. (1997) *Assessing Student Learning in Higher Education*. London: Routledge.

Brown, I. (1971) The dispersed polytechnic. *Higher Education Review*, 3 (2), 25–45.

Brown, R. H. (1994) Reconstructing social theory after the postmodern critique. In H. W. Simons and M. Billig (eds) *After Postmodernism: Reconstructing Ideology Critique*. London: Sage Publications.

Brown, S. and Knight, P. (1994) *Assessing Learners in Higher Education*. London: Kogan Page.

Brown, S., Race, P. and Smith, B. (1996) *500 Tips on Assessment*. London: Kogan Page.

Bryson, J. M. (ed.) (1995) *Strategic Planning for Public and Non-Profit Organizations*. San Francisco, CA: Jossey-Bass.

Burgess, T. (1977) *Education After School*. London: Victor Gollancz.

Burgess, T. (1979) New ways to learn. *The Royal Society of Arts Journal*, CXXVII (5271), 143–57.

Burgess, T. and Adams, E. (1980) *The Outcomes of Education*. London: Macmillan Education.

Burgess, T. and Pratt, J. (1970) *Policy and Practice: The Colleges of Advanced Technology*. London: Allen Lane, The Penguin Press.

Burgess, T. and Swann, J. (forthcoming) *Improving Learning – Improving Schools: The Art and Science of Education*. London: Kogan Page.

Campbell, D. T. (1959) Methodological suggestions from a comparative psychology of knowledge processes. *Inquiry*, 2 (3), 152–83.

Carr, W. and Kemmis, S. (1986) *Becoming Critical: Education, Knowledge and Action Research*. London: Falmer Press.

Cazden, C. B. (1989) Richmond Road: a multilingual/multicultural primary school in Auckland, New Zealand. *Language and Education*, 3 (3), 143–66.

Chalmers, A. F. (1982) *What Is This Thing called Science?: An Assessment of the Nature*

and Status of Science and Its Methods. Milton Keynes: Open University Press.
Chalmers, A. F. (1990) *Science and Its Fabrication.* Milton Keynes: Open University Press.
Chown, A. and Last, J. (1993) Can the NCVQ model be used for teacher training? *Journal of Further and Higher Education,* 17 (2), 15–26.
Clark, C. M. and Yinger, R. J. (1987) Teacher planning. In J. Calderhead (ed.) *Exploring Teachers' Thinking.* London: Cassell Educational.
Cohen, L. and Manion, L. (1994) *Research Methods in Education.* London: Routledge (first edition 1980).
Cohen, L., Manion, L. and Morrison, K. (1996) *A Guide to Teaching Practice.* London: Routledge.
Connolly, P. (1995) Racism, masculine peer-group relations and the schooling of African/Caribbean infant boys. *British Journal of Sociology of Education,* 16 (1), 75–92.
Corson, D. J. (1981) Social dialect, the semantic barrier and access to curricular knowledge. London: University of London (unpublished PhD thesis).
Corson, D. J. (1985a) Educational research and Popper's theory of knowledge. *Universities Quarterly: Culture, Education and Society,* 40 (1), 73–89.
Corson, D. J. (1985b) Popper on education. *Access: Contemporary Themes in Educational Inquiry,* 4 (1), 41–61.
Corson, D. J. (1986) Policy in social context: a collapse of holistic planning in education. *Journal of Education Policy,* 1 (1), 5–22.
Corson, D. J. (1987) An approach to research in educational administration. *Journal of Educational Administration and Foundations,* 2 (1), 20–36.
Corson, D. J. (1989a) The social epistemologies of education: a response to McHoul and Luke. *Social Epistemology: A Journal of Knowledge, Culture and Policy,* 3 (1), 19–37.
Corson, D. J. (1989b) A radical learning theory for education. *Cogito,* 3 (3), 224–30.
Corson, D. J. (1990a) Old and new conceptions of discovery in education. *Educational Philosophy and Theory,* 22 (2), 26–49.
Corson, D. J. (1990b) Applying the stages of a social epistemology to school policy making. *British Journal of Educational Studies,* 38 (3), 259–76.
Corson, D. J. (1990c) *Education for Work: Background to Policy and Curriculum.* Clevedon, Avon: Multilingual Matters.
Corson, D. J. (1991a) Educational research and Bhaskar's conception of discovery. *Educational Theory,* 41 (2), 189–98.
Corson, D. J. (1991b) Bhaskar's critical realism and educational knowledge. *British Journal of Sociology of Education,* 12 (2), 223–241.
Corson, D. J. (1995a) *Discourse and Power in Educational Organizations.* Toronto: University of Toronto Press.
Corson, D. J. (1995b) *Using English Words.* London: Kluwer Academic.
Corson, D. J. (1997) Reclaiming reality: laying the ideology of cultural compatibility. *International Journal of Intercultural Relations,* 21 (1), 105–11.
Corson, D. J. (1998) *Changing Education for Diversity.* Buckingham: Open University Press.
Corson, D. J. (1999) *Language Policy in Schools: A Resource for Teachers and Administrators.* New York: Lawrence Erlbaum Associates.
Cottingham, J. (1984) *Rationalism.* London: Paladin Books.
Crosland, A. (1965) Speech by the Secretary of State for Education and Science, Woolwich Polytechnic, Tuesday 27 April 1965.
Croydon Education Authority (1985) *Primary Education in Croydon: A Guide for Parents.* Croydon: Croydon Education Authority and the Voluntary School Authorities.
Dale, R. R. (1974) *Mixed or Single-Sex School? Volume III: Attainment, Attitudes and Overview.* London: Routledge & Kegan Paul.
Dearden, R. F. (1976) *Problems in Primary Education.* London: Routledge & Kegan Paul.

Department of Education and Science (1966) *A Plan for Polytechnics and Other Colleges: Higher Education in the Further Education System.* London: Her Majesty's Stationery Office, Cmnd 3006.

Department of Education and Science (1972) *Education: A Framework for Expansion.* London: Her Majesty's Stationery Office, Cmnd 5174.

Department of Education and Science (1975) *Curricular Differences for Boys and Girls (Education Survey 21).* London: Her Majesty's Stationery Office.

Department of Education and Science (1991) *Higher Education: A New Framework.* London: Her Majesty's Stationery Office, Cm 1541.

Department for Education (1995) *Key Stages 1 and 2 of the National Curriculum.* London: Her Majesty's Stationery Office.

Department for Education and Employment (1998a) *The Learning Age: A Renaissance for a New Britain.* London: Her Majesty's Stationery Office, Cm 3790.

Department for Education and Employment (1998b) *Teaching: High Status, High Standards (Circular Number 4/98).* London: Department for Education and Employment.

Doyal, L. and Harris, R. (1986) *Empiricism, Explanation and Rationality: An Introduction to the Philosophy of the Social Sciences.* London: Routledge & Kegan Paul.

Driver, R. and Oldham, V. (1986) A constructivist approach to curriculum development in science. *Studies in Science Education,* 13, 105–22.

Dror, Y. (1968) *Public Policymaking Reexamined.* New York: Intext Educational Publishers.

Dror, Y. (1971) *Ventures in Policy Sciences: Concepts and Applications.* New York: Elsevier.

Dror, Y. (1986) *Policymaking Under Adversity.* New Brunswick, NJ: Transaction.

Durkheim, E. (1966) *The Rules of Sociological Method.* New York: The Free Press (translated by S. A. Solovay and J. H. Mueller, and edited by G. E. G. Catlin) (first French edition 1895).

Ecclestone, K. (1996) *How to Assess the Vocational Curriculum.* London: Kogan Page.

Ecclestone, K. (1999) Ensnaring or empowering?: the implications of outcome-based assessment in higher education. *Higher Education Quarterly,* 53 (1), 29–48.

Ecclestone, K. and Swann, J. (1999) Litigation and learning: tensions in improving university lecturers' assessment practice. *Assessment in Education: Principles, Policy & Practice,* 6 (3), forthcoming.

Edwards, M. L. (1999) Getting it right. London: Centre for Institutional Studies, University of East London (unpublished MSc thesis).

Einstein, A. (1950) *Out of My Later Years.* London: Thames and Hudson.

Equal Opportunities Commission (1979) *Do You Provide Equal Educational Opportunities?: A Guide to Good Practice in the Provision of Equal Opportunities in Education.* Manchester: Equal Opportunities Commission.

Eraut, M. (1994) *Developing Professional Knowledge and Competence.* Lewes: Falmer Press.

Eve, R. A., Horsfall, S. and Lee, M. E. (eds) (1997) *Chaos, Complexity and Sociology: Myths, Models and Theories.* London: Sage Publications.

Feyerabend, P. (1988) *Against Method: Outline of an Anarchistic Theory of Knowledge.* London: Verso (first published 1975).

Fransella, F. and Bannister, D. (1977) *A Manual for Repertory Grid Technique.* London: Academic Press.

Garry, A. and Pearsall, M. (eds) (1989) *Women, Knowledge and Reality: Explorations in Feminist Philosophy.* London: Routledge.

Gellner, E. (1992) *Postmodernism, Reason and Religion.* London: Routledge.

Gibbs, G. (ed.) (1994) *Improving Student Learning through Assessment and Evaluation.* Oxford: Oxford Centre for Staff Development.

Gibson, R. (1986) *Critical Theory and Education.* London: Hodder and Stoughton.

Gitlin, A., Bringhurst, K., Burns, M., Cooley, V., Myers, B., Price, K., Russell, R. and Tiess, P. (1992) *Teachers' Voices for School Change: An Introduction to Educative Research*. London: Routledge.
Glaser, R. and Chi, M. T. H. (1988) Overview. In M. T. H. Chi, R. Glaser and M. Farr (eds) *The Nature of Expertise*. Hillsdale, NJ: Lawrence Erlbaum Associates.
Griffin, C. (1987) *Adult Education as Social Policy*. Beckenham: Croom Helm.
Griffiths, M. and Tann, S. (1992) Using reflective practice to link personal and public theories. *Journal of Education for Teaching*, 18 (1), 69–84.
Habermas, J. (1970) Towards a theory of communicative competence. *Inquiry*, 13 (4), 360–75.
Habermas, J. (1976) The analytical theory of science and dialectics. In T. W. Adorno, H. Albert, R. Dahrendorf, J. Habermas, H. Pilot, and K. R. Popper *The Positivist Dispute in German Sociology*. London: Heinemann (translated by G. Adey and D. Frisby) (first German edition 1969).
Habermas, J. (1979) *Communication and the Evolution of Society*. London: Heinemann Educational Books (translated by T. McCarthy) (first German edition 1976).
Habermas, J. (1984) *The Theory of Communicative Action, Volume 1 – Reason and the Rationalization of Society*. Boston, MA: Beacon Press (translated by T. McCarthy) (first German edition 1981).
Habermas, J. (1987) *The Theory of Communicative Action, Volume 2 – Lifeworld and System: A Critique of Functionalist Reason*. Boston, MA: Beacon Press (translated by T. McCarthy) (first German edition 1981).
Harding, S. (1986) *The Science Question in Feminism*. Ithaca, NY: Cornell University Press.
Hargreaves, D. H. (1996) Teaching as a research-based profession: possibilities and prospects, Teacher Training Agency annual lecture 1996. London: Teacher Training Agency.
Higher Education Funding Council for England (1995) *Review of Higher Education: Submission by the Higher Education Funding Council for England*. Bristol: Higher Education Funding Council for England, M495.
Higher Education Quality Council (1996) *Understanding Academic Standards in Modular Frameworks*. London: Higher Education Quality Council.
Higher Education Quality Council (1997) *The Graduate Standards Programme: Final Report*. London: Higher Education Quality Council.
Hillage, J., Pearson, R., Anderson, A. and Tamkin, P. (1998) *Excellence in Research on Schools*. London: Department for Education and Employment.
Hillier, Y. (1994) *Informal Practitioner Theory in Adult Basic Education*. London: University of East London (unpublished PhD thesis).
Hobsbawm, E. (1993) The new threat to history. *New York Review of Books*, 16 December, 63.
Hogwood, B. W. and Gunn, L. A. (1984) *Policy Analysis for the Real World*. Oxford: Oxford University Press.
Hughes, J. A. (1990) *The Philosophy of Social Research*. London: Longman (first edition 1980).
Hutcheon, L. (1989) *The Politics of Postmodernism*. London: Routledge.
Hyland, T. (1993) Professional development and competence-based education. *Educational Studies*, 19 (1), 123–31.
James, R. (1980) *Return to Reason: Popper's Thought in Public Life*. Shepton Mallet, Somerset: Open Books Publishing.
Kant, I. (1960) *Education*. Ann Arbor, MI: University of Michigan Press (translated by A. Churton) (first German edition 1803, first English edition 1899).
Keddie, N. (1980) Adult education: an ideology of individualism. In J. L. Thompson (ed.) *Adult Education for a Change*. London: Hutchinson.
Kelly, G. A. (1955a) *The Psychology of Personal Constructs, Volume 1 – A Theory of Personality*. New York: W. W. Norton and Co.

Kelly, G. A. (1955b) *The Psychology of Personal Constructs, Volume 2 – Clinical Diagnosis and Psychotherapy.* New York: W. W. Norton and Co.

Kelly, G. A. (1969) Man's construction of his alternatives. In B. Maher (ed.) *Clinical Psychology and Personality: The Selected Papers of George Kelly.* New York: John Wiley & Sons (paper first published 1958).

Kelly, G. A. (1970) A brief introduction to personal construct theory. In D. Bannister (ed.) *Perspectives in Personal Construct Theory.* London: Academic Press.

Kemmis, S. and McTaggart, R. (eds) (1988) *The Action Research Planner.* Victoria, Australia: Deakin University Press.

Kerr, J. F. (1968) The problem of curriculum reform. In J. F. Kerr (ed.) *Changing the Curriculum.* London: University of London Press.

Knight, P. (ed.) (1995) *Assessment for Learning in Higher Education.* London: Kogan Page.

Krick, E. V. (1969) *An Introduction to Engineering and Engineering Design.* New York: John Wiley and Sons.

Krige, J. (1980) *Science, Revolution and Discontinuity.* Brighton: Harvester Press.

Labov, W. (1982) Objectivity and commitment in linguistic science: the case of the Black English trial in Ann Arbor, *Language in Society*, 11 (2), 165–201.

Lampinen, O. (1992) *The Utilization of Social Science Research in Public Policy.* Helsinki: VAPK-Publishing.

Lather, P. (1994) Staying dumb? Feminist research and pedagogy with/in the postmodern. In H. W. Simons and M. Billig (eds) *After Postmodernism: Reconstructing Ideology Critique.* London: Sage Publications.

Latour, B. and Woolgar, S. (1979) *Laboratory Life: The Construction of Scientific Facts.* Albany, NY: State University of New York Press.

Lindblom, C. E. (1959) The science of 'muddling through'. *Public Administration Review*, 19 (2), 79–88.

Lindblom, C. E. (1979) Still muddling, not yet through. *Public Administration Review*, 39 (6), 517–26.

Little, G. R. (1981) Social models: blueprints or processes? *Impact of Science on Society*, 31 (4), 439–47.

Locke, M. (1978) *Tradition and Controls in the Making of a Polytechnic: Woolwich Polytechnic 1890–1970.* London: Thames Polytechnic.

Locke, M., Pratt, J. and Burgess, T. (1985) *The Colleges of Higher Education 1972 to 1982: The Central Management of Organic Change.* London: Critical Press.

Lord President of the Council (1946) *Scientific Man-Power: Report of a Committee Appointed by the Lord President of the Council.* London: Her Majesty's Stationery Office, Cmd 6824.

Lyotard, J.-F. (1984) *The Postmodern Condition: A Report on Knowledge.* Minneapolis, MI: University of Minneapolis Press (translated by G. Bennington and B. Massumi) (first French edition 1979).

McCarthy, T. (1984) *The Critical Theory of Jürgen Habermas.* Cambridge: Polity Press (first edition 1978).

McGaw, B., Boud, D., Poole, M., Warry, R. and McKenzie, P. (1992) *Educational Research in Australia: Report of the Review Panel.* Canberra, Australia: Australian Government Publishing Service.

McIntyre, D. (1997) The profession of educational research. *British Educational Research Journal*, 23 (2), 127–40.

Maclure, S. (1989) *Education Re-formed: A Guide to the Education Reform Act.* London: Hodder and Stoughton.

Magee, B. (1973) *Popper.* London: Fontana Press.

Majone, G. (1980) Policies as theories. *Omega*, 8 (2), 151–62.

Marsh, D. (ed.) (1998) *Comparing Policy Networks.* Buckingham: Open University Press.

Marsh, D. and Rhodes, R. A. W. (eds) (1992) *Policy Networks in British Government.* Oxford: Oxford University Press.

Matthews, M. R. (1994) *Science Teaching: The Role of History and Philosophy of Science*. New York: Routledge.

May, S. (1994) *Making Multicultural Education Work*. Clevedon, Avon: Multilingual Matters.

Medawar, P. B. (1969) *Induction and Intuition in Scientific Thought*. London: Methuen.

Meighan, R. and Siraj-Blatchford, I. (1997) *A Sociology of Educating*. London: Cassell (first edition 1981).

Mill, J. S. (1989) *On Liberty and Other Essays*. Cambridge: Cambridge University Press (first edition of *On Liberty* 1859).

Miller, D. (1982) Conjectural knowledge: Popper's solution of the problem of induction. In P. Levinson (ed.) *In Pursuit of Truth: Essays on the Philosophy of Karl Popper on the Occasion of His 80th Birthday*. Atlantic Highlands, NJ: Humanities Press.

Miller, D. (1985) Editor's introduction. In D. Miller (ed.) *Popper Selections*. Princeton, NJ: Princeton University Press.

Miller, D. (1994) *Critical Rationalism: A Restatement and Defence*. Peru, IL: Open Court Publishing.

Ministry of Education (1945) *Higher Technological Education: Report of a Special Committee Appointed in April 1944*. London: Ministry of Education Reports.

Ministry of Education (1956) *Technical Education*. London: Her Majesty's Stationery Office, Cmd 9703.

Musgrave, A. (1993) *Common Sense, Science and Scepticism: Historical Introduction to the Theory of Knowledge*. Cambridge: Cambridge University Press.

Nagel, T. (1997) *The Last Word*. New York: Oxford University Press.

National Committee of Inquiry into Higher Education (1997) *Higher Education in the Learning Society: Report of the National Committee of Inquiry into Higher Education*. London: Her Majesty's Stationery Office.

Neill, A. S. (1968) *Summerhill*. Harmondsworth, Middlesex: Penguin Books (first edition 1962).

Organisation for Economic Co-operation and Development (1995) *Educational Research and Development: Trends, Issues and Challenges*. Paris: Organisation for Economic Co-operation and Development.

Paechter, C. (1995) Subcultural retreat: negotiating the design and technology curriculum. *British Educational Research Journal*, 21 (1), 75–87.

Paterson, R. W. K. (1989) Philosophy and adult education. In B. Bright (ed.) *Theory and Practice in Adult Education: The Epistemological Debate*. London: Routledge.

Pawson, R. and Tilley, N. (1997) *Realistic Evaluation*. London: Sage Publications.

Perkinson, H. J. (1971) *The Possibilities of Error: An Approach to Education*. New York: David McKay.

Perkinson, H. J. (1980) *Since Socrates: Studies in the History of Western Educational Thought*. New York: Longman.

Perkinson, H. J. (1984) *Learning from our Mistakes: A Reinterpretation of Twentieth-Century Educational Theory*. Westport, CT: Greenwood Press.

Perkinson, H. J. (1993) *Teachers Without Goals/Students Without Purposes*. New York: McGraw-Hill.

Peterson, P. L. (1998) Why do educational research?: rethinking our roles and identities, our texts and contexts. *Educational Researcher*, 27 (3), 4–10.

Phillips, D. C. (1987) *Philosophy, Science, and Social Inquiry: Contemporary Methodological Controversies in Social Science and Related Applied Fields of Research*. Oxford: Pergamon Press.

Phillips, D. C. (1992) *The Social Scientist's Bestiary: A Guide to Fabled Threats to, and Defenses of, Naturalistic Social Science*. Oxford: Pergamon Press.

Pinker, S. (1998) *How the Mind Works*. London: Allen Lane.

Popham, W. J., Eisner, E. W., Sullivan, H. J. and Tyler, L. L. (1969) *Instructional Objectives*. Chicago, IL: Rand McNally and Company.

Popper, K. R. (1925) Über die Stellung des Lehrers zu Schule und Schüler: Gesellschaftliche oder individualistische Erziehung? *Schulreform*, 4 (4), 204–8.

Popper, K.R. (1927) Zur Philosophie des Heimatgedankens. *Die Quelle*, 77 (10), 899–908.

Popper, K. R. (1931) Die Gedächtnispflege unter dem Gesichtspunkt der Selbsttätigkeit. *Die Quelle*, 81 (6), 607–19.

Popper, K.R. (1932) Pädagogische Zeitschriftenschau. *Die Quelle*, 82 (3), 301–3.

Popper, K. R. (1934) *Logik der Forschung*. Vienna: Springer Verlag.

Popper, K. R. (1961) *The Poverty of Historicism*. London: Routledge & Kegan Paul (first edition 1957).

Popper, K. R. (1966a) *The Open Society and its Enemies, Volume 1 – The Spell of Plato*. London: Routledge & Kegan Paul (first edition 1945).

Popper, K. R. (1966b) *The Open Society and its Enemies, Volume 2 – The High Tide of Prophecy: Hegel, Marx, and the Aftermath*. London: Routledge & Kegan Paul (first edition 1945).

Popper, K. R. (1972a) *The Logic of Scientific Discovery*. London: Hutchinson (first German edition 1934, first English edition 1959).

Popper, K. R. (1972b) *Conjectures and Refutations: The Growth of Scientific Knowledge*. London: Routledge (first edition 1963).

Popper, K. R. (1974) The myth of the framework. In E. Freeman (ed.) *The Abdication of Philosophy: Philosophy and the Public Good*. La Salle, IL: Open Court Publishing.

Popper, K. R. (1976a) The logic of the social sciences. In T. W. Adorno, H. Albert, R. Dahrendorf, J. Habermas, H. Pilot and K. R. Popper *The Positivist Dispute in German Sociology*. London: Heinemann (translated by G. Adey and D. Frisby) (first German edition 1969).

Popper, K. R. (1976b) Reason or revolution? In T. W. Adorno, H. Albert, R. Dahrendorf, J. Habermas, H. Pilot and K. R. Popper *The Positivist Dispute in German Sociology*. London: Heinemann (translated by G. Adey and D. Frisby) (first German edition 1969).

Popper, K. R. (1979) *Objective Knowledge: An Evolutionary Approach*. Oxford: Oxford University Press (first edition 1972).

Popper, K. R. (1985a) The problem of induction (1953, 1974). In D. Miller (ed.) *Popper Selections*. Princeton, NJ: Princeton University Press.

Popper, K. R. (1985b) The problem of demarcation (1974). In D. Miller (ed.) *Popper Selections*. Princeton, NJ: Princeton University Press.

Popper, K. R. (1985c) Piecemeal social engineering (1944). In D. Miller (ed.) *Popper Selections*. Princeton, NJ: Princeton University Press.

Popper, K. R. (1992) *Unended Quest: An Intellectual Autobiography*. London: Routledge. (First published as Autobiography of Karl Popper. In P. A. Schilpp (ed.) (1974) *The Philosophy of Karl Popper, Book I*. La Salle, IL: Open Court Publishing.)

Pratt, J. (1976) What's wrong with the study of public administration? London: Centre for Institutional Studies, North East London Polytechnic (unpublished paper).

Pratt, J. (1997) *The Polytechnic Experiment 1965–1992*. Buckingham: The Society for Research into Higher Education and Open University Press.

Pratt, J., Bloomfield, J. and Seale, C. (1984) *Option Choice: A Question of Equal Opportunity*. Windsor: NFER-Nelson.

Pratt, J. and Burgess, T. (1974) *Polytechnics: A Report*. London: Sir Isaac Pitman and Sons.

Pratt, J. and Hackl, E. (forthcoming) Breaking the mould in Austrian Higher Education. *Higher Education Review*.

Pratt, J. and Silverman, S. (1988) *Responding to Constraint: Policy and Management in Higher Education*. Buckingham: The Society for Research into Higher Education and Open University Press.

Pressman, J. L. and Wildavsky, A. (1973) *Implementation: How Great Expectations in Washington are Dashed in Oakland*. Berkeley, CA: University of California Press.

Quade, E. S. (1975) *Analysis for Public Decisions*. New York: American Elsevier.

Quality Assurance Agency for Higher Education (1998a) An agenda for quality. *Higher Quality: The Bulletin of the Quality Assurance Agency for Higher Education (Consultation Issue)*, 1 (3).

Quality Assurance Agency for Higher Education (1998b) *Quality Assurance: A New Approach*. Gloucester: Quality Assurance Agency for Higher Education.

Quine, W. V. (1966) *The Ways of Paradox and Other Essays*. New York: Random House.

Quine, W. V. (1969) *Ontological Relativity and Other Essays*. New York: Columbia University Press.

Rabinow, P. (1986) Representations are social facts: modernity and post-modernity in anthropology. In J. Clifford and G. E. Marcus (eds) *Writing Culture: The Poetics and Politics of Ethnography*. Berkeley, CA: University of California Press.

Raven, J. (1977) *Education Values and Society: The Objectives of Education and the Nature and Development of Confidence*. London: H. K. Lewis.

Raven, J. (1982) Broadening the base of educational assessment: some reasons, some problems, some suggestions. *Bulletin of the British Psychological Society*, 25, 332–44.

Reay, D. (1995) 'They employ cleaners to do that': habitus in the primary classroom. *British Journal of Sociology of Education*, 16 (3), 353–71.

Redding, P. (1986) Habermas, Lyotard, Wittgenstein: philosophy at the limits of modernity. *Thesis Eleven*, 14, 9–25.

Reynolds, D. (1998) Teacher effectiveness: better teachers, better schools. *Research Intelligence*, 66, 26–9.

Robbins, Lord (1963) *Higher Education: Report of the Committee appointed by the Prime Minister under the Chairmanship of Lord Robbins 1961–63*. London: Her Majesty's Stationery Office, Cmnd 2154.

Robinson, E. E. (1968) *The New Polytechnics*. London: Cornmarket Press.

Robinson, V. (1993) *Problem-based Methodology: Research for the Improvement of Practice*. Oxford: Pergamon Press.

Rorty, R. (1980) *Philosophy and the Mirror of Nature*. Oxford: Basil Blackwell.

Rorty, R. (1994) Does academic freedom have philosophical presuppositions?: academic freedom and the future of the university. *Academe*, November–December, 52–63.

Ruse, M. (1986) *Taking Darwin Seriously: A Naturalistic Approach to Philosophy*. Oxford: Basil Blackwell.

Rutherford, F. J. and Ahlgen, A. (1990) *Science for All Americans: Project 2061*. New York: Oxford University Press (first edition 1989).

Ryan, A. (1992) Princeton diary. *London Review of Books*, 26 March, 21.

Sagan, C. (1996) *The Demon-Haunted World: Science as a Candle in the Dark*. New York: Random House.

Sayer, A. (1992) *Method in Social Science: A Realist Approach*. London: Routledge.

Schilpp, P. A. (ed.) (1974) *The Philosophy of Karl Popper, Books I and II*. La Salle, IL: Open Court Publishing.

Schön, D. A. (1983) *The Reflective Practitioner: How Professionals Think in Action*. London: Temple Smith.

Schön, D. A. (1987) *Educating the Reflective Practitioner: Towards a New Design for Teaching and Learning in the Professions*. San Francisco, CA: Jossey-Bass.

Schools Council Publications (1972) *With Objectives in Mind: Guide to Science 5–13*. London: MacDonald Educational.

Scott, P. (1987) *A Constructivist View of Learning and Teaching in Science*. Leeds: Centre for Studies in Science and Mathematics Education, University of Leeds.

Scott, P. (1995) *The Meanings of Mass Higher Education*. Buckingham: The Society for Research into Higher Education and Open University Press.

Seville, A. and Tooley, J. (1997) *The Debate on Higher Education: Challenging the Assumptions*. London: Institute for Economic Affairs.

Shore, C. and Wright, S. (eds) (1997) *Anthropology of Policy: Critical Perspectives on Governance and Power*. London: Routledge.

Shotter, J. (1993) *Conversational Realities: Constructing Life through Language.* London: Sage Publications.

Silver, H. (1990) *A Higher Education: The Council for National Academic Awards and British Higher Education 1964–1989.* London: Falmer Press.

Simon, H. A. (1947) *Administrative Behavior: A Study of Decision-Making Processes in Administrative Organizations.* New York: Macmillan.

Simon, H. A. (1957) *Models of Man: Social and Rational Mathematical Essays on Rational Behavior in a Social Setting.* New York: John Wiley and Sons.

Simon, H. A. (1960) *The New Science of Management Decision.* Englewood Cliffs, NJ: Prentice Hall.

Simons, H. W. (1994) Teaching the pedagogies: a dialectical approach to an ideological dilemma. In H. W. Simons and M. Billig (eds) *After Postmodernism: Reconstructing Ideology Critique.* London: Sage Publications.

Sokal, A. and Bricmont, J. (1998) *Intellectual Impostures: Postmodern Philosophers' Abuse of Science.* London: Profile Books.

Sparkes, A. C. (1994) Self, silence and invisibility as a beginning teacher: a life history of lesbian experience. *British Journal of Sociology of Education,* 15 (1), 93–118.

Stenhouse, L. (1975) *An Introduction to Curriculum Research and Development.* London: Heinemann Educational Books.

Stephenson, J. (1980) Higher education: School for Independent Study. In T. Burgess and E. Adams (eds) *Outcomes of Education.* London: Macmillan Education.

Stephenson, J. (1981) Student planned learning. In D. Boud (ed.) *Developing Student Autonomy in Learning.* London: Kogan Page.

Stewart Howe, W. (1986) *Corporate Strategy.* Basingstoke: MacMillan.

Swann, J. (1983) Teaching and the logic of learning. *Higher Education Review,* 15 (2), 31–57.

Swann, J. (1988) How can classroom practice be improved?: an investigation of the logic of learning in classroom practice. London: Council for National Academic Awards (unpublished PhD thesis).

Swann, J. (1995) Realism, constructivism, and the pursuit of truth. *Higher Education Review,* 27 (3), 37–55.

Swann, J. (1997) How can we make better plans? *Higher Education Review,* 30 (1), 37–55.

Swann, J. (1998a) What doesn't happen in teaching and learning? *Oxford Review of Education,* 24 (2), 211–23.

Swann, J. (1998b) A Popperian theory of learning and teaching. Paper presented at the annual conference of the Scottish Educational Research Association, University of Dundee, 24–26 September.

Swann, J. (1999) What happens when learning takes place? *Interchange, A Quarterly Review of Education,* 30, forthcoming.

Swann, J. and Arthurs, J. (1999) Empowering lecturers: a problem-based approach to improve assessment practice. *Higher Education Review,* 31 (2), 50–74.

Swann, J. and Brown, S. (1987) The implementation of a national curriculum and teachers' classroom thinking. *Research Papers in Education,* 12 (1), 91–114.

Swann, J. and Ecclestone, K. (1999) Improving lecturers' assessment practice in higher education: a problem-based approach. *Educational Action Research,* 7 (1), 87–108.

Swartz, R. M. (1974) Education as entertainment and irresponsibility in the classroom. *Science Education,* 58 (1), 119–25.

Swartz, R. M. (1999) Education for freedom from Socrates to Einstein and beyond. In G. Zecha (ed.) *Critical Rationalism and Educational Discourse.* Amsterdam, The Netherlands: Rodopi BV Editions.

Swartz, R. M., Perkinson, H. J. and Edgerton, S. G. (1980) *Knowledge and Fallibilism: Essays on Improving Education.* New York: New York University Press.

Tarnas, R. (1991) *The Passion of the Western Mind: Understanding the Ideas that have Shaped our World View.* New York: Ballantine Books.

Technician Education Council (1976) *TEC Guidance Notes No. 1: The Presentation of*

Educational Objectives in TEC Units. London: Technician Education Council.

Thomas, G. (1998) The myth of rational research. *British Educational Research Journal*, 24 (2), 141–61.

Thompson, J. B. (1990) *Ideology and Modern Culture: Critical Social Theory in the Era of Mass Communication.* Stanford, CA: Stanford University Press.

Tooley, J. (1995) *Disestablishing the School: Debunking Justifications for State Intervention in Education.* Aldershot: Ashgate Publishing.

Tooley, J. (1996) *Education Without the State.* London: Institute for Economic Affairs.

Tooley, J. (1999a) New versus old Barber: an unfinished revolution. *British Journal of Educational Studies*, 47 (1), 28–42.

Tooley, J. (1999b) *The Global Education Industry.* London: Institute for Economic Affairs.

Tooley, J. (forthcoming) *Reclaiming Education.* London: Cassell.

Tooley, J. with Darby, D. (1998) *Educational Research: A Critique – A Survey of Published Educational Research.* London: Office for Standards in Education.

Tunley, P., Travers, T. and Pratt, J. (1979) *Depriving the Deprived: Finance and Educational Provision in a London Borough.* London: Kogan Page.

Tyler, R. W. (1949) *Basic Principles of Curriculum and Instruction.* Chicago, IL: University of Chicago Press.

University of East London (1993) Modular Masters Programme definitive document. London: University of East London.

Usher, R. and Bryant, I. (1989) *Adult Education as Theory, Practice and Research: The Captive Triangle.* London: Routledge.

Utley, A. (1998) Benchmark plans 'are unworkable'. *Times Higher Education Supplement*, 11 December, 8.

Van Maanen, J. (1988) *Tales of the Field: On Writing Ethnography.* Chicago, IL: University of Chicago Press.

von Glasersfeld, E. (1985) Reconstructing the concept of knowledge. *Archives de Psychologie*, 53 (204), 91–101.

Webb, G. (1995) Reflective practice, staff development and understanding. *Studies in Continuing Education*, 17 (1 and 2), 70–7.

Webster, L. (1995). A language policy for 'Huron' School. Toronto: University of Toronto (unpublished research paper).

Weinberg, S. (1993) *Dreams of a Final Theory.* London: Hutchinson Radius.

Wilson, E. O. (1998) *Consilience: The Unity of Knowledge.* London: Little, Brown.

Wittgenstein, L. (1953) *Philosophical Investigations.* Oxford: Blackwell (translated by G. E. M. Anscombe).

Wittgenstein, L. (1961) *Tractatus Logico-Philosophicus.* Atlantic Highlands, NJ: Humanities Press International (translated by D. F. Pears and B. F. McGuinness) (first German edition 1921).

Woodhead, C. (1998) Foreword. In J. Tooley with D. Darby *Educational Research: A Critique – A Survey of Published Educational Research.* London: Office for Standards in Education.

Yin, R. K. (1994) *Case Study Research: Design and Methods.* London: Sage Publications (first edition 1984).

Index

academic drift 82, 86–7
action research *see* problems, researching practical
Adams, E. 144
Adorno, T. W. 31
Advisory Council for Scientific Policy 81
Agassi, J. 102–3, 107, 108
Ahlgen, A. 101–4, 106
American Association for the Advancement of
　　Science 101, 105
American Educational Research Association 3
Argyris, C. 146, 149
assessment of student attainment 53, 56, 58, 59, 65,
　　109, 114, 117, 118, 119, 172
　in adult and further education 90–1
　by examination bodies 55, 90, 91, 103, 109, 145
　in higher education 85, 89–100, 117, 157–61, 162
　in secondary education 143, 145
Australian Research Council 3
authoritarianism 58, 90, 101, 103–8, 115

Bailey, R. 9, 110
Bannister, D. 147, 150
Barber, M. 177–8
Barrett, S. 44, 46
Bassey, M. 6
BERA *see* British Educational Research
　　Association
Bhaskar, R. 69–75, 121
Billig, M. 30–1, 33
Blenkin, G. M. 55, 56
Bloom, A. 3, 30
Bloom, B. S. 55, 56, 60
Boudon, R. 52
Bourdieu, P. 72, 9, 74, 75, 174–6, 178
Bricmont, J. 32, 37
Bright, B. 146, 148, 149
British Educational Research Association 3, 167

Brookfield, S. D. 148, 149, 155
Brown, I. 88
Brown, R. H. 37
Bryant, I. 146, 148, 149, 154
Burgess, T. 47, 60, 64, 81, 82, 83, 87, 109, 110, 113,
　　114, 115, 116, 117, 118, 144

Campbell, D. T. 68
Carr, W. 64, 96–7, 98, 149
Cazden, C. B. 128
Centre for Institutional Studies 40, 45, 46, 50, 80,
　　157
Chalmers, A. S. 36, 146
Chi, M. T. H. 122
CIS *see* Centre for Institutional Studies
CNAA *see* Council for National Academic
　　Awards
Cohen, L. 6, 54
conditions (in science) 6, 18, 26, 28, 43, 73, 74; *see
　　also* explanation, scientific; prediction
confidence
　crisis of
　　in educational research 3
　　in Western conceptual system 31
　and learning 25, 61, 113–15, 118–19
conjecture and refutation, simplified schema of 23,
　　46, 48, 68, 111–12
Connolly, P. 171–2
consequences, unexpected and/or unintended 28,
　　29, 42–3, 51–2, 57–8, 62–3, 65, 69, 81, 90,
　　92–3, 95–6, 99, 119
constructivism 17, 112
corroboration 7, 11, 21, 24–5, 27, 68, 180
Corson, D. J. 8, 9, 40, 45, 178
Council for National Academic Awards 50, 82,
　　84–5, 87
Crosland, A. 82

Croydon Education Authority 54
curriculum 34, 55, 58, 88, 128, 129, 130, 135–45, 176;
    see also planning, planning, development
    and synoptic module; science in the
    curriculum; teaching
  development 53, 55, 133, 143
  prescribed 41, 101–8, 113–14, 140, 144
    national 48, 50, 55, 56, 58, 90, 91, 114, 119, 135,
    145, 160
  for the professional educator 157–63
  student-centred 116–17, 144

Darby, D. 3, 9, 10, 11, 167, 170, 177, 178
Darwin, C. R. 67, 179, 180
Dearden, R. F. 55, 56
Dearing, Sir Ron *see* National Committee of
    Inquiry into Higher Education
deconstruction 7, 32–3, 37, 38 n. 2, 49
democracy 4, 40, 47, 56, 74, 90
  in schools 107–8, 130
Department for Education 55
Department for Education and Employment 3, 11,
    48, 56, 91, 177
Department of Education and Science 47, 79, 82,
    83, 85–8, 135, 136, 137, 138
Derrida, J. 30, 32, 36
DES *see* Department of Education and Science
DfEE *see* Department for Education and
    Employment
discovery of error and/or inadequacy 8, 9, 10, 15,
    21–5, 28–9, 61, 66, 104, 111–14, 115, 169; *see
    also* trial and error
  penalizing 114, 115
Donnison, D. 40
Doyal, L. 146–7
Dror, Y. 42, 43, 48
Durkheim, E. 72–3

education
  adult 55, 91, 148
  basic 146, 148–55
  further 55, 79, 80–2, 85–6, 90, 91
  higher 3, 4, 40, 49, 50, 55–6, 79–88, 89–100, 101
  postgraduate 156–63
  see also assessment of student attainment;
    curriculum; objectives-based approaches;
    planning; problems, problem-based
    approaches; research, educational;
    schools/schooling; science of education;
    teaching
Education Reform Act (1988) 135, 145
Edwards, M. L. 6
Einstein, A. 36, 102, 103, 107, 108
empiricism 19–20, 21, 45, 70, 103, 110
Enlightenment 31, 33
EOC *see* Equal Opportunities Commission

equal opportunities 130, 154; *see also* policy,
    education, equal opportunities in; teaching,
    multicultural
Equal Opportunities Commission 135–7, 138
Eraut, M. 5, 40, 149
ethics 18, 40, 60, 74, 89, 93, 96–7, 122, 154, 159, 161
Eve, R. A. 7, 41
explanation 7–8, 64, 153
  historical 48–9
  scientific 7, 26–7, 40–1, 45–6, 70–1, 117–19, 136,
    179; *see also* science
  schema of 26

falsification *see* refutation
Feyerabend, P. 35, 104
Foucault, M. 30, 36, 178
Fransella, F. 150
Fudge, C. 44, 46
Further and Higher Education Act (1992) 79, 80,
    84, 86

Gellner, E. 31, 32, 35, 37
General National Vocational Qualifications 55, 90
generalizations 5, 6, 20–1, 29, 35, 47, 83, 173–4;
    see also universal statements/theories
Glaser, R. 122
Griffiths, M. 149
Gunn, L. A. 43, 44, 45, 80

Habermas, J. 7, 44, 72, 73–4, 75
Harding, S. 30, 33, 38 n. 5
Hargreaves, D. H. 167
Harris, R. 146–7
Harte, W. 46–7
HEFCE *see* Higher Education Funding Council
    for England
higher education *see* education, higher; policy,
    education, higher
Higher Education Funding Council for England 4
Higher Education Quality Council 91, 92
Hillage, J. 3, 10, 11, 177
Hogwood, B. W. 43, 44, 45, 80
Hughes, J. A. 72
Hume, D. 21–2, 178, 180
'Huron' Elementary School 126–7
Hutcheon, L. 32
hypotheses 21, 26, 29, 32, 43, 103
  auxiliary 25
  creating/generating 10, 46, 63, 146, 153, 171, 173
  testing 24, 39, 46, 49–51, 83, 86–7, 111, 137, 139,
    146, 153, 169–74
  prohibitive 27–8, 118–19

idealism 17, 70, 72
implementation *see* policy
induction 5, 6, 11, 20–2, 25, 28–9, 48, 70, 110, 112,
    113, 180

instrumentalism 4,98
Irigaray, L. 32

James, R. 112

Kant, I. 102
Kelly, A. V. 55,56
Kelly, G. A. 146–7,150,154
Kemmis, S. 64,96–7,98,149
knowledge
  body of 10,11,170,177
  certain and/or secure 10,11,18,20,21,28,37,57,
    110,113
  commonsense 126
  conjectural 10,11,18,19,20,25,28,49,146; *see
    also* conjecture and refutation; knowledge,
    growth of
  growth of 8,9,10,15,16,18,19–25,28,29,35,36,
    63,67–9,102,103,109,110,146–7,162,
    168–9,177–8
  kinds/forms of 4–7,31,75
  locally embedded 5,6,41,44,99,122,128,129
  objective 17,19,35,46,111
  practitioner and/or expert 122,131,149,153,
    155,157,158–9
  propositional 5,6,7,8,40,47,49,146,153–4
  from research 3,40–1,72,87,125,167–8
  scientific and/or technical 8,10,20,42,101,102,
    103,146–7
  sources of 102–4
  subjective 19,32,35,149–50
  see also conditions (in science); curriculum;
    empiricism; generalizations; rationalism;
    science; universal statements/theories
Krick, E. V. 50
Krige, J. 38 n. 4

Lampinen, O. 41
language
  games 31–2,33,37,75
  language learning 118–19,137–8,148
    bilinguality 125–30,131,132–3
  role of 7,17,19,31,35,71,72,74,111,123,124,
    179
  argumentative 19,111,115
  descriptive 17,19,111,179
  see also literacy; metalanguage
Lather, P. 31,32,38 n. 2
Latour, B. 34,37
learning
  assessment of 90,91,117,118,157–8,159
  impediments to 9,11,29,48,53,59–60,66,90–1,
    100,109,114,115–16,118; *see also*
    objectives-based approaches
  lifelong 11,148
  logic of 8–9,10,11,15,20,22–5,48,59,60,66,92,
    109–20,144,156,159,161–3,169

planning for 53–5,59–60,61,63,66,116–17,154,
    157–8
  Popperian approach to 8,9,107,109; *see also*
    learning, logic of
  and research 5,10,28,40,48,52,63–4
  rote 112,126
  society 11,88
  testable theory of 117–19
  see also confidence and learning; curriculum;
    literacy, reading, learning from; teaching
learning outcomes, intended *see* objectives
Lindblom, C. E. 42,43–4,46,47
literacy 119
  literacy hour 48,119
  reading
    learning from 21,22,24–5
    in the postgraduate curriculum 160–1
    postmodern deconstruction 32
    in the school curriculum 127,129
    scientific 37,101,103,108 n.
  see also language
Locke, M. 86
Lord President of the Council 80
Lyotard, J.-F. 5,35,178

McCarthy, T. 153
McGaw, B. 3
McIntyre, D. 167
Maclure, S. 48
McTaggart, R. 97
Magee, B. 39,46,47,51,52
Majone, G. 46
Marcuse, H. 31
Marsh, D. 44
Matthews, M. R. 102,104–5
May, F. 128,130
Meighan, R. 58,115
metalanguage 19
metaphysics 15–17,70; *see also* research,
    metaphysical research programmes
Miller, D. 15,21,29
Ministry of Education 79,80,81
Musgrave, A. 38 n. 3

Nagel, T. 35
National Committee of Inquiry into Higher
    Education (chaired by Sir Ron Dearing) 88,
    92
National Vocational Qualifications 55
numeracy hour 119

objectives 82–3,90,93,109,127,143
  -based approaches 42–3,46,51,53–60,63,64–6,
    115,119
observation 20–2,26,28,32,34,59,102,103,104,
    118,144,146
  statements 16,20,22

theory-free 7, 21, 110–11
theory-laden 7, 22, 24, 34, 110–11, 179
OECD *see* Organisation for Economic Co-
operation and Development
Office for Standards in Education, report on
educational research 3, 9, 167–78
Ofsted *see* Office for Standards in Education
Organisation for Economic Co-operation and
Development 3, 5–6, 11, 39, 40

Paechter, C. 172–3
Pawson, R. 7, 45, 46, 80, 88, 136
PDAS *see* planning, planning, development and
synoptic module
Perkinson, H. J. 110
personal construct theory 146–8, 150–1; *see also*
repertory grid technique
Peterson, P. L. 3
Phillips, D. C. 17
piecemeal social engineering 47, 50
Pinker, S. 36
planning 42, 51, 53–66, 69, 90, 93, 97, 125, 126–7
planning, development and synoptic module
157, 159, 161
see also objectives; policy-making; problems,
problem-based approaches
Plato 38, 101, 106
policy
analysis/evaluation 42–52, 53, 57, 62, 76, 80, 81,
83–4, 86, 125
education 3, 4, 5, 11, 15, 29, 39–41, 46, 47, 48, 50,
51, 52, 53, 55, 56, 58, 59, 65, 69, 75–6, 115, 148,
167–8
equal opportunities in 135–45; *see also* 'Huron'
Elementary School; Richmond
Road School; teaching, multicultural
higher 49, 50, 79–88, 89–92, 100
implementation 42–6, 48, 49, 50, 58, 76, 90, 95,
96, 115, 124, 125
-making 3, 4, 5, 29, 39–52, 53, 55–9, 65, 68–72, 74,
75–6, 79, 84, 86, 87, 93, 115, 121–34
and research 3, 4, 5, 29, 39–41, 45–52, 124, 125,
167–8
testing 39–52, 69, 79, 81, 82–3, 96, 124–5, 135–45
Popham, W. J. 54, 55
Popper K. R. (and Popperian) 7–11, 15–29, 40, 43,
45–50, 52, 57, 60, 67–71, 86, 89, 92–3, 101,
103–4, 106–8, 109–13, 117, 120, 146–7, 161,
167–80
positivism 4–5, 6, 7, 20, 67, 68, 104
postmodernism 7, 8, 30–8, 48, 179
Pratt, J. 58, 167, 168–9, 177, 179
prediction 5, 25–8, 44, 46, 50–2, 59, 71, 118, 146, 147,
151, 153
unpredictability 10, 41, 51–2, 59, 70; *see also*
consequences

see also explanation, scientific schema of;
hypotheses
Pressman, J. L. 42
problems
different types of 6, 40, 50, 60, 63–4, 123, 161
formulation of 11, 47, 48, 50, 52, 57, 60–1, 63, 64,
89, 92, 115, 116, 117, 123, 144, 160, 161–2
identification of 76, 122–3, 130–3
practical 23–4, 60–4, 116
problem-based approaches 5, 45–52, 53, 56–66,
76, 80, 89, 92–100, 115–17, 121–34, 161–3
researching practical 63–4, 89, 92–100, 109
of the solution 48, 145
theoretical 23–4, 60, 63–4
see also conjecture and refutation; knowledge,
growth of; learning, logic of

QAAHE *see* Quality Assurance Agency for
Higher Education
Quade, E. S. 42, 43
Quality Assurance Agency for Higher Education
56, 90–1, 92
Quine, W. V. 71, 180

Rabinow, P. 31
rationalism 19–20, 30, 43, 46
rationality 6, 8, 17, 31, 33–4, 35–6, 43, 45, 48, 49,
56–7, 66, 71–2, 80, 101, 168–9, 179
'rational' model 42–3, 48, 56; *see also*
objectives-based approaches
Raven, J. 143, 144
reading *see* literacy
realism 7–8, 17–18, 46, 146–7, 168–9, 179, 180
commonsense 16, 17, 179
critical 9, 67–75
postmodern alternative to 7, 31–2
Reay, D. 174–6
Redding, P. 33
reflective practice 5, 41, 97–8, 100, 149–50, 152,
154–5, 157, 159
refutation 16, 22–3, 25, 27–9, 67–8, 110, 115, 146–7,
169; *see also* conjecture and refutation
reinventing the wheel 115
relativism 7–8, 17, 25, 30–8, 43, 75, 179, 180
repertory grid technique 150–5; *see also* personal
construct theory
research 42, 44, 45, 47, 48, 49, 50, 68–9, 72, 74, 150
degrees 5, 156
educational 3–11, 16, 28–9, 38 n. 2, 39–41, 44, 48,
68, 80, 87, 91, 100, 109, 115, 119, 120, 125,
135–41, 149–50, 151–5, 167–80
small-scale 11, 27, 29, 76, 119, 124, 125, 126
educational/social research, kinds of 4–7
funding 4, 10, 28, 177, 178
metaphysical research programmes 16
methods 18, 121, 125, 154–5, 169–70, 172; *see
also* triangulation

purposes of 4–5,10,39–40,70–1
see also problems, researching practical; science
Research Assessment Exercise 100
Reynolds, D. 10
Rhodes, R. A. W. 44
Richmond Road School 128–34
Robbins, Lord 79,81,82
Robinson, E. E. 82,87
Rorty, R. 30,31,179
Ruse, M. 179
Rutherford, F. J. 101–4,106
Ryan, A. 36

Sagan, C. 36
Sayer, A. 7
Schön, D. A. 146,149
School for Independent Study 116–17
schools/schooling 48,52,55,58,59–60,70,76,87,
    102,105,109,114,117,119–20,123–5,171
  primary/elementary 116,118–19,126–34,135
  secondary 46,101,135–45
  see also curriculum; democracy, in schools;
    research, educational; teaching
science 5,8,9,15–17,21,23,30–1,34,35–7,38 n. 2,
    41,42,43,46,50,51,67,178,179,180
  boldness in 16–17,25,27,28,29,146,169,170
  and critical preference 25
  in the curriculum 101–6,108
    and equal opportunities 137–8,139–40,142,
    144,145
  deconstruction of 32–3
  of education 15–29,120
  logical analysis of 15,26–7
  natural 6,15,28,40,41,45,46,71
  scientific knowledge 8,10,20,42,69,103–4,
    146–7
  scientific theory 16,25–8,34,41,45,104
  social 4–5,6,7,8,9,15–16,28,34,40,41,42,43,
    45,46,51
    critically realist approach to 67–76
  see also explanation, scientific; knowledge,
    growth of; literacy, scientific; technical
    application; universal statements/theories
Science for All Americans: Project 2061 101–6
Scott, Peter 84
Scott, Philip 112
Sex Discrimination Act (1975) 135,136,137,138,
    139,141
Shotter, J. 73
Silver, H. 85
Silverman, S. 49
Simon, H. A. 42,43
Simons, H. W. 30–1,33,38 n. 2
Siraj-Blatchford, I. 58,115

situational analysis/logic 48–50,53,79,86
Socrates 106
Sokal, A. 32,37
Sparkes, A. C. 173–4
Stenhouse, L. 55,56
Swann, J. 144,167,168–9,177,179–80
Swartz, R. 110,144

Tann, S. 149
targets *see* objectives
Tarnas, R. 31,33,35,38 n. 1
teacher education/training 4,79–80,149,163
  initial 55–6,85–6,87,91,105,138,149
teaching 10,53,59,67,90,102,106,143,156
  careers 140,142
  logic-of-learning approach to 109–20,161–3
  multicultural 128–9,131; *see also* 'Huron'
    Elementary School; Richmond Road
    School
  postmodern 37,38 n. 2,48
  see also assessment of student attainment;
    curriculum; democracy, in schools;
    education; learning; objectives-based
    approaches
technical application 10,26–7,50
Thomas, G. 6,149–50
Thompson, J. B. 121
Tilley, N. 7,45,46,80,88,136
Tooley, J. 3,9,10,11,137
trial and error 23,40–1,42,46,47,48,50–2,60,62,
    67–9,76,89,92,95,99,111–13,115,117,
    124–5,128,133,161–2; *see also* discovery of
    error and/or inadequacy
triangulation 121,137,168,169,170,172–3
truth 7,16,18–19,22,24,30,35,68,103,110,113
  as correspondence 18–19
  pursuit of 15,16–18,25,28,31–2,36
Tyler, R. W. 55,60

universal statements/theories 6,7,16,18,20–2,25,
    26–8,179; *see also* generalizations
Usher, R. 146,148,149,154

Van Maanen, J. 38 n. 2
verification 6,22,26,68,110
von Glasersfeld, E. 17

Webster, L. 126
Weinberg, S. 34
Wildavsky, A. 42
Wilson, E. O. 37
Wittgenstein, L. 67,72,75
Woodhead, C. 4,167,168
Woolgar, S. 34